CW01261061

Irish Women Poets
Rediscovered

Irish Women Poets Rediscovered

Readings in poetry from the eighteenth to the twentieth century

Maria Johnston and Conor Linnie

EDITORS

CORK UNIVERSITY PRESS

First published in 2021 by
Cork University Press
Boole Library
University College Cork
Cork
T12 ND89
Ireland

© the contributors 2021

Library of Congress Control Number: 2021934718
Distribution in the USA: Longleaf Services, Chapel Hill, NC, USA

All rights reserved. No part of this book may be reprinted or reproduced or utilised in any electronic, mechanical, or other means, now known or hereafter invented, including photocopying and recording or otherwise, without either the prior written permission of the publishers or a licence permitting restricted copying in Ireland issued by the Irish Copyright Licensing Agency Ltd, 25 Denzille Lane, Dublin 2.

British Library Cataloguing in Publication Data
A CIP record for this book is available from the British Library.

ISBN: 978-1-78205-479-5

Printed in Malta by Gutenberg Press
Print origination & design by Carrigboy Typesetting Services
www.carrigboy.co.uk

COVER IMAGES – 'My Mind is Frazzled' (1992), courtesy of the artist, Janet Mullarney.

www.corkuniversitypress.com

In memory of
Janet Mullarney (1952–2020)
and
Lynda Moran (1948–2020)

Contents

ACKNOWLEDGEMENTS ix

NOTES ON CONTRIBUTORS xi

INTRODUCTION: Acts of Attention 1
   Maria Johnston and Conor Linnie

1. Olivia Elder (1735–80) 13
   Andrew Carpenter

2. Ellen Taylor (years unknown; one extant publication, 1792) 20
   Sarah Prescott

3. Dorothea Herbert (c.1767–1829) 27
   Bernadette Gallagher

4. Emily Lawless (1845–1913) 36
   Seán Hewitt

5. Charlotte Grace O'Brien (1845–1909) 43
   Nora Moroney

6. Dora Sigerson Shorter (1866–1918) 52
   Jack Quin

7. Lola Ridge (1873–1941) 58
   Tara McEvoy

8. Florence Mary Wilson (1874–1946) 66
   Carol Baraniuk

9. May Morton (c.1880–1957) 76
   Stephen O'Neill

10. Blanaid Salkeld (1880–1959) 84
   Michelle O'Sullivan

11.	Ethna MacCarthy (1903–59) *Maria Johnston*	92
12.	Freda Laughton (1907–95) *Jaclyn Allen*	103
13.	Madge Herron (1915–2002) *Jane Robinson*	110
14.	Patricia Avis (1928–77) *Conor Linnie*	119
15.	Angela Greene (1936–97) *Susan Connolly*	129
16.	Lynda Moran (1948–2020) *Kenneth Keating*	138
17.	Cathleen O'Neill (b. 1949) *Emma Penney*	147

AFTERWORD: The Future of Irish Women Poets: A new language   156
Lucy Collins

ENDNOTES   163

INDEX   183

Acknowledgements

The impetus for this book originated in the one-day seminar *Missing Voices: Irish women poets of the 18th–20th centuries* hosted by Poetry Ireland in October 2018. We would therefore like to thank Poetry Ireland for making possible this landmark event that brought into focus ongoing issues of diversity and inclusion in relation to Irish poetry and the canon. Many of the papers delivered at *Missing Voices* have been rewritten as essays for this volume and we are delighted to capture some of the conversational spirit of the seminar in these pages. We are personally indebted to Gerald Dawe and Lucy Collins for their encouragement and guidance. It has been our great pleasure to work with Cork University Press and we sincerely thank Mike Collins and Maria O'Donovan for their support of this project. We are also enormously grateful to the readers at Cork University Press for their careful and considered readings of the book as it evolved. We were fortunate enough to attract a range of immensely talented scholars and readers to contribute to this book and we wish to thank each and every one of them here for their expert and attentive readings. Their scholarly passion and dedication will no doubt be an inspiration to all who read this volume.

We have benefited from the generosity of many people, publishers and institutions to secure permissions for the range of poetry, prose excerpts and archival material featured in the book. For permission to quote from the work of Dorothea Herbert we are grateful to Frances Finnegan and Congrave Press, and for permission to view Herbert's archival material we extend our thanks to the staff of Manuscripts and Archives, Trinity College Dublin. Daniel Tobin, Andrew Latimer and Little Island Press kindly allowed us to quote from the published work of Lola Ridge. For permission to reproduce Florence Wilson's archival material we are grateful to the Linen Museum, Lisburn, and Belfast Central Library. For permission to quote from the unpublished correspondence of May Morton, we are grateful to the National Library of Ireland. For permission to publish the poetry of Blanaid Salkeld, we thank Blanaid Behan. For permission to quote from the published and unpublished work of Ethna MacCarthy, we are deeply grateful to Andrew Woolfson, and we wish also to extend our thanks to Jane Maxwell, Manuscripts and Archives, Trinity College Dublin, for her generous assistance, and to Eoin O'Brien for his kind and helpful response to queries. For permission to publish the poetry of Freda Laughton, we are grateful to the Freda Laughton estate and to Emma Penney. For permission to publish the poetry of Madge Herron, we thank Patricia Herron. For permission to publish the poetry of Patricia Avis, we are grateful to Emily Riordan. For permission to publish the poetry of Angela Greene, we thank Salmon Poetry. For permission to publish the poetry of Lynda Moran, we are grateful to the family of Lynda Moran. We thank Cathleen O'Neill for giving permission to publish her poetry. For permission to publish material from the Women's Community Press, we thank the Arts Council of Ireland Archives. We would also like to thank Claire Cunningham of Rockfinch Productions for her interest in and support of this project and for inviting many of the book's contributors to speak on national radio about their chosen poet. Warm thanks to Wendy Mooney for essential technical support. Finally, we are deeply grateful to the late Janet Mullarney for so generously providing us with the cover image for the book. We dedicate the book to her memory and to the memory of the late Lynda Moran.

Notes on Contributors

Jaclyn Allen is a final-year doctoral candidate at University College Dublin (UCD). Her thesis focuses on English and Irish women poets publishing between 1930 and 1950 and their navigation of hostile literary cultures. She is a resident scholar at UCD's Humanities Institute.

Carol Baraniuk has lectured and published widely on Ulster literature in the Scottish tradition. Her monograph on the County Antrim United Irishman James Orr was published in 2014 as *James Orr, Poet and Irish Radical*. Having previously lectured on Scottish Literature at Ulster University, she is currently a research associate in Robert Burns studies at the University of Glasgow and is preparing an essay on Burns and his biographers for the forthcoming *Oxford Handbook to Robert Burns*.

Andrew Carpenter is emeritus professor of English at University College Dublin and a member of the Royal Irish Academy. He works on Irish poetry in English from the seventeenth and eighteenth centuries. His most recent anthology (joint-edited with Lucy Collins) is *The Irish Poet and the Natural World: An anthology of verse in English from the Tudors to the Romantics* (Cork University Press, 2014).

Lucy Collins is associate professor of English at University College Dublin. Her books include *Poetry by Women in Ireland: A critical anthology 1870–1970* (2012) and a monograph, *Contemporary Irish Women Poets: Memory and estrangement* (2015), both from Liverpool University Press. She has published widely on contemporary poets from Ireland, Britain and America, and is co-founder of the Irish Poetry Reading Archive, a national digital repository.

Susan Connolly is the author of three collections of poetry: *For the Stranger* (Dedalus Press, 1993), *Forest Music* (Shearsman Books, 2009) and *Bridge of the Ford* (Shearsman Books, 2016). She was awarded the Patrick and Katherine Kavanagh Fellowship in Poetry in 2001.

Bernadette Gallagher is a writer. Her poems have been published in various journals and recorded by the University College Dublin Poetry Archive. She has been invited to read her work in Ireland, the United Kingdom, the United States and at the Sahitya Akademi, New Delhi.

Seán Hewitt is a Government of Ireland research fellow at University College Cork and a book critic for *The Irish Times*. His first monograph is *J.M. Synge: Nature, politics, modernism* (Oxford University Press, 2021), and his first collection of poetry is *Tongues of Fire* (Jonathan Cape, 2020).

Maria Johnston is a poetry critic who has held lecturing roles in a number of universities. Her essays and reviews have appeared in a wide range of publications including, most recently, *Poetry Review*, *The Cambridge Introduction to Irish Poets*, *The Oxford Handbook of Modern Irish Poetry* and the *Cambridge History of Irish Women's Poetry* (forthcoming). She is co-editor, with Philip Coleman, of *Reading Pearse Hutchinson* (Irish Academic Press, 2012).

Kenneth Keating is the author of *Contemporary Irish Poetry and the Canon: Critical limitations and textual liberations* (Palgrave Macmillan, 2017). Kenneth has held research and lecturing roles in University College Dublin and University College Cork. He has published widely on modern and contemporary poetry, and is the editor of Smithereens Press. He is co-founder of Measuring Equality in the Arts Sector (MEAS).

Conor Linnie is a Government of Ireland postdoctoral fellow at University College Dublin. He is curator of the digital humanities project *The Poetics of Print: The private press tradition and Irish poetry* with the Library of Trinity College Dublin. He is the author of various articles and chapters on Irish print culture, modernism, and the intersections of literary and visual culture in Britain and Ireland during the mid-twentieth century.

Tara McEvoy is a PhD candidate at Queen's University Belfast. Her doctoral research concerns poetry, politics and publication culture. She co-founded and edits *The Tangerine*, a Belfast-based magazine of new writing.

Notes on Contributors

Nora Moroney is an Irish Research Council postdoctoral fellow at Trinity College Dublin and Marsh's Library. She is working on a cultural history of collecting in twentieth-century Ireland in relation to the Benjamin Iveagh Library. Her doctoral research focused on Irish writers and the late-Victorian periodical press. She has published on Irish women writers abroad in the *Victorian Periodicals Review*, and has a chapter forthcoming on the twentieth-century Belfast press in *The Edinburgh History of Newspapers and Periodicals in Britain and Ireland, Volume III*.

Stephen O'Neill was the National Endowment for the Humanities Fellow for 2019–20 at the University of Notre Dame's Keough-Naughton Institute for Irish Studies. He is currently writing a book about partition and Irish culture.

Michelle O'Sullivan is a poet and the author of three poetry collections from the Gallery Press, the most recent being *This One High Field* (2018).

Emma Penney recently completed her PhD thesis entitled 'Class Acts: Working-class feminism and the women's movement in Ireland' at University College Dublin (UCD). She is co-founder of the UCD Decolonial Platform and a member of the Equality, Diversity and Inclusion committees at the UCD College of Arts and Humanities and at the International Association for the Study of Irish Literatures.

Sarah Prescott is principal and dean of the College of Arts and Humanities at University College Dublin and fellow of the Learned Society of Wales, specialising in seventeenth- and eighteenth-century British and Irish women's writing and pre-1800 Welsh writing in English. She is the author of a number of books including *Women, Authorship, and Literary Culture, 1690–1740*; *Women and Poetry, 1660–1750*; *Eighteenth-Century Writing from Wales: Bards and Britons* and *Writing Wales from the Renaissance to Romanticism*. Her co-authored volume *Writing Wales in English, 1536–1914: The first four hundred years* is to be published in 2020. Her current project is as the principal investigator and general editor of a Leverhulme Trust funded collaborative project, 'Women's Poetry 1400–1800 from Ireland,

Scotland, and Wales. A multilinguistic poetry anthology based on this project and an accompanying critical study, entitled *Women's Poetry from Ireland, Scotland, and Wales, 1400–1800: Critical and Comparative Contexts*, are forthcoming from Cambridge University Press.

Jack Quin has held positions as an Irish Research Council fellow and Leverhulme postdoctoral fellow at Trinity College Dublin. He is the author of various articles and chapters on W.B. Yeats, Irish poetry and the visual arts.

Jane Robinson is a poet and scholar. Her poetry collection *Journey to the Sleeping Whale* (Salmon Poetry, 2018) won the Shine-Strong Award for debut collection of the year. She is a recipient of the Strokestown International Poetry Award 2014 and the Red Line Book Festival Poetry Prize 2015. Her recorded poems have appeared on RTÉ's Lyric FM, the Poetry Jukebox, the Poetry Programme, and the Poetry Ireland podcast series. She was the Irish Writers Centre's 2019 writer in residence in Norway, as well as 2019 poet in residence at the National Centre for Biological Sciences in Bangalore, India.

INTRODUCTION

Acts of Attention

Maria Johnston and Conor Linnie

> In a world
> where God is 'He'
> and everyone else
> 'mankind',
>
> what chance
> do we have for
> a bit of attention?[1]

The seventeen essays in this volume are titled with the names of seventeen women poets. As you look through the list, some of the names will be familiar and others you may vaguely recognise, but many will be completely unknown. Each essay is prefaced with a poem you may never have read but which signals a vivid voice in the story of anglophone Irish poetry across three centuries. Each of these seventeen essays is an act of attention. Written by a diverse range of established and emerging scholars and practising poets, they rediscover familiar voices and reclaim those that have suffered marginalisation or neglect. *Irish Women Poets Rediscovered* enters into the reinvigorated critical field of Irish women's literary studies that is bringing into new and necessary focus the work of writers who are 'either forgotten or, if remembered, are framed within a limited critical discourse'.[2] The primary focus of this essay volume is on the poetry itself. Each poet is first presented to the reader in their own words with a stand-alone poem or poem extract that launches an engaging and informative essay response, thereby illuminating the details of the poet's life and work through a combination of close reading and broader contextualisation. In this way, the essays move from the particular to the general, introducing the selected poet to the reader before situating her within a wider view of Irish culture from the eighteenth to the twentieth centuries.

Irish Women Poets Rediscovered invites the reader to delight in the newly found poem, but also to consider why many of its represented poets have struggled for visibility. The essays collected here reflect on the conditions and contexts by which Irish women poets have been historically denied their readers. They raise significant questions about class and inequality through the individual stories of eighteenth-century servants and labourers to those struggling with unemployment and marginalisation in modern-day Dublin. They chart the political beliefs and activism of women poets amid the social upheaval and revolutionary fervour of the nineteenth and early twentieth centuries. New insights into the field of Irish literary production reveal the myriad difficulties faced by women in a male-dominated publishing sphere, and how they contested their predicament through the cultivation of independent publishing contexts and social networks. The essays highlight the liberating social space of the local writing group, of epistolary correspondence, and the varying opportunities afforded in Irish periodical culture and the private press tradition. The collection speaks of the constant and varied impediments faced by women poets, but also of how they navigated these challenges to find their way into print.

Recent major studies in the tradition of Irish women's writing have highlighted the 'powerful occlusion of women's role in literary production in Ireland'.[3] The perpetuation of this narrative of occlusion in our own time has been reflected in a number of high-profile publishing controversies. The landmark three-volume *Field Day Anthology of Irish Writing*, published in 1991, received widespread criticism for its lack of representation of women writers, leading to the publication of two supplementary volumes in 2002 that focused exclusively on women's writing and traditions. These two volumes marked what their editors described as 'the first attempt to bring together a substantial body of written documents produced by and about women since writing began

Introduction: Acts of Attention

in Ireland'.[4] While the volumes have stimulated much important research and writing in the intervening years, the vexed issue of the under-representation of Irish women poets remains. Many, though not all, of the essays included in the present volume were developed from papers delivered at the 2018 seminar *Missing Voices: Irish women poets of the 18th–20th centuries*.[5] The seminar was organised by Poetry Ireland as a way to address the critical issues raised in the wake of the publication of *The Cambridge Companion to Irish Poets* (2017) concerning the lack of female poets represented in its pages.[6] The seminar provided a vital public forum to engage with issues of diversity and inclusion in the Irish canon. These issues have been brought to similar attention in the digital sphere. Two online collective initiatives, *Fired! Irish Women Poets and the Canon* and the *Irish Women's Writing (1880–1920) Network*, have established dynamic digital platforms committed to stimulating action and engagement, creating accessible resources and facilitating interdisciplinary exchange in the field of Irish women's writing.[7] The digital space has encouraged a diversity of participation and achieved a public impact extending beyond the formal bounds of academia. *Irish Women Poets Rediscovered* fosters a similar diversity in its contributing authors, presenting the diverse perspectives of poets and scholars.

The seventeen essays included in this book bring into dialogue the distant but echoing stories of Irish women poets writing in English across three centuries. *Irish Women Poets Rediscovered* is at the same time consciously more modest in scope than the 'comprehensive overview' provided by recent publications.[8] The essays are intimately framed by the individual reader responding to the individual poet and poem, before extending outward into broader themes and contexts. A consequence of this narrower remit is that this book features only English-language poets, though Irish-language quotations, translations and traditions are illuminatingly referenced in various essays in the collection. The fact remains, however, that a separate study would be required to trace the development of women poets writing and publishing in the Irish language across the extensive time-frame covered by this collection of essays. The value of a more limited frame of reference has been asserted by Lucy Collins in her landmark anthology, *Poetry by Women in Ireland*. 'Rather than seeking the broadest possible representation of women poets', her anthology presents 'the range and complexity of the work of individual women'.[9] The seventeen essays collected here find similar richness in the individual voice.

And so, *Irish Women Poets Rediscovered* begins by taking us back to Coleraine in the eighteenth century as Andrew Carpenter presents the satirical poet (or 'poor poetess', as she styled herself) **Olivia Elder (1735–80)**. Elder's fearless pen spared no one and as one who lived 'between the mean and the sublime', she was particularly effective at capturing the frustration of the woman writer in the face of domestic chores and servitude: 'I oft forsake both Pope and Swift / The house to sweep and pots to lift!' A house-keeper throughout her life, Elder's reading was enriched by poets such as Alexander Pope and John Milton and, as Carpenter's essay reveals, her sparkling poetry comprises a range of poetic forms, styles and subjects: from satires and deeply felt elegies to verse-letters and caricatures of friends and enemies. Copied into a notebook during her lifetime, her poems represent 'the only verses written by a woman living and working in eighteenth-century Ulster that have survived the ravages of time'. As such, the artful, spirited work of this dynamic poet is significant both for its literary finesse and fine-tuned socio-cultural insights.

Also born in eighteenth-century Ireland, the enigmatic **Ellen Taylor (years unknown; one extant publication, 1792)** is brought into the light by Sarah Prescott. Her life, as documented in her poetry as well as in the scant biographical details that have survived, was tragic and poverty-stricken. Prescott identifies Taylor as an important example of an Irish labouring-class woman poet of her time. Her work, which amounts to ten poems published in 1792 by an anonymous 'editor' under the title *Poems, by Ellen Taylor, the Irish Cottager*, is significant for the way that it articulates and controls great feeling while writing against the bitter realities of life as a destitute domestic servant. Taylor's poetry voices a range of opinions on class and education. She is a fascinating presence, and her remarkable, resilient poems are deserving of greater study not only in the context of Irish literary and social history but also in the wider context of working-class literature in Ireland and Britain.

Unpublished in her lifetime, **Dorothea Herbert (*c*.1767–1829)** nonetheless considered herself a writer or 'authoress' and is best known for her two-volume memoir *The Retrospections of Dorothea Herbert, 1770–1806*, described by the late Eileen Battersby as a 'Jane Austen-style social diary capturing the essence of rural Ireland'.[10] Herbert was also a committed poet who revelled in satirical and pastoral styles and who produced a formally diverse poetic oeuvre that ranged from short ephemeral pieces to the sprawling mock-heroic epic. As a writer, a skilled painter and musician, and one who considered herself an 'outcast' from society, Herbert remains a complex and compelling figure. Drawing on her examination of Herbert's papers at the Manuscript and Archives Library at Trinity College Dublin and inspired by Herbert's talents, poet Bernadette Gallagher broadens our view of Herbert and her world.

'I have a relish, I might almost say a passion, for obscurity', **Emily Lawless (1845–1913)** declared, in a way that seems to foretell her inclusion in a book such as this but that also says something about the freedom that women writers may enjoy, and perhaps even exploit, as they forge their art under the radar. As a 'forgotten writer' Lawless the novelist has been the worthy subject of scholarly attention, but her poetry continues to suffer from limited critical attention despite her having achieved some popularity in her lifetime. Seán Hewitt presents a dimension to Lawless' work that few readers will have encountered before and which is urgently necessary in this contemporary age of environmental and ecological crisis. 'Her time is with us', Hewitt asserts, reminding us of Lawless' omission from fields of study, such as eco-criticism, that her work so illuminatingly pre-empts. Lawless in fact exemplifies the woman poet from the past who should be studied not only in the context of her own historical moment but also because her poetry speaks to the artistic climate and existential concerns of our own times and into the future.

The political world of the nineteenth century registers with force in the poetry of **Charlotte Grace O'Brien (1845–1909)**. Daughter of the illustrious Young Ireland figure, William Smith O'Brien, her life was steeped in the political and social activism that imbues much of her writing. As a poet, O'Brien remains almost unknown in the annals of Irish writers, yet, as Nora Moroney uncovers, she maintained a steady publishing presence in both Ireland and England, producing two full works of poetry and many periodical pieces. Moroney's essay brings O'Brien's poetry to light for the first time, focusing in particular on her poetic addresses of the political state of Ireland and commentaries on William Gladstone's social and economic policies. O'Brien was directly involved in campaigns for political and social change through her writing, proving that Irish women were active in the nineteenth-century public sphere in a variety of ways. She is an exemplar of the woman writing back, discussing and intertwining the political and poetic discourses of her day.

Dora Sigerson Shorter (1866–1918) represents another vivid example of the politicised woman poet of the nineteenth and early twentieth century. The poet, artist and journalist remains an ill-fated and enigmatic figure in accounts of the Irish Literary Revival. Sigerson Shorter was born in Dublin, where she met several key revivalist writers including W.B. Yeats, Rose Kavanagh and Katharine Tynan, before moving to London. After the Easter Rising and the execution of its leaders, Sigerson Shorter suffered from depression and chronic physical illness until her death in 1918, which several contemporaries attributed to her grief. Jack Quin brings new attention to the craft and import of Sigerson Shorter's political elegies and self-elegies published in the collection *The Sad Years* (1918), considering her experiments with style and her aesthetic dialogue with contemporaries such as Yeats, even as she grappled with the traumatic consequences of the Rising. Quin delves into the darker side of Sigerson Shorter's poetics, where a rich arboreal imagery and lyricism are woven into the mourning of public figures and the private self.

Born in Dublin and living in America, Australia and New Zealand, **Lola Ridge (1873–1941)** belongs to more than one poetic tradition and her work defies easy categorisation. Tara McEvoy presents the poet as an elusive transnational émigré whose work is energised by the movement of immigration and multiculturalism and who is needed now more than ever in this age of debate around national borders and globalisation. Again, as with Lawless, it is her 'contribution to our current poetic landscape' that proves her enduring and increasing importance. In a review of Ridge's *Collected Early Works* (2018), David Wheatley admires the 'prismatic patterns cast by her beguiling lyrics', and the growing number of publications dedicated to Ridge in recent years testifies to the increasing academic and readerly interest in her work. McEvoy's essay joins the rising tide of scholarly engagement with this dynamic poet.[11]

The poetry of **Florence Mary Wilson (1874–1946)** also crosses borders of time, place and genre. Born in Antrim, she published one volume of poems, *The Coming of the Earls and Other Verse*, in 1918, which draws on both Irish folk traditions and the Scots-influenced dialect of Ulster. As an expert in the field of Ulster literature in the Scottish tradition, Carol Baraniuk brings a wealth of research to enrich her reading of Wilson as a woman writer within an Irish Protestant tradition of literary and political nationalism, thus enlarging our understanding of the poetic heritage of Ireland north and south, and complicating simplistic political oppositions.

The collection's northern perspective is continued with **May Morton (c.1880–1957)**, the Limerick-born poet who settled in Belfast in the first years of the twentieth century, where she worked as a teacher. Morton is remarkable in that she only began to seriously develop her poetic craft late in life, with her three published collections coming after her retirement from the 1930s onwards. Despite this, as Stephen O'Neill charts, she became a central presence in Irish literary circles and societies of the mid-century, chairing the Belfast Centre of PEN International and regularly corresponding with poets including John Hewitt and Austin Clarke. Morton also enjoyed commercial and critical success with her late poetry collections. O'Neill discusses her poem 'Spindle and Shuttle', which won the Northern Ireland Prize for poetry as part of the festival of Britain in 1951. Tasked with writing a poem on the subject of 'Northern Ireland' for the competition, Morton explores the craft and labour of the linen industry as a form of remembrance of tradition and history.

The struggle for visibility for women poets was acute in the beleaguered decades of the mid-twentieth century. The supreme authority of the Catholic Church and the calcifying legacy of revolutionary nationalism restricted the public perception of the Irish woman to iconic maternal figure rather than equal and engaged citizen. As Heather Ingman and Clíona Ó Gallchoir observe, Irish women remained fatally wedded to the grand patriarchal symbols of the revolutionary period: 'with the example of the Virgin Mary set before them, [they] were to embody the purity of the Irish nation'.[12] Hegemonic gender divisions obscured and indeed obstructed the activities of women across the spectrum of mid-century Irish social and cultural life, sanctioning a narrative of occlusion that has persisted into our own time. For Anne Mulhall, the reputation of women writers of the mid-twentieth century has 'fallen victim to the particular political investments involved in the constitution of an Irish national culture'.[13] Yet, when we return to the periodicals, private press publications, pamphlets and letters of the period, the cultural field is suddenly animated by the vigorous industry of women poets. Though the identity of the modern Irish woman was suppressed in the official discourse of the new state, as Gerardine Meaney, Mary O'Dowd and Bernadette Whelan argue, 'Irish women persistently engaged with modernity' and to recover the wealth of this primary material is to realise that women's 'resistance to the dominant ideology of womanhood in this period has frequently been underestimated'.[14]

The second half of *Irish Women Poets Rediscovered* situates the reader in this newly recovered terrain. Poet Michelle O'Sullivan responds to the experimental voice of **Blanaid Salkeld (1880–1959)**, who transformed her unassuming Dublin home at 43 Morehampton Road into a site of independent publishing activity in the 1930s and 1940s. Salkeld founded the Gayfield Press with her son Cecil in 1937 and the focus of O'Sullivan's essay is on Salkeld's first collection of poems published under the Gayfield imprint, *…the engine is left running*. The freedom of the private printing press encouraged Salkeld's experiments in all aspects of the publishing process. As O'Sullivan shows, Salkeld's innovative approach to typography and design was integral to her creative praxis: the radical presentation of poems on the page stages an unconventional and unruly aesthetic where word and image collide in rhythmic exchanges of friction and flow. The sensitivity to the materiality of the book anticipates Salkeld's attention to the female body and its precarity. In *…the engine is left running*, transgressions of style and social commentary combine to project a daring poetic voice from the margins.

Born in 1903 in Coleraine, poet and physician **Ethna MacCarthy (1903–59)** represents a rebellious and outward-looking generation in Irish literary history. A lifelong friend of Samuel Beckett, whom she met as a student at Trinity College Dublin in the 1920s, MacCarthy is known, when she is remembered at all, as the model for Beckett's 'Alba'. Yet, as the publication of her *Poems* by Lilliput Press in 2019 confirmed, MacCarthy was a poet in her own right and one who, in the words of Eiléan Ní Chuilleanáin, 'has not received her proper scope and attention'.[15] Although she never published a full-length collection, her poems appeared in the pages of the *Dublin Magazine* and *The Irish Times*. As the editors of MacCarthy's *Poems* assert: 'MacCarthy was an intellectual presence in an age that did not often promote, if at all acknowledge, the woman's voice', and the publication of her poems decades after her death finally makes possible 'the reclamation of her missing poetic voice'.[16] Maria Johnston's essay makes use of the Leventhal-MacCarthy archive at Trinity College Dublin to reveal something of the range and force of MacCarthy's literary legacy and introduces her to a new readership as a poet and writer of cosmopolitan flair and formidable intelligence.

Irish Women Poets Rediscovered follows the blueprint of 'generous inclusion' established by the editors of *The Cambridge History of Irish Literature* and *A History of Modern Irish Women's Literature*, holding to a liberal conception of the 'Irish poet' that encompasses women born in Ireland along with those who lived for significant periods of time on the island.[17] This extension of the geographical coordinates of Irish poetry continues with Jaclyn Allen's essay on **Freda Laughton (1907–95)**. Born in Bristol, Laughton moved to Ireland in 1932, where she became a prominent poet in Dublin's vibrant periodical scene. As Allen illustrates, Laughton's only published collection, *A Transitory House* (1945), establishes the centrality of nature in her poetry, where the imagery of the natural world offers a symbolic resource for feminine experience and the unconscious expression of the psyche. This expression had, inevitably, to contend with the prejudices of a male-dominated literary sphere of the mid-twentieth century. Allen interrogates the gendered conventions of Irish critical culture and the challenges faced by women poets in print.

A central theme running through this collection is the enduring capacity of Irish women poets to challenge and subvert inherited social, cultural and political boundaries. Donegal-born poet **Madge Herron (1915–2002)** encapsulated this spirit of resistance in a late interview with the simple statement: 'I hated being told what to do.' Poet Jane Robinson affirms Herron as a performance poet before her time, revealing how her poetic craft was infused with the live energies of spoken word and drama, and the bilingualism of her native Irish and English. Herron drifted between the theatrical and broadcasting worlds of Dublin and London throughout the mid-century, performing on the Abbey Theatre stage and across the national airwaves in the 1930s, and later featuring on the BBC Third Programme. By the 1960s, Herron was living in London and beginning to channel her stage and broadcasting experience into her poetry. Robinson draws from rare live BBC recordings of Herron reading in London to recover the force of her poetry in performance.

Mobility was often essential to the developing careers of women poets in a time of limited opportunity. Born in Johannesburg to an Irish mother and a Dutch-Afrikaans father, **Patricia Avis (1928–77)** orbited literary circles in post-war Dublin, London and Paris. Conor Linnie recovers Avis' poetry from the British and Irish periodical and anthology cultures of the 1950s and 1960s, while also foregrounding her role as editor and publisher of the Dublin cultural review *nonplus*. Avis' posthumous literary reputation has been obscured by her romantic relationships with poets Philip Larkin and Richard Murphy – a fate typically suffered by women writers at the hands of male biographers. Linnie addresses her problematic representation in recent biographies and refocuses critical attention on her poetry and publishing. Avis thereby sheds her crude characterisation as the object of male desire to become instead an active and influential presence among her literary contemporaries.

Angela Greene (1936–97) followed a similar trajectory to Freda Laughton as a poet born in England who eventually settled and found her voice in Ireland. Poet Susan Connolly's personal response to her work draws from her first meetings with Greene at the Barbican Writers' Group in Drogheda in 1983. Connolly foregrounds the often unacknowledged role played by writers' groups in local communities, with the Barbican connecting its poets to a resurgent periodical scene that included *Poetry Ireland Review*, *The Honest Ulsterman* and the 'New Irish Writing' page of the *Irish Press*, edited by David Marcus. Greene seriously turned to writing poetry after long years spent raising her four children. The family home and garden consequently set the intimate domestic setting for many of the poems collected in *Silence and the Blue Night*, published by Salmon Poetry in 1993. In poems such as 'Enniskillen', however, the private and personal concerns of the poet extend dramatically out into the wider community and the violent rupturing of social life during the Troubles.

Violence and its consequences for the female body is a theme that pervades the poetry of **Lynda Moran (1948–2020)**, whose 1985 collection *The Truth About Lucy* is brought to new recognition by Kenneth Keating. 'I'm a butcher myself', the speaker of Moran's 'Something Else' states starkly, subjecting the body to a literal and metaphorical dissection that is presented unflinchingly to the reader. The explosive transition from the intimate lyric to the urgent communal voice evident in Angela Greene is similarly triggered by Moran in her poetry, which deals with both the precarities and possibilities faced by women in the public arena. Keating situates Moran among an emerging generation of Irish women poets determined to establish the lived reality of the female body and sexuality as a rightful subject for poetry in 1980s Ireland. Yet, Moran's promising early career was curtailed by the absence of a second poetry collection that could have established her reputation. Keating is a founder, with Ailbhe McDaid, of Measuring Equality in the Arts Sector (MEAS), an organisation that monitors and reports on equality in the arts sector in Ireland.[18] His essay draws from the example of Moran to interrogate the systemic gender inequalities in the publishing and funding landscape of present-day Ireland, revealing the often invisible institutional and commercial barriers faced by the marginalised.

Social class remains one of the invisible barriers in Irish society and culture. Born in 1949, **Cathleen O'Neill**, the concluding poet of the collection, gives exhilarating voice to the working class during the economic depression of the 1980s and the uneven recovery of the 1990s. For Emma Penney, working-class women's poetry 'is often collective in that you are more likely to encounter an "us" or a "we", than an "I"', and her essay demonstrates the radical communality of O'Neill's writing. Echoing Susan Connolly's insight into the Barbican Writers' Group, Penney highlights the importance of outlets provided by women's writing groups in Dublin such as KLEAR and SAOL. She situates O'Neill and her work in these groups and the industrious independent publishing culture that emerged from them, producing a diverse archive of working-class women's writing and testimony. As Penney argues, KLEAR and SAOL provided spaces where women writers could share their experiences of the class system and begin to creatively engage with 'the double-burden ... of their gender and their poverty'.

'They want to corral us off as "women poets", as if that were a form of inferior being', Nuala Ní Dhomhnaill once remarked to Medbh McGuckian.[19] As readers of modern and contemporary poetry will know, the category, or sub-category, of 'women's poetry' is a contested one that brings with it its own thorny ambivalence. The American poet Elizabeth Bishop famously refused her inclusion in an anthology of women poets, remarking in 1974 that 'art is art and should have nothing to do with gender'.[20] In some ways, it is hard not to agree with this outlook: such a categorisation can be reductive. However, there is no arguing against the fact that the light of attention must be shone with discrimination in order to enable and sustain acts of inquiry and retrieval. Added to this, the fact remains that women poets, even in twenty-first-century Ireland, do not feel equal in status to their male counterparts. 'You are less likely to be reviewed by a male critic if you are a woman writer. Sexism is alive and well in literary circles', the poet and critic Caitríona O'Reilly remarked in a 2008 newspaper article titled 'Tackling the Poetry Patriarchy'.[21] Organisations such as MEAS are currently playing a central role in identifying the systemic inequalities that continue to define the Irish publishing landscape.

In her afterword to this volume, Lucy Collins assesses the current state of Irish women's poetry and maps the necessary future direction of the field. 'Much has changed in the past ten years in how this field has been defined', she observes, 'and much remains to be done to represent the differing creative processes, and varying access to power, that women demonstrate in Ireland today.' We must, in Collins' words, 're-make our criticism' to encompass this diversity of perspective and experience. To read this book is to have much of what is known and taught about Irish poetry and Irish writing altered and expanded. There is no single tradition in Irish poetry, and there is more than one story. This timely collection of readings continues the recent efforts by which the name and nature of Irish poetry is being challenged, widened and enriched.

Olivia Elder (1735–80)

Andrew Carpenter

from **To Mrs A.C.H., an account of the Authors manner of spending her time**

> I oft forsake both Pope and Swift
> The House to sweep, and Pots to lift;
> With Princely Queensb'ry leave his Gay,
> To call the folks from making hay;
> Or Young upon the morning Star
> To help the boy down with a Car;
> Quit Tragick Queens in all their clutter,
> And help to churn, or dress the Butter.
> Oft from my Hand the Pen I whisk out,
> And in its place take up the Dishclout;
> For spite of all sublimer wishes,
> I needs must sometimes wash the Dishes.[1]

The poems written by Olivia Elder, the daughter of a New Light Presbyterian[2] minister from Aghadowey near Coleraine, seem to be the only verses written by a woman living and working in eighteenth-century Ulster that have survived the ravages of time. Certainly, verse was written in the eighteenth-century Ulster Presbyterian community, and we know that some of it circulated in the form of verse letters between women friends. But, apart from the poems Olivia Elder preserved in her copybook, nothing else has survived.[3] For those seeking the missing poetic voices of the women of Ireland as a whole, and of Ulster in particular, Olivia Elder carries special significance.

Olivia Elder never married – the result of having been 'cruely deceiv'd in Love', she wrote – and spent her life in Aghadowey helping her father with the small farm he ran to supplement his income. Though she would have much preferred to have spent time reading or writing poetry, she fully involved herself in the everyday chores of home and farm. The lines presented above are taken from one of the lively verse letters Olivia Elder exchanged with her female friends in 1769, here explaining her 'manner of spending her time'; other verse letters contained requests for flower roots, invitations to visit and snippets of local news. Her friends seem to have been of the same social standing as herself, daughters of farmers or small landowners. Once she had decided she was a 'poetess' (which seems to have happened in her thirties), Elder wrote verse regularly and on all sorts of occasions, often placing lines from her favourite English poets – Milton, Gay, Thomson or Pope – as an epigraph to a poem. She was an adventurous and energetic writer, not afraid to try her hand at almost any form of poetry – elegies, odes, songs, verse epistles, occasional poems and, perhaps most surprisingly, satires. These 'carrikaturas', as she called them, were aimed at specific individuals, among them Old Light Presbyterian ministers and clergy of the Church of Ireland; Elder accused these men of the cloth of many vices including sloth, dishonesty, corruption, cynicism, drunkenness and sexual misconduct. One of her most virulent attacks – on the rector of Coleraine – was, astonishingly, published in *The Freeman's Journal* in Dublin, though this was her only appearance in print. Otherwise, her verse remained in manuscript until its recent publication.

The outspokenness of Olivia Elder's satiric attacks can startle the modern reader, and it is not surprising to find that the relatives of one of the clergymen who was the victim of a poetic attack by Olivia Elder 'took great offence at it'.[4] However, there is no record of the response of the recipient of the verse letter that follows. Her name is hidden behind the initials M.B., but she was probably Margaret Blair of Laurel Hill, Coleraine. The poem, 'To the Same [i.e. Miss M. B.] Novbr 29th', is one in a series of poetic exchanges dated November 1769 and it opens with a quotation from Swift:

Raillery gives no offence
where truth has not the least pretence
nor can be more securely placed
than on a Nymph in Stellas taste[5]
                              Swift

Since in my last I did deceive ye
Of Panigyrick on your Davy[6]
I make amends, you lazy elf
I'll send you one upon yourself[.]
When you by T---s[7] were so slighted
No doubt you thought he was near sighted
Or when the men forebore to chat
You wou'd insinuate by that
As silence reign'd throughout the Room
They by your charms were all struck dumb
And that hereafter they'll be telling
How they mistook you for a Helen.

You taken for the Grecian Queen!
Was e'er a Ton of Beauty[8] seen?
For with the likeness none will quarrel,
If I compare you to a Barrel:[9]
Your little Neck so like a Tosset,[10]
A passage for your pint of Posset,
That nightly at your mouth you tun,
And like a torrent down does run.
A spiggot rounded at the top,
The fosset,[11] somehow, form'd to stop,
May best describe your Pigmy head;
Of which no more need now be said:
But to this Head, and Neck, and waste,
Suppose an Arm on each side placed,
Then give the whole a rocking motion,
Of Pugg we'll have a proper notion.
Your Arm indeed and eke your hand,
Might well become a better stand;

No doubt the source of mighty <all your> pride,
But let me swathe[12] them by your side,
And if comparisons are scant,
The Malthouse shall supply my want;
Or bring them from the homely Barn,
And say your [*recte* you're] like a sack of corn.

But here perhaps you'll tell me pat,
The Grecian Beauties all were fat;
It's true, but yet we must suppose
Dame Helen did not fill her Hose,
Nor yet her Stays, so well by half,
Or she had only raised a laugh
Instead of raising Greece's Ire,
And setting Men and Gods on fire.

Perhaps you'll say your radient Eyes
Are of the *Hue* that paints the Skys; --
But not the *Blue*, I needs must say;
They're only like the morning gray.
'Tis true your skin is white and sleek,
And store of Roses in your cheek;
But now and then a Spitefull Rose
Leaps up and takes you by the Nose
Or sometimes in your forehead blows.
O yes! if any one can find,
A charm to which the Muse is blind,
Then let it be produced with Speed,
Or else to sentence we proceed.

Now here your mind I woud describe,
But fear my Muse has got a Bribe
O'er this to draw a friendly veil,
Or from yourself at least, conceal
What, --- but sure nothing e'er was harder!
She will not move an hairbreadth farther.

A few points on this strange poem: this is not the text as Elder sent it to Miss M.B. It is a fair copy made by the poet after writing the poem and before sending: as she says in a footnote to the poem that appears just before this one in the manuscript: 'this and ye following were written extempore save a few lines here & there'. Thus, though the poems may look spontaneous, they have been worked over and amended. This is not sudden, impromptu verse, which the sender might later wish she had not sent, but a text that she had worked on and was sufficiently proud of to copy into her notebook. Though it may have started as private banter, the poem as copied out has become something that the poet expected other readers to see.

Secondly, the register is one of affectionate irony, from the term 'Panigyrick' in the second line onwards – in other words, the victim is not meant to take offence. The footnote definitions the poet gives of a 'carrikatura' make it clear that she thought this poem, like others in her book, was a particular kind of a joke or a 'jest'. A useful comparison is with late eighteenth-century political cartoons, which often portray their victims in ways that can seem cruel to us – particularly when the images are obscene or scatological. However, the cartoonists' victims seem to have taken the insults in good part. Though one does not think of rural Ulster as being a fertile ground for cutting personalised satire, that is what we have in this poem. Satire is always, to some extent, unkind, since it exaggerates aspects of the victim's behaviour or appearance and is intended to raise a laugh from the viewer or reader at his or her expense. The vision it presents is so extreme that the victim looks ludicrous: in this case, even if, as Elder's footnote puts it, Miss M.B. was 'inclined to be fat', the way her appearance is ridiculed seems unkind. In other poems, Olivia Elder praised friendship, particularly between women, and one hopes that her friendship with Miss M.B. survived this poem.

Olivia Elder often personified her muse – as she does towards the end of the poem above, blaming the muse for outspokenness and excusing some of what the muse tells her to say on the grounds that it is 'ironic'.[13] An authorial footnote to the poem that contains the 'carrikatura' of Davy reads: 'This may be looked on as a carrikatura of the gentleman, a strong but distorted likeness; he is rather Handsom, genteel and agreable than otherwise.' The reader needs the footnote since the text of that particular poem has described Davy as having a face 'like a frog all o'er speckled', a habit of staring like 'a stuck pig', and eyes that are 'bloodshot and Muddy' due to his fondness for spending time in hostelries. The poem about Davy is, indeed, no 'Panigyrick' on him and the reader who does not have the advantage of Elder's footnote on Davy might easily misread the text.

Since we have nothing with which to compare the verse written by Olivia Elder, it is hard to know exactly what to make of the poem above, or indeed of other poems in a similar vein in her collection. Clearly, there is a substantial gulf between the serious theological disputes being written about in rural Ulster by the Presbyterian prose writers of the time (including Olivia's father, John Elder [1693–1769])[14] and the energetic, domestic verse being written by at least one of their womenfolk. The poem above is not an isolated instance of a poem in this register in the oeuvre of Olivia Elder: there are several poems expressing surprisingly outspoken thoughts considering Elder's Presbyterian background; one of the best of these is a wickedly pointed attack on the hypocrisy of Old Light Presbyterian ministers.[15] On the other hand, Olivia Elder was the author of several gentle, meditative poems on death and the passing of time, some interesting poems of religious faith and an eloquent elegy on Mary Ann Knox, a local girl shot dead by the famous 'half-hang'd' MacNaghten.[16] Several poems address her own life – her unhappiness in love, her depression and her sorrow at the death of her parents. Other poems contain lively descriptions of imagined scenes, such as 'Matrimony at the Throne', which visualises Elder and one of her sober-minded friends being married to two drunken louts; Elder's use of dialogue in that poem is particularly memorable.

A revealing poem is the one she wrote to Anna Laetitia Barbauld asking if she could become one of Barbauld's friends and correspondents; in that poem, Elder describes her miserable plight as a woman poet in 'bleak Hibernia's stormy Isle' where not only is the weather unpropitious but civil liberty 'droops' and 'August religion' – that is, New Light Presbyterianism – is shackled by the penal laws. 'Hard war' and 'bigot rage' rule society in Ulster, she tells Barbauld. This poem, and several other long pieces, are impressive in their handling of complex matters with elegance and skill. In fact, one of the most admirable aspects of Olivia Elder's poetry is its range in subject matter, tone and form. A good example of her sensitivity can be seen in her 'Verses to Mrs A.C.H. on the death of her only daughter, a child of five years old, who died of a mortification in the smallpox, April 1771'.[17] These well-crafted stanzas compare very favourably with other poems by other women poets of the age on similar themes.

We have about fifty poems by Olivia Elder, poems that she was sufficiently proud of to copy carefully into a notebook, hoping that future readers would see, not only her verse letters and her 'carrikaturas', but also her serious, meditative poems on friendship and on death. By any standards, she was a poet of range and originality, showing herself at various times to be a sharp social critic; a tender, affectionate friend; a mischievous parodist and the author of verse of deep feeling. Hers has been, indeed, a missing voice in poetry written in Ireland; it is time it was heard.

Ellen Taylor (years unknown; one extant publication, 1792)

Sarah Prescott

Written by the BARROW side, where she was sent to wash LINEN

Thy banks, O Barrow, sure must be
    The Muses choicest haunt,
Else why so pleasing thus to me,
    Else why my Soul enchant!

To view thy dimpled surface here,
    Fond fancy bids me stay,
But Servitude with brow austere,
    Commands me straight away:

Were Lethe's virtues in thy stream,
    How freely wou'd I drink,
That not so much as on the name
    Of Books, I e'er might think.

I can but from them learn to know
    What's misery compleat,
And feel more sensibly each blow,
    Dealt by relentless fate.

In them I oft have pleasure found,
    But now it's all quite fled,
With fluttering heart, I lay me down,
    And rise with aching head.

For such a turn, ill suits the sphere
   Of life in which I move,
And rather does a load of care,
   Than any comfort prove.

Thrice happy she condemned to move
   Beneath the servile weight,
Whose thoughts ne'er soar one inch above,
   The standard of her fate.

But far more happy is the soul,
   Who feels the pleasing sense,
And can indulge without control,
   Each thought that flows from thence.

Since nought of these my portion is,
   But the reverse of each,
That I shall taste but little bliss,
   Experience doth me teach.

Cou'd cold insensibility,
   Thro' my whole frame take place,
Sure then from grief I might be free,
   Yes, then I'd hope for peace.[1]

All we know about Ellen Taylor, the eighteenth-century 'Irish Cottager' poet, is that she was alive in 1792 when ten of her poems were prepared for subscription publication by an anonymous writer who supplied an introduction with a few tantalising biographical details of her life. From this introduction, and as the opening poem suggests, it is clear that Taylor lived a life of extreme poverty and emotional distress. The introduction recounts what is known of her origins in County Laois:

> It appears that she was the daughter of an indigent Cottager, in a remote part of The Queen's County, who had barely the ability to afford common sustenance to her and a numerous family during his life-time.[2]

On the death of her father, Taylor lived with her beloved younger brother (whose death and her grief upon it features in her poetry) and tended him in 'a lingering disorder'. To do so, she had to sell all her belongings, including 'some favourite books which were given her by a friend in the neighbourhood'. Due to her even further reduced circumstances, she then took a place as a domestic servant for a nearby gentry family (internal evidence from the poems indicates that the family name was Porter), but she was dismissed due to the melancholy caused by her brother's death, which 'rendered her unfit for a service where activity and labour were actually necessary'. Since this time, she has lived in dire poverty 'which she now experiences in a poor Hut on the Commons of Lyons, where to earn a scanty livelihood she keeps a small day school'. The unnamed 'Editor' has collected the poems for publication, without her knowledge, in order to raise money 'to assist Genius when sinking under poverty and distress'.

Despite her obscurity, both in her own time and since, Ellen Taylor is an important example of an Irish 'labouring-class' eighteenth-century woman poet, examples of which are also found in England and Scotland in the period and with whom there are some interesting parallels as well as national differences. In Scotland, for example, Jean Adam (1704–65) and Janet Little (1759–1813), 'The Scottish Milkmaid', both published collections of poetry by subscription and with the assistance of a female mentor acting in a similar way to Taylor's 'Editor'. Both women were domestic servants at some stage in their lives and Jean Adam, like Taylor, also kept a day school but eventually died in a Glasgow workhouse in destitution. Janet Little came to the notice of Robert Burns, as her employer and mentor, Mrs Frances Dunlop, was a friend and correspondent. The most well-known English example is probably Ann Yearsley (bap. 1753–1806), the 'Bristol Milkwoman' or 'Lactilla', whose patron was the high-profile writer and woman of letters Hannah More. The introduction to Taylor's poems suggests that the writer of the introduction is aware of these precedents as Taylor is presented to the reader through the frame of the popular eighteenth-century trope of the untutored genius, signalled by the quotation from Thomas Gray's 'Elegy Written in a Country Churchyard' on the title page: 'Full many a flower is born to blush unseen / And waste its sweetness on the desert air'.

The introduction relates how a gentleman visitor to the house came upon Ellen as she was finishing her cleaning. Taylor is described as weeping over a print of a similarly weeping female figure leaning on an urn, and clutching a piece of paper wet with her tears. To the gentleman's 'astonishment', the paper turns out to be a poem, destined to be the opening poem of the collection: 'On seeing the Print of a Female Figure in a weeping Attitude, leaning on an Urn'. As a result, it is seen as a 'duty' to bring her genius to public attention to save her from the poverty into which she has fallen even deeper: 'It now becomes almost a duty of the generous public, to prevent this beautiful field flower from being buried (like Burns' mountain daizy [sic]) beneath the oppressive Ploughshare of poverty.' Although seemingly unaware of her female counterparts, the introduction evokes Robert Burns as an example of non-elite genius, although the full import of Burns' poem 'To a Mountain Daisy' (1786) – which declares 'Stern Ruin's ploughshare drives elate, / Full on thy bloom, / Till crush'd beneath the furrow's weight / Shall be thy doom' – tragically negates the editor's optimism that the collection of poems will alleviate Taylor's economic woes.

In a rare critical appraisal of Taylor's poetry, Leith Davis suggests that it is precisely Taylor's suffering that leads to her 'poetic discovery', as exemplified by the tear-strewn poem found in her hand by the 'Gentleman'.[3] Davis argues that the sentimental and affective nature of her distress reinforces her worth as a poet representing emotion, even as it makes her unfit for domestic labour. She also suggests that in the poem which heads this essay, 'Written by the BARROW side', Taylor performs a similar manoeuvre whereby, despite the loco-specific title of the poem, she switches focus 'from the external world to the internal world, from physical to personal affect'.[4] The poem is indeed very fitting for thinking about how Taylor tries to balance her life as a domestic servant, her domestic labour, and her life as a poet, the life of the mind and the emotions. However, this poem is also very useful as a starting point for thinking about Taylor as a labouring-class poet and about the context from which she wrote. Taylor opens the poem by apostrophising the river – 'O Barrow' – and thus signals a local readership and a relationship to a known and specified place. The title of the poem reinforces this effect as the poem itself is actually written on the banks of the river in question: the Barrow is both the site as well as the subject of composition. Furthermore, Taylor's social position is firmly signalled by the title: she has not wandered to the riverbank of her own volition to indulge poetic fancy but has been '*sent* to wash linen' (emphasis added). Rather than seeing Taylor as turning away from these external constraints, I would suggest that the poem continually plays on the tension between her position as a local servant, and the menial and physical task before her, and the life of the mind, a luxury usually only afforded to the wealthy and educated. Taylor evokes, for example, the classical precedent of the Hippocrene spring on Mount Helicon as the source of poetic inspiration to frame her experience: the site of her linen washing becomes 'The Muses choicest haunt', which enchants her soul.

In the next stanza, 'Fond fancy' directly battles with 'Servitude with brow austere', 'commanding' (just as she was 'sent' to wash linen) her to get on with her chores. The poem overall seems to convey deep frustration with her position as Taylor again evokes classical allusion to frame her frustration: she wishes that the Barrow was now the River Lethe (symbolic of oblivion and forgetfulness in Greek mythology), and thus by drinking of that water she could forget that she had ever read a book; her education is presented as leaving her in the impossible situation of being even more aware of the misery she must endure, 'And feel more sensibly each blow, / Dealt by relentless fate'. Taylor concludes the poem by wishing that her thoughts would 'ne'er soar one inch above, / The standard of her fate', that is, that she had not had her ambitions and her expectations raised when her physical situation is so different from her aspirations. In the poignant last stanza, she wishes for the opposite of affective emotion: she calls on 'cold insensibility' to take her over, as only then can she be free of grief and 'hope for peace'.

The poem is very striking in its depiction of what we might term class alienation, a battle between stark circumstance and educated sensibility that makes poverty and suffering harder to bear. The poem reveals the almost impossibility of Taylor becoming a poet, or the personal cost in trying, which makes it even more remarkable that she did and that her poems were preserved. However, what the editor also mentions in passing is that Taylor has been published before:

A few lines written by her appeared some time ago in one of our News-papers, in which were such strong effusions of feeling and sensibility, as induced the Editor to make minute enquiries into the life and situation of the Writer.

I have not as yet been able to locate the newspaper in which Taylor's lines appeared, but it is clear from this statement that, in fact, she had a previous life as a poet that predates the publication of *Poems*. This insight complicates the view of her as an obscure 'beautiful field flower' waiting to be discovered. It would appear that, on reading the lines in the newspaper, the writer of the introduction tracked Taylor down to her previous employment where, presumably, the family had a copy of her poems in their possession. There are also other poems in the collection that are not as bleak as the one discussed here, for example she writes some lively verse on female friendship 'to a Fellow Servant, who went to Dublin to get a Place or to visit her Friends', although the bulk of her oeuvre of ten poems are indeed heartfelt elegies (including one to her mistress, Miss Porter). On a brighter note, the collection also includes a poem thanking a gentleman 'who had lent her some Books', where, in contrast to the Barrow poems, she sees books as a source of comfort: 'That I, when time permit – can sit and read / O'er all the elegance of mind, and pen / Of these most learned celebrated men'.

The obscurity of Ellen Taylor herself is almost matched by the mystery surrounding the writer of the introduction and the editor of her work. There remains much more research to be done here, but some immediate clues are in the subscription list, described in the introduction as 'confined to a small circle'.[5] The subscribers do indeed seem to be a small and select circle, not only in terms of geographical reach (there seems to be a nexus crossing Kildare, Kilkenny, Laois, Carlow; all places associated with Taylor), but also in terms of the literary and cultural interests of the mainly Irish subscribers, and those from Dublin literary society in particular. For example, the list includes 'Mrs. Vesey' who may be the literary intellectual Elizabeth Vesey, (she may have subscribed just prior to her death in 1791), who was an associate of the English Bluestockings, including Elizabeth Carter, Hannah More and Elizabeth Montagu.[6] The appearance of the 'Countess Mt Cashell' (Lady Mount Cashell), another well-connected

Irish intellectual aristocrat (and previous pupil of Mary Wollstonecraft when the latter was a governess in Ireland), again suggests that Taylor's work was presented to established and highly regarded literary circles, who may have been intrigued by her lowly class origins.[7] Indeed, the countess' husband was a close relative of the Whig salon hostess, Lady Moira, who presided over a number of important literary gatherings at Moira House, Dublin, and was a great influence on the countess herself as well as a supporter of other Irish women writers such as Henrietta Battier and Mary Tighe.[8]

There is also the tantalising name of 'Mrs Lefanu', who may or may not be Alicia Sheridan Lefanu, sister of Richard Sheridan, who was also an active participant in Dublin literary circles of the time. The name of the antiquarian and Shakespeare editor Isaac Ambrose Eccles further compounds the literary credentials of the group.[9] Moreover, a Richard Griffith and Mrs Griffith also appear on the list and are most likely the writer Elizabeth Griffith and her son, Richard (her husband, also Richard, died in 1788). Although she was born in Wales, Elizabeth's father was the actor-manager of Smock Alley Theatre in Dublin, her mother was from Portarlington, and her husband Richard Griffith was a farmer from Kilkenny. The Griffiths lived between Dublin and London but had retired to their son's estate in Kildare by the 1790s when Taylor's poems were published.[10]

Finally, but not exhaustively, there is Thomas Tickell, a very well-known (if minor) English poet and man of letters who happened to have married Clotilda Eustace, daughter and co-heiress of Sir Maurice Eustace of Harristown, County Kildare, in 1726. There is thus a curious mismatch between Ellen Taylor's obscurity and a small and select subscription list that reflects the cream of the Irish literary elite, although the intellectual and political interests of the group may have made them more open to Taylor's predicament. It is possible that one of these writers, many of whom were voluminous journal and letter writers, mentioned Taylor in their work. It would be gratifying to think that they did and that she left more traces of her existence than we have yet discovered.

Dorothea Herbert (c.1767–1829)

Bernadette Gallagher

Lines to a Friend

Lines addressed to a Friend who used laughingly wish the Author Married to some Peer or Bishop that she might give her Husband a good fat Living

Come my laughter loving Friend
Seriously for once attend
And say if these Words be true
You love me as I love you
For most truly I can swear
Ne'er was Friendship more sincere
More unmix'd more pure than Mine
My dear Bess for Thee and Thine.
      Oh that I by deeds cou'd prove
How sincerely I thee love
But those nasty selfish Lords
Won't let me fulfil my Words
Nor will e'en a sleek fat Bishop
Leave it in my power to dish up
A good Living to your Clarke
For in fact I do remark
Not one titled Wretch doth shew
A penchant to be my Beau
Clifden, Cork already gone
Callan's heart a perfect stone
For myself I cou'd endure
Their neglect if they'd procure

> One good Living for my Brother
> And for my friend Clarke another
> Choak them not one tender glance
> Tells me we've the smallest chance
> Well what can befall us worse
> Than to have an empty purse
> Which when drain'd we'll e'en turn Writers
> And curse Coronets and Mitres.[1]

Dorothea, or 'Dolly' as she was known to her family, was the daughter of a Protestant clergyman, Nicholas Herbert, and mother Martha (Cuffe).[2] She was born in c.1767, the eldest of nine children, and lived with her siblings and parents in the rectory at Carrick-on-Suir and Knockgrafton (New Inn), County Tipperary. Jane Austen and Maria Edgeworth were contemporaries, although we have no knowledge that they knew or were aware of each other.

Herbert, in her own handwriting, tells us that she wrote four volumes consisting of poems, plays and novels. The volumes containing plays and novels have not been discovered. One hundred years after her death saw the first publication of her autobiography *Retrospections* (volume 4).[3] It took almost another century before her volume of poetry was published. Readers are indebted to Frances Finnegan for discovering the location of Herbert's poetry manuscript and for publishing the poems in 2011 along with additional journal entries in *Introspections: The poetry & private world of Dorothea Herbert*, from which most of Herbert's poems referenced here are taken.[4] Herbert completed *Retrospections* and likely a good number of her poems by 1809. From 1810 until her death in 1829 she seems to have disappeared from public view. Her poetry ranges from a five-line satirical poem 'The Bundle' to the sweeping epic poem, *The Buckiad, a Mock-Heroic Poem*.

The poem 'Lines to a Friend' by Dorothea Herbert (presented above) is a favourite of mine. The opening line is welcoming, inclusive and disarming and pulls one into the poem: 'Come my laughter loving Friend'. In the first stanza she talks directly to her friend Bess as if to a character in a play. In somewhat theatrical fashion, she expresses her love for Bess and asks her friend to confirm that this feeling is mutual.

In the second stanza it is as if she were talking in a monologue. She would like to prove her love for Bess by procuring, 'One good Living for my Brother / And for my friend Clarke another'. The only way she has of achieving this is by marrying well. Her primary concern is for others: 'For myself I cou'd endure / Their neglect'. Towards the end of the poem she admits that they have 'the smallest chance', yet she finishes on a high note. Even if they end up penniless: 'we'll e'en turn Writers / And curse Coronets and Mitres'. Here, she is indicating that they will have the final word and put it in print. The poem employs, with some deviation, a seven syllabic metre accentuated by iambic tetrameter in rhyming couplets.

Three poems in *Retrospections of Dorothea Herbert* (2004) that do not appear in her poetry manuscript are 'Dirge', written after the death of her father; a separate 'Dirge' for her brother who died young and a thirteen-verse pastoral elegy, 'The Village Adieu: A Farewell Poem'. The latter is a farewell not just to the village of Knockgrafton but to her unrequited love, John Roe. These poems appear to be addressed to a different audience than that of her manuscript of poetry. She prefaces 'The Village Adieu: A Farewell Poem' by saying: 'The thoughts of bidding a final Adieu to those beloved Scenes set me absolutely distracted and I continually Wanderd about the Glebe anticipating the dreadful Blow I was to receive in being torn for ever from it and John Roe — My Heart was convulsed with Sorrow and having no other way of venting my internal Conflicts I composed the following Poem in my Melancholy Saunters and felt some Relief in thus giving loose to my Despair.'[5]

A more accomplished long poem that also harks back to her younger days is 'The Villa', influenced by Oliver Goldsmith, whose father and brother were both Anglican vicars. In *Retrospections* Herbert describes the trigger for the writing of this poem. Having left the busy seaside house at Bunmahon, as she relates: 'I went to Carrick for a week beforehand and as Summer was now in its prime the Sweet Serenity of our rural Abode struck me so much … that my muse produced my poem calld the Villa.'[6] Goldsmith's influence is evident in Herbert's repeated use of 'Auburne' from his *The Deserted Village* and the poem mentions him by name: 'Alas no Goldsmith dwells within thy Bowers'.[7] Herbert scholars Frances Finnegan and Mary Catherine Breen provide further examples of allusions to Goldsmith and other poets. Furthermore, Breen sheds light on the dedication of a poem to Herbert by Edward Mandeville and how Herbert's poetry inspired his own writing.[8] 'The Villa' is not just a pastoral ode. Herbert, perhaps acknowledging the destruction of the Bardic tradition and downplaying her own ability, is the poet at this time and place: 'Since no great Bard no skilful Poet's Lays / Shall sing in living Numbers thy soft praise / Yet let th'Effusions of a flowing Heart / Thy num'rous Charms in modest Lines impart'. The muse relents: 'Each pitying Muse my pardon has decreed / Oh let me then our rural Villa sing' but as a young and inexperienced poet 'Tho' tremblingly I soar on unfledg'd wing'. Later in the poem, Herbert tells us not to blame her for delighting in the garden spaces and the memories these evoke in her: 'Nor let proud surly Criticism blame / If still allur'd by the delightful Theme / I should on those lov'd Scenes too fondly dwell / And past the Critic's Bounds Description swell'. Goldsmith wrote of the changes wrought by boundary building and gentrification from tillage to pasture and the effects on the peasants. It may be that Herbert too was intimating that the gentry were at fault: 'Who pourest Blessings on each guilty Head'. She ends her poem thinking of life's end: 'To those blest Realms where Time shall be no more'.

Herbert lived during the penal times, the French Revolution and the Napoleonic wars. In 1770s Ireland, and in particular County Tipperary, the Whiteboy opposition to the payment of tithes to the Church of Ireland was widespread, with casualties on both sides. During this period and beyond, women of a certain social standing were educated for marriage or locked in a limbo of old-maidism, preventing them from moving within that society as men did. Herbert deals with this topic in her poem 'The Rights of Woman'. The following is an extract of the first six lines, which would appear to indicate that Herbert was a supporter of equality for women:

> Whilst Man is so busy asserting <u>his</u> Rights
> Shall Woman lie still without gaining new lights
> Our Sex have been surely restrain'd enough
> By stiff prudish Dress and such old fashion'd stuff
> Too long have been fetter'd and tramelld I wot
> With Cumbersome Trains and the Strict petticoat[9]

The first line references Thomas Paine's *The Rights of Man* (1791), which predates this poem by two years. It is likely that Herbert had also read Mary Wollstonecraft's *A Vindication of the Rights of Woman* (1792) as Herbert's line 'No longer will Woman to Satire be Dupe' touches on a line from Wollstonecraft: 'ridiculed or pitied by the writers who endeavour by satire or instruction to improve them'.[10] Elsewhere in the poem, she alludes to the players of the French Revolution: 'but soon will become e'en a true Sans-Culote'.

It may be that Herbert, in this poem, is writing satirically against rather than for the idea of equality and in opposition to the French Revolution. Towards the end of her poem 'And Flourish away e'er the Ending of Spring / Sans Jupe, Sans Culote, in short – sans any thing' she alludes to Jacques' final words in Shakespeare's *As You Like It* (Act II, Scene VII), 'All the world's a stage':

> Last scene of all,
> That ends this strange eventful history,
> Is second childishness and mere oblivion,
> Sans teeth, sans eyes, sans taste, sans everything.

Throughout Herbert's journal and poetry we get an insight into the social history of the period from the perspective of the landed gentry. Describing the Maypole celebrations: 'All the people of the lower Class round us Assembled dressd in May dresses and we had two Days of continual Dancing in the Field whilst they were ordered a suitable treat'.[11] In her poem 'Sally the Waiting Maid's Complaint', she portrays a native servant in a comic mode as was typical of the time. Herbert adds a note at the end of the poem in a satiric verse telling us: 'That most of what's written above is a Lie'.[12] She makes fun of her own family too, as in 'The Parson's Fireside', when she tells us of the evening ritual of keeping the fire alight and the 'scuffle' that usually ensued between her father and mother:

> His nightly Task of shutting Doors
> Now ended, he profoundly snores
> Then waking from his Evening Nap
> Says positively there's some Gap

> Through which the Wind its entrance makes
> For He's all over pains and Achs
> And then addressing thus his Wife
> My Dear it may cost me my Life[13]

Alexander Pope also has a poem in imitation of 'Dr. SWIFT The Happy Life of a Country Parson', and Pope, whom Herbert references in her journal, was a key influence: "Hope springs Eternal in the human Breast" (says Pope) and I do suppose it crept imperceivably into mine or disappointment would have killd me.'[14] In the preface to her book of poems she writes satirical verse about her own poems, in the manner of Pope, as if they were children inadvertently given away by a parent.[15] The poems having escaped into the world, she is relieved that they have been received well by friends. She ends the poem 'Preface' with a call out to future critics:

> Oh spare me Critic spare a helpless Woman
> For Mercy only Mercy do I sue Man
> I never meant my Pages should be rude
> Or that they should on others time intrude
> But since exposed to other Eyes by Chance
> May Satire on their great Defects ne'er glance
> And be it only on the proud Severe
> Bend the rough Oak the humble Bulrush spare.[16]

While satires predominate across her oeuvre, there are some fine poems in other styles, for example her poem 'The Storm'. This poem may have been a response to a real weather event in 1789 which, as Herbert describes, 'was not only felt all over Europe but we afterward found the same tempest had desolated the West Indies and other parts with unprecedented Horrors'.[17]

> But if on Land those Storms so dreadful seem
> With what grim terrors must dire Ocean teem
> Whilst violent squalls its troubled surface sweep
> Millions of Vessels founder in the Deep[18]

From *Retrospections*, we learn of events external to her home but also intimate details of her personal life. The title page of *Retrospections* reads thus: *Retrospections Of An Outcast Or the life of Dorothea Herbert Authoress Of The Orphan Plays And Various Poems And Novels Written in Retirement Volume the Fourth Adorned with Cuts*; it informs us that she saw herself as an 'Outcast'. Reading *Retrospections*, one would believe that she lived an estranged existence, especially after John Roe's marriage to another in 1804. By contrast with her personal circumstances, her poetry is controlled, as evidenced by her epic poem *The Buckiad* and the remainder of her poetry manuscript. The title of her manuscript, 'Poetical Eccentricities / Written by an / Oddity / And humbly inscribed to all those who are / Lovers of Whimsical Performances / By their most obedient / Humble Servant / Dorothy Strangeways', belies what Michael Coady describes as work 'of considerable literary interest'.[19] In addition to her writing and painting, she was also an accomplished player of the harpsichord and was well versed in the Classics and in French. According to Hughes, Herbert's social position as a member of the minor gentry mitigated against her having a more active role in her community like her contemporary, the writer and poet Mary Leadbeater.[20]

Poets, like painters and other makers, learn from what has come before. Homer has been an inspiration for poets from Sappho to Elizabeth Jennings to Louise Glück.[21] Herbert was no exception, referencing Homer three times in her notes to *The Buckiad*. Homer's influence comes through the translation of the *Iliad* by Alexander Pope.[22] In her own index for her manuscript of poems, Herbert calls out to Pope in the preface and in her final poem, *The Buckiad*.[23] Pope's epic *The Dunciad* deals with his numerous literary quarrels and 'often he descended to violent scurrility'.[24] Herbert's epic, which requires an essay all to itself, introduces us to the antics of the lives lived by those around her, we suppose, her brothers (Bucks) and their peers. The Pandemonium Club referenced in *The Buckiad* harks back to the stories from the Hellfire Club in Dublin. The club want Goddess Frolic to take charge but first they have to offer sacrifices to the Goddess Vice and change their ways by taking instructions from Goddesses Vulgarity, Justice, Folly, Cowardice and, finally, Bribery. Thomas Paine's *The Rights of Man* also gets a mention in *The Buckiad (Book the Second)*.

Herbert informs us in the 'Argument to Book the Fourth' that: 'The poem ends with the Coronation and full establishment of the Goddess, the Installation of the Knights and the promotion of Scape Grace as Prince of Bucks and Clubs.'[25]

What remains of Herbert's handwritten manuscripts are her poetry, autobiography and journal entries. Her poetry manuscript, to my knowledge, remains in private hands.[26] The manuscript of *Retrospections* along with the additional *Journal Notes 1806–07* are held by Trinity College Dublin. The manuscript is bound and illustrated by Herbert using pencil drawings and watercolours. The frontispiece is titled 'The Outcast', below which Herbert has inscribed a quotation from Oliver Goldsmith. There are thirteen illustrations (plates) in all, from landscapes of Carrick-on-Suir, Bonmahon and Killarney to self-portrait and other titles such as 'The Mourning Muse' and 'The Lone Wanderer'. Her handwriting is clear with a well-crafted script slanted to the right. She uses capital letters with some abandon and uses the dash, but there is minimal use of other punctuation.

Parts one and two of *Retrospections* deal with her early years and the day-to-day activities of her immediate and extended family, friends and neighbours and of her falling in love with John Roe.[27] That love seems to have been encouraged by him at first and later withdrawn. In *Retrospections* she writes openly about her unrequited love and obsession for John Roe. Her journal tells us that she was kept a prisoner by her family and that they wanted to murder her.[28] Finnegan suggests that Herbert alludes to John Roe in *The Buckiad* and that part three of *Retrospections* was burned by John Roe's daughter, Elizabeth Roe, due to offensive references to her mother.[29] (Elizabeth was married to a nephew of Herbert's.) Her poetry has no direct reference to John Roe but a great deal of attention to living a life apart, evident in poems such as 'Solitude', 'An Address to Old-Maids', 'Epitaph on an Old-Maid' and 'Miss Herbert's Last Will'.

Herbert's poetry provides us with a link to writers like Constantia Grierson (1705–32), Mary Barber (1685–1755) and Mary Monck (1677–1715) and her contemporary Mary Alcock (1742–98). Another contemporary but of an oral Irish tradition was Máire Bhuí Ní Laoire, a poet from Inchigeelagh, County Cork.[30] *The Field Day Anthology of Irish Writing V* and the recently published *A History of Modern Irish*

Women's Literature reference Herbert's *Retrospections* but not her poetry. It seems that the ongoing restoration of women poets is like a river, where some things get lost in backwaters, later to be found, or not.

As a poet, and as a reader of poetry, I have enjoyed the range of themes across Herbert's work and her use of the language of the time. I have laughed, and heard others laugh, listening to her words. Herbert's writings have given me a deeper appreciation of the value of satire. Her poems are worthy of inclusion in the canon of poetry in Ireland. One hopes that the original poetry manuscript may be added to the material already available at Trinity College Dublin or presented to the Irish Poetry Archive at University College Dublin. Perhaps the final word should go to Dorothea Herbert: 'My Poems were shewn to all the Circle of our Friends in Dublin who honourd them with great Applauses, but I soon grew tired of trite Eulogiums.'[31]

Emily Lawless (1845–1913)

Seán Hewitt

To that Rare and Deep-Red Burnet-Moth only to be met with in the Burren

>Sparkle of red on an iron floor,
>In the fiercest teeth of this gale's wild roar,
>What has brought thee, oh speck of fire,
>Speaking of love and the heart's desire,
>   To a land so dead?
>
>Rocks gaunt and grim as the halls of Death,
>Sculptured and hewn by the wind's rough breath,
>Fortress-shaped, fantastic things,
>Reared for some turbulent race of Kings,
>   Kings long since dead.
>
>Wind-blown pools where no herbs grow,
>Streams lost and sunk in the depths below,
>Where scant flowers bloom, where few birds sing,
>Thou, *thou* fliest alone, thou fire-winged thing!
>   Small speck of red![1]

Emily Lawless (1845–1913) is now perhaps best remembered for her novels, though they are all (with the exception of *Grania* (1892) a proto-feminist tale set on the Aran Islands) out of print. Her poetry, however, was very popular, though her apparent reluctance to publish many of her verses without an introductory note explaining their historical and cultural provenance shows that she recognised just how particularly rooted they are in their Irish context. Offering readers supplementary information on the poems' references and settings, Lawless not only provided a scaffold for their interpretation, but also emphasised their Irishness.

Lawless was the fourth and eldest daughter of the third Lord Cloncurry and his wife Elizabeth Kirwan, who had an estate at Castle Hackett, County Galway. Lord Cloncurry's principal home was Lyons Castle, County Kildare, and it was between that large demesne and her mother's home at Castle Hackett that Emily Lawless grew up, taking full advantage of all opportunities for adventure and exploration. Lyons Castle, which was an historic residence full of artworks and boasting a large park, also had a ruined castle on its grounds, no doubt sparking the young Emily's sense of a Romantic and dramatic history. On her mother's side, Lawless' family boasted an eminent scientist, John Kirwan (1733–1812), and it was on their Castle Hackett estate that she developed her love for wild creatures and natural historical study.[2]

Lawless' poems can be found mainly in four published volumes, the privately printed *Atlantic Rhymes and Rhythms* (1898), the popular *With the Wild Geese* (1902), a small work produced for the benefit of 'some of the fishing people' of Galway, called *The Point of View: Some talks and disputations* (1909), and the posthumous *The Inalienable Heritage, and Other Poems* (1914), though *The Point of View* and *Atlantic Rhymes* are difficult to access even in Ireland. Padraic Fallon's 1965 edition of her *Poems* is a slender compendium, and his introduction makes a compelling case for Lawless' influence on W.B. Yeats. As Gerardine Meaney notes, Lawless is a writer 'notoriously difficult to categorise'.[3] A Unionist who was criticised by *The Nation* for looking down on the Irish peasantry from 'the pinnacle of her three-generation nobility', she also rejected calls for suffrage and did not take part in many of the public-facing cultural activities (such as the theatre movement) that made up the Irish Literary Revival.[4] However, with her cousin Horace Plunkett, Lawless took a keen interest in the Agricultural Cooperative Movement in Ireland, supported the 'United Irishwomen' and was a proud patriot.

The Point of View, as Lawless' subtitle suggests, is given over mainly to poems dealing with the author's personal philosophy, including a number of poems that stress the unity of all life, and the chain of evolution; however, the majority of Lawless' verses are lyrical or narrative in mode. Often, they have a note of melancholy, in which the reader hears the ebb and flow of the sea, the ghosts of emigrants, a country haunted by misrule and ecological destruction. But there are also moments of joy, often taking the form of rare plants and insects sighted in reverie and wonder. If the historical and Romantic tendencies of Lawless' poetry now appear old-fashioned, their ecological aspect – especially when they are placed in the context of her prolific work in botany, entomology and marine zoology – is fascinatingly modern. The skill with which Lawless weaves history, colonial heritage and nature study in the daring exclamations of 'To that Rare and Deep-Red Burnet-Moth' is indicative of the ways in which natural history was to her both a lens and a font of imagery.

'To that Rare and Deep-Red Burnet-Moth' is both symbolic and ecologically real; it is an image of revival and life in a landscape damaged by loss of biodiversity and in a historical context of colonial misrule. Lawless' stanza structure (AABBC), where the final rhyme only finds its completion in the following stanza, means that both the ecological and historical 'deaths' ('a land so dead' and 'Kings long since dead') are aurally regenerated by the 'small speck of red'. Likewise, the sparseness of the landscape is emphasised by a rhythmic disruption. Generally, the lines have four beats each, but, when we get to 'scant flowers bloom' and 'few birds sing', the stressed syllables disrupt the insistent rhythm and draw attention to themselves. Lawless' rapture in this poem is typical of her emphasis on wonder in the natural world. But her nature is never only symbolic: in 'To the Winged Psyche, Dying in a Garden', from *The Point of View*, Lawless pines to 'narrow my gaze to an insect's eye', seeking an ecological perspective that might grant access to 'that riddle of riddles', 'what it is to *be*'.[5]

Emily Lawless' first publication, in 1867, at the young age of twenty-one, was a contribution to *Entomologist's Monthly Magazine*, and she details in various essays her life as a natural historian. In *Traits and Confidences* (1898), she describes the insects and frogs that she let loose in her house and nursery as a girl, relates the primary importance of entomology to her young self (way above music or art or literature), and bemoans the fact that 'by no possible stretch of indulgence, would this Cuvier or Buffon in short frocks ever be entrusted with a gun'.[6] Later, she would quarrel with her hired cook, one Mrs O'Donnell, after Lawless filled pie dishes, frying pans, fish pans, stew pans and jam jars from the kitchen with all manner of creatures that she had dredged from the sea: 'every wriggling, writhing, prickly, slimy, glassy, brittle-rayed, tentacle-armed, spine-protected, or weed-resembling creature that their depths afforded'.[7] The bog, and the Burren, were for her places of a gothic and Romantic atmosphere: 'a region full of bewitching suggestions, of haunting mystery, of dim, untravelled possibilities. A region from which no amount of after-familiarity ever entirely succeeded in stripping away the glamour.'[8] This endless fascination, and the way in which these wild landscapes left Lawless (despite her expertise) with no sense of 'after-familiarity', is central to the success of her poems, many of which are addressed from, or even to, these places.

An accomplished scientific woman, Lawless approached the natural world as real, physical and material, rejecting the dominant mode of *fin-de-siècle* literature, which tended to refer to nature largely in symbolic terms. As Heidi Hansson, Lawless' most attentive critic, notes, 'Lawless was a Darwinist, and on one level her nature poetry is the literary corollary of her scientific interests.'[9] In fact, her 'smallest of notes', which 'hazarded' (in a self-effacing tone) the 'mere hypothesis' that burnet moths had roles as pollinators in the Burren, was picked up on by Charles Darwin, who initiated correspondence with her and encouraged her to submit her findings for publication in the journal *Nature*.[10] This did not, however, temper critics of her novels in questioning her ability to accurately explore scientific themes. Before she began to set her novels in Ireland, Lawless wrote *A Chelsea Householder* (1882), in which the main character enjoys mothing, and later wrote *Major Lawrence, F.L.S.* (1887), in which the protagonist is (as the letters after his name suggest) a Fellow of the Linnaean Society. In a review of the latter, the *Pall Mall Gazette* questioned Lawless' authority, suggesting that 'When a lady undertakes to make her hero a man who is a rising Indian officer and a naturalist, the wary reviewer looks out for a chance of setting his authoress right on several points connected with soldiering and science … Her application of proper names in science is not always quite happy, particularly when they are given to creatures of the sea.'[11] Such a wary reception reflects the added hostility that Lawless was subject to as a woman scientist, though (unsurprisingly) the reviewer was unable to suggest any failings in either her military or scientific knowledge.

In her essays, her novel *The Book of Gilly: Four months out of a life* (1906) and poems such as 'To a Tuft of White Bog-Cotton, Growing in the Tyrol', Lawless uses her naturalist knowledge to emphasise a sort of uncanny enchantment. If the general narrative has been that scientific progress has led to a disenchanted secularism, most pithily summed up in the twentieth century by Horkheimer and Adorno in the idea that 'the project of Enlightenment was the disenchantment of the world', then Lawless offers a counter-narrative, one in which scientific knowledge is allied to an increasing sense of wonder and an awareness of the numinous.[12] Whereas her contemporary W.B. Yeats, as part of the Celtic Twilight movement, had criticised 'that "externality" which a time of scientific and political thought has brought into literature', in Lawless' work we find a close focus on the material, on the 'external', only fitting for a poet who was also a keen scientific observer.[13] In her preface to the poems collected posthumously in *The Inalienable Heritage*, Edith Sichel noted that Lawless, in her poetry, demonstrated 'a twofold relation to Nature':

> There was the external aspect; the physical tie by which she became part of the earth and its teeming life; which made her in younger years adore movement – the rush through the air on a horse, the cleaving of the waves as she swam; which made her also a passionate naturalist, a moth-hunter who knew under which tree-root the grey moths lived, or where to stop the boat upon the sea and dredge for creatures unknown even to the fishermen.[14]

There was also an 'inward relation to Nature', the 'wisdom and comfort she drew from it', its connection with history and with the intellect. Sichel summarised Lawless' attractions as being to 'the visible pagan nature of the senses, and the search into Nature which means science, and the search concerning Nature which means thought'. Drawing attention to physical nature, and searching into nature through science, is fundamental to the thought of her poetry.

Introducing us to the landscape of the Burren, where she undertook much work as a naturalist, Lawless writes of a place with

> No hint, no touch of grim utility,
> Earth's busy functions sleep abandoned here;
> Corn-grower, root-grower, nourisher of grain,
> All are forgotten; nakedly austere.
> Nought but herself, her inmost core, survives,
> Stripped to the elements; enskyed and pure,
> Remote, and stern, and coldly sanctified;
> Pale as a ghost, yet rock-fast to endure.[15]

Nature stripped of utility, existing for 'Nought but herself', is central to Lawless' vision, which draws our attention to ecosystems, environmental relations and environmental destruction. Though there may be more than a touch of privilege in valuing a natural world that exists outside of 'utility' (a position that is much easier to take if one does not rely on the land for one's livelihood), Lawless here brings the focus back to a nature that is material, physical and not solely a literary device for the expression of the speaker's mind, or a symbol of a metaphysical idea.

That does not, of course, mean that Lawless refuses to use nature as a way of thinking. In her poem addressed 'To a Tuft of White Bog-Cotton, Growing in the Tyrol', written in 1886, the appearance of this familiar plant in Austria becomes a way of discussing emigration, exile and belonging.

> And is it *thou*? small playmate of the fens,
> Child of damp haunts, and pallid sea-borne fogs,
> Light flutterer over dank and oozy glens,
> White-tufted, starry friend of Irish bogs!
> What dost *thou*, tossed upon this mountain here,
> Flaunting thy white crest in this alien air?
> ...
> Shall brawling torrent, lost to every beam,
> White with its spoil of glacier and moraine,
> Serve thee as well as some slow-moving stream,
> Brown with its brimming toll of recent rain.[16]

Likewise, as in her historical novel *Maelcho* (1894), in which deforestation is linked symbolically with the defeat of the Irish in the Desmond rebellion in the late sixteenth century, Lawless' poem, the 'Dirge of the Munster Forest, 1581', explores the rich connections between national history and natural history. Speaking unusually in the voice of the forest itself, Lawless focuses on the felling of the woodland and its impact on the ecosystem. Referring to the other plants and animals that call the woodland home, the forest laments 'For shortly I must die as they have died / And lo! My doom stands yoked and linked with theirs'.[17]

Lawless' work has yet to gain its due critical attention, and even the major studies of the relationship between science and literature, and between evolutionism and literature more particularly, have failed to discuss her, despite the obvious interest her works have for such inquiries. Even more pressingly, ecocritical studies (which examine the relationship between nature and the human in literature) have rarely featured her name. Addressing the tuft of bog-cotton in her poem, Lawless coaxes it to 'uplift thy modest crown, / Nor here alone exalt that snow-white head': 'For time is with us. Time who gilds the wheat, / And rounds the year, and stays the raving blast.' In this moment of new and urgent interest in environmental studies, when ecological visions that link history and humanity without pushing aside the autonomy of the natural world are needed more than ever, it is fitting for us to turn back to the works of Emily Lawless. Her time is with us.

Charlotte Grace O'Brien (1845–1909)

Nora Moroney

GLADSTONE (1884)

His Confession that he did not Recognise the Crisis 1879, 1880.

>He did not know — he did not heed this thing
>That all our land was moistened with the tears
>Of blue-lipped, haggard women, mad with fears
>For the poor babes that at their bare breasts cling.
>He did not know — he did not hear the ring
>Of words that yet re-echo in our ears.
>Nor see the brand that famine fever sears
>On human hearts crouched low beneath its wing.
>And yet he dare to rule us, dare to thrust
>Those very men who led us in full light
>Into strong prison-bands, nor let the trust
>And love of their own nation give respite
>Ah, me! how foolish are the very wise,
>How weak the good, how blind the clearest eyes![1]

GLADSTONE (1886)

>Once more thou art our friend, and we are glad.
>Once more thy wavering needle points to truth;
>True in thine age as erst in thy strong youth!
>Thou speakest, and straightway fierce thoughts, wild and bad,
>Flee to dark realms, and where were musings mad,
>Are love's revenge, warm hearts and Christian ruth;

Yea, and shall be, for now in very sooth
Shall they rewrite our page, blood-stained and sad.
Thou drawest England, too, with strenuous bands:
And not in vain, for we who hold this thing.
As wrought of God, and safe within His hands.
Hear the Divine voice through the human ring.
And pray that He who gave thee this great grace
In freedom, trust, and peace will crown thy race.[2]

The writer and activist Charlotte Grace O'Brien was born in Cahirmoyle, County Limerick, the youngest daughter of the nationalist William Smith O'Brien, a prominent member of Daniel O'Connell's Repeal movement. O'Brien was one of seven children who were raised by their mother during William Smith's imprisonment and exile in Tasmania following the Young Ireland uprising of 1848. She was educated at home by tutors, and, following her mother's death in 1861, spent her time between the family house in Cahirmoyle and accompanying her father on his travels until his death in 1864. She spent much of her later life in her house near Foynes, County Limerick, where she lived alone, beset by periods of ill-health and her lifelong struggle with deafness.

O'Brien first found her footing as an author with the 1870 novel *Dominick's Trials*. It was not, however, until the publication of her second novel, *Light and Shade*, in 1878 that she became widely recognised for her literary work. *Light and Shade* dealt with the Fenian uprising of 1867, and although it received mixed reviews in the British press it garnered praise for its realistic depiction of Irish nationalist fighters – many of whom O'Brien would have known (and sympathised with) through her father's networks. She went on to publish three poetry collections and one play and achieved a considerable degree of success with her journalistic writings, which appeared in titles such as *The Nation* and *Dublin University Review*. Many of these articles focused on what was to become her abiding concern from 1880 onwards: namely, the issue of Irish emigration and conditions facing those travelling to America. Her advocacy for the needs of poor Irish emigrants, particularly single women, found its most forceful expression in a *Pall Mall Gazette* article of May 1881 entitled 'Horrors of an Emigrant Ship'. In it, she condemned the lamentable state of steerage conditions and problems of overcrowding on the White Star Shipping Line, describing vividly 'the evidences of fresh sorrow on almost every face ... with a hopeless submission to daily want'.[3] The outcry caused by the article prompted the British government to conduct a review of steamship companies and, although the report eventually found against O'Brien, it won her a number of important political admirers, including Charles Stewart Parnell and T.P. O'Connor. Alongside similar high-profile pieces published in British monthly literary magazine the *Nineteenth Century*, this article highlighted O'Brien's continued ability to utilise various sectors of the press and media outlets in her activism.

She is perhaps best known for this work, as well as her continuing role in raising awareness of emigrant conditions both prior and subsequent to the transatlantic voyage. In 1881 she established a lodging house for young women in Queenstown, aimed at providing some measure of comfort prior to departure. A series of lectures across the United States in the years following enabled her to further publicise her reforming agenda, and brought her into contact with a number of early members of the Gaelic League, as well as supporters of both the Young Ireland and Fenian movements. The contemporary view of her was summed up by M.C. Keogh in an obituary in the *Irish Monthly*: in a discussion of O'Brien's poetry, Keogh described her as 'good to the heart's core; pious, loyal, unselfish, and sincere. A foe to conventionality, careless in dress, awkward in movement, unmethodical, eccentric – and thoroughly lovable.'[4]

O'Brien's political leanings have tended to come under scrutiny in light of her father's involvement with nationalist organisations in the mid-nineteenth century. Her development of a similar viewpoint in her writings was, however, due less to family loyalty than to her own experiences and observations. Despite being raised as a member of the land-owning aristocracy, O'Brien sided firmly with the plight of the tenants during the Land War. She also opposed many of the British government's policies aimed at quashing non-parliamentary agitation and assisting emigration throughout the 1880s. She remained a supporter of Parnell, and became a firm advocate of the work of the Gaelic League. Sometime around 1887 she converted to Catholicism, perhaps influenced by the nationalist-Catholic milieu in which she was most comfortable.

Her poetry, as well as her prose work, was shaped by these various political currents across Britain and Ireland. The Gladstone sonnets which preface this essay are emblematic of O'Brien's responsiveness to fluctuations in the public sphere. She wrote four of them in total, between 1869 and 1886, a grouping often referred to as her 'Gladstone quartet'. Her changing view of the statesman can be mapped on to his vicissitudes in these years over the question of Irish Home Rule. In particular, her political sympathies attach themselves to him as a symbolic – and indeed quite real – hero of the constitutional nationalist movement in Westminster. The earlier two poems, of 1869 and 1877, are hopeful in tone, proclaiming a deep and loving relationship between him and the Irish people and pledging faith in the 'bonds of trust' that underpin the Irish 'welcome' of his policies. They were also written in the midst of the Land War upheavals and the disestablishment of the Irish Anglican church in 1869. The two poems featured above, however, are more strikingly personal. They enact a drama of betrayal and redemption, speaking to the poet's real-time and visceral reaction regarding developments in the Irish nationalist cause and amounting to an almost Yeatsian admittance of previous error. For Charlotte Grace O'Brien, at least, it could be claimed that Gladstone too has 'been changed in his turn'.[5]

For both pieces, an awareness of context is crucial. The year 1884 was one where food scarcity and destitution continued to affect the Irish rural population, and the failure of successive British governments' policies led to a growing frustration among many writers and politicians. O'Brien's poem directly references the famines of the early decade, the 'blue-lipped, haggard women, mad with fears' an emotive appeal to the sympathies of her audience, both British and Irish. The stark imagery of the 'poor babes' that cling to the 'bare breasts' similarly invites readers to imagine the plight of Ireland's young, as well as conjuring up broader allusions to the dependent relationship between Britain and Ireland during the nineteenth century. It was a trope with which O'Brien would not have been unfamiliar – she was born in 1845, at the outset of the Great Famine, and though somewhat cushioned from the worst of it on her family's estate, she remained painfully aware of its effects on the Irish peasantry throughout her life.[6] The recurrence of famine imagery in this poem – the 'brand that … sears / On human hearts crouched low beneath its wing' – therefore implicates Gladstone in some of the darkest events of Ireland's recent history. As well as this historical resonance, moreover, the poem also references the Land War and agrarian unrest of 1879 and 1880. It points to the growing divergence between popular opinion and Gladstone's policies in wilfully opposing Irish reform, particularly the treatment of 'those men' (presumably leaders such as Michael Davitt) whose 'prison-bands' only yoked them more firmly to the public imagination and admiration.

But if O'Brien was both saddened and angered by Gladstone's actions in 1884 – decrying 'how foolish are the very wise' – she displays a remarkably more positive attitude by 1886. The third-person descriptions of the earlier sonnet have morphed into a more direct second-person address in the latter. Contrast the opening lines, for example: 'He did not know – he did not heed' has by 1886 softened to, 'Once more thou art our friend', the 'blind' actions transformed into 'strong' and 'true' leadership. Indeed, the depiction of senses is a striking feature of the two poems, and an important signifier for a poet who was deaf for most of her life. The personal redemption of Gladstone in this second poem is linked, however, to more profound matters. The call to 'rewrite our page, blood-stained and sad' reflects the nationalist legacy and historical narrativisation that was to gain momentum in the years leading up to 1900. Pre-empting the literary machinations of the Gaelic Revivalists, the poem also employs language replete with religious overtones: Gladstone, in a quasi-saviour role, speaks with a 'Divine voice' and holds Ireland's fate 'safe within His hands'. Irish republicanism as an overtly religious ideology is not, of course, a strictly novel idea – its apotheosis was to be reached in the stark rhetoric of the 1916 proclamation – but what is notable here is the context in which the poem was composed.[7] O'Brien, as mentioned above, converted from Protestantism to Catholicism in 1887, a decision that undoubtedly influenced her choice of references in this poem. The last two lines give voice to this forceful religious conviction, where the people of Ireland 'pray that He who gave thee this great grace / In freedom, trust, and peace will crown thy race'.

It is tempting, therefore, to see a relationship here between two individual moral journeys – that of O'Brien's imminent religious conversion and the much more public 'conversion' of Gladstone in 1886. The politician's decision in that year to back Home Rule for Ireland was perhaps one of the most important turning points for Irish nationalism in the second half of the nineteenth century, and indeed for British Liberalism as a whole. O'Brien was writing not only at a watershed in terms of Anglo-Irish relations but also at a time of vastly increased publicity for both proponents and opponents of Irish nationalism. As Eugenio Biagini reminds us, the 'claim that neither [Britain] nor the politicians wanted to know about Ireland in 1885 is hardly reconcilable ... with the attention devoted to the Irish question by journalists, political economists and land reformers'.[8] Indeed, it is no overstatement to say that Irish history (in its constitutional guise) happened in Britain during these years, and to a large degree happened in the journals of the British liberal establishment. The crises of land ownership and tenant rights in the early 1880s brought to public attention the injustices and political neglect that laid the groundwork for Gladstone's adoption of Home Rule as a cause. It is a meaningful reflection of O'Brien's political alertness, then, that she chooses to focus in these sonnets on two critical junctures in both Gladstone's and Ireland's historical trajectory. The 'wavering needle' of Gladstone's politics not only reminds readers of her previous poetry on the subject, but also of the historical contingency that had marked British political attitudes towards Ireland throughout the nineteenth century.

It is notable also that O'Brien chose the sonnet form for these poems. It follows her preference for what Stephen Gwynn would call a 'rigid convention', or the formal style of poetry that predominates her three collections. In Gwynn's biography of his aunt, he observes that 'the looser lyrics have their charm and their grace, but I find her distinctive and individual character only in the sonnets'.[9] Indeed, she engaged with the style on a formal level elsewhere. In another poem, published in the *Irish Monthly* magazine in November 1887 (as part of a piece entitled 'Two Sonnets About Sonnets'), O'Brien portrays the sonnet as a 'determinate sweet form of speech'.[10] With reference to the inward 'aching senses' (it should be noted that an earlier poem on 'Deafness' also took sonnet form), she describes how

> the sonnet then across our brain's mad wars
> Draws near to us as some soft-handed leech,
> Giving our thoughts deliverance, setting each
> Free and alone, self-centred as the stars.

These Gladstone poems also display a kind of elevated, archaic language that gestures to O'Brien's literary upbringing – in other poems from *Lyrics*, she acknowledges her debt to William Shakespeare, Friedrich Schiller and other canonical forebears. This avowed cultural legacy and allegiance to the 'great man' view of literature (as, indeed, of politics) positions her firmly in the high-Victorian tradition, as do her other writings that affirm a belief in the righteousness and moral good standing of art and politics in the public sphere.[11]

Yet, in other ways O'Brien was self-consciously modern in her outlook. Her publishing strategies point to a shrewd awareness of the late-nineteenth-century literary market and, especially, an awareness of genre and transnational reach and how they interact. It is perhaps significant that her poetry, much of which was either about Ireland or overtly nationalist in nature, was mostly published in Ireland, while her prose and essay pieces, which dealt with broader issues of poverty and emigration, were largely aimed at British and American audiences. The *Irish Monthly*, in particular, was an important vehicle for her early poetry, with its editor Matthew Russell championing O'Brien's sonnets and 'true Irish heart'.[12] Although her 1880 collection *A Tale of Venice: A Drama, & Lyrics* was something of a non-starter for her literary career, she had rather more success with the 1888 collection *Lyrics*, which reprinted many of the previous book's poems – and included the two Gladstone sonnets reproduced here.

She was also a writer who used her relative social mobility among the Irish upper classes to her advantage. Although few of her own papers remain, Gwynn quotes a number of her letters to Douglas Hyde, Aubrey de Vere and others in which she comments on literary matters and offers publishing advice.[13] In this way, she sustained networks that were crucial to her public image abroad, although how successful this was is a matter of uncertainty. Gwynn claims that a transatlantic appeal was evident in how 'she entertained, as all Irish writers do, the delusive dream of a sale in America. [John] Boyle O'Reilly [the nationalist

Irish-American author], writing to her in February 1887, dispelled that illusion: – "We Irish in America are a great power for work and politics … but we do not buy books. My books are sold, but not to my own people."[14] It was, ultimately, O'Brien's activism regarding emigrant rights and Irish poor houses that would cement her connection with the United States, while her literary efforts were most successful in the British and Irish press.

But the interaction of poetry and polemics within her work was also reflective of the 'generic promiscuity' that characterised many Irish writers at the time. As one study has put it, the late Victorians did not necessarily regard literariness and polemic as mutually exclusive, and frequently moved between the two in the same piece.[15] Irish writers and politicians, particularly those who aimed to reach an audience beyond Ireland, were remarkably attuned to the cultural capital that a range of styles could accrue. Figures such as Justin McCarthy, Horace Plunkett and George Moore contributed essays, books and pamphlets dedicated to politics on Ireland during these years – but also published pot-boiler novels (in the case of Justin McCarthy), poetry and literary criticism. It is perhaps unsurprising, then, that Gladstone was such a presiding subject for O'Brien's political poetry. The British Liberal statesman, indeed, was a central and recurring figure in the literary and political discourse on both sides of the Irish Sea for the last two decades of the century, not least for the writers mentioned above. His imaginative significance for the currents of popular Liberalism made itself felt in journals such as the *Nineteenth Century* and *Fortnightly Review* (where he often engaged in debates with intellectuals and political writers of all stripes) but also in the literary response to current affairs. Matthew Campbell has discussed Algernon Swinburne's outraged reaction to Gladstone's 1886 actions in his poem 'Commonweal', 'not so much a party political broadside as one based in a single constitutional issue, the Irish Question'.[16] G.K. Chesterton, too, was to pay tribute to Gladstone in poetic form following the politician's death, describing him in *The Speaker* as 'a giant-bearing star'.[17] O'Brien was therefore reflecting a trend in late-Victorian intellectual life of interweaving political ideals, cultural representation and the continued worship of the 'great man'.

Yet, however culturally relevant and critical Charlotte Grace O'Brien was in her own time, she remains mostly unremembered over a century later. This may be because of her awkward positioning in literary histories: neither a particularly successful novelist nor poet, much of her success lay in polemical periodical contributions that do not always fit well in accounts of women's writing. Like her contemporaries Emily Lawless and Alice Stopford Green, she moved across genres and subjects that were often marked by 'hybridity', but maintained a sceptical distance from the burgeoning cultural nationalist movement in the last decades of the century.[18] (It is worth noting too that, like Lawless, much of her later life was spent out of the public eye and largely dedicated to gardening and botany, about which she published a number of articles and which remained abiding passions.)[19] These Gladstone sonnets, with their debt to Victorian literary form and language, speak to a certain time in the poet's life and political preoccupations, but also to a specific point in time and nationalist politics. In this way, they are characteristic of O'Brien's unique poetic outlook: one that was rooted in an ideological conviction and underpinned by a sharp and ultimately accurate reading of the 'wavering needle' of a nation's pulse.

Dora Sigerson Shorter (1866–1918)

Jack Quin

The Patchwork Quilt

Bring to me white roses, roses, pinks, and lavender,
Sweet stock and gillyflowers, poppies mauve and red,
Bee-flowers and mignonette, with blue forget-me-not –
I would make a coverlet for my narrow bed.

Bring me no silken cloth, velvet sheen or satin shine,
Gossamer of woven lace, gold and silver thread,
Purple deep and dove, and grey, through my idle fingers fall,
Bidding me in patient hours make a patchwork spread.

Since I must go forth alone, far beyond the roof-tree's shade,
Out into the open soon lonely there to lie,
What want I of silken cloth woven by the hands of men?
Time would soon despoil me there as he passed me by.

Bring to me white roses then, roses, pinks, and lavender,
Sweet stock and gillyflowers, poppies gold and red,
Bee-flowers and mignonette and blue forget-me-not,
So I have a coverlet for my narrow bed.[1]

The poet, artist and journalist Dora Sigerson Shorter (1866–1918) remains a tragic and enigmatic figure in accounts of the Irish Literary Revival. Sigerson Shorter was born in Dublin, the daughter of the Gaelic scholar George Sigerson. She befriended several key revivalist writers during her time in Dublin, including W.B. Yeats, Rose Kavanagh and Katharine Tynan. She moved to London when she married the literary editor Clement K. Shorter in July 1896. After the Easter Rising and the execution of the Rising leaders, she suffered from depression and chronic physical illness until her death, which several contemporaries attributed to her grief. Tynan wrote that she died of a broken heart, while Edward Thompson concluded that 'she remained passionately with Ireland', despite living in London through much of the Second World War, 'and the events of Easter, 1916, were an agony of which she died on January 6, 1918'.[2] Sigerson Shorter penned a series of political elegies and self-elegies reflecting on the Rising and its aftermath in her aptly named collection *The Sad Years* (1918). Her quatrain poem 'The Patchwork Quilt' from this collection courts domestic imagery but quickly dispenses with the needle and thread to contemplate a darker vein of arboreal and burial imagery.

Sigerson Shorter's imaginary botanical weave draws comparison with W.B. Yeats' dreamlike embroideries in 'He Wishes for the Cloths of Heaven', while subverting many of the old Romantic tropes. In Yeats' poem, the use of repetitions in place of end-rhymes loops the poem back circuitously into the same patchwork of words and images: cloths / light / cloths / half-light / feet / dreams / feet / dreams.[3] Similarly, Sigerson Shorter's first and final quatrains are almost identical, drawing together the same white roses, 'roses, pinks and lavender', bee-flowers, mignonette and blue forget-me-not. 'The Patchwork Quilt' also mirrors the internal rhyming of Yeats' eight-line poem with its own intricate internal rhymes threaded through: silken / woven and mignonette / coverlet each recur twice in the sixteen-line poem. However, there is a rejection of man-made materials in the second and third quatrains of Sigerson Shorter's poem: 'Bring me no silken cloth, velvet sheen or satin shine, / Gossamer of woven lace, gold and silver thread'. Yeats' heavenly embroidered cloths, '[e]nwrought with golden and silver light', are an unsuitable material for the speaker of Sigerson Shorter's poem, who asks, 'What want I of silken cloth woven by the hands of men?' In an early poem by Sigerson Shorter, 'A Vagrant Heart', the speaker resists several gendered vocations, including the expectation that she must settle down and sew: 'Thrust a cloth between her fingers, and tell her she must sew; / Must join in empty chatter, and calculate with straws – / For the weighing of our neighbour – for the sake of social laws.'[4] In 'The Patchwork Quilt', the speaker – alone and out in the open – requests a more natural, botanical quilt for her 'narrow bed'.

The speaker of modern elegies often assumes the role of funeral director, as Jahan Ramazani states in *Poetry of Mourning* (1994), by choreographing the procession, memorial service or burial.[5] In Sigerson Shorter's 'The Patchwork Quilt', the speaker goes so far as to assume the roles of undertaker and corpse, crafting her own burial surrounded by flowers. Matthew Campbell has noted that Sigerson Shorter's last poems transport the reader 'from the slightly safer surrounds of the Victorian and Edwardian domestic elegy' into 'something much more violently internalised, something that leaps across from living to dead'.[6] Among Sigerson Shorter's floral inventory the pun on 'blue forget-me-not' alludes to her wider self-elegising streak in poems from *The Sad Years*, while the choice of flower might stem from Christina Rossetti's 'A bed of Forget-Me-Nots', in which the speaker ponders what might endure when love is 'so prone to change and rot'.[7] In 'The Patchwork Quilt', the narrow bed outdoors implies a grave and the floral 'coverlet' becomes a means of self-burial. Another Yeats poem, 'To A Shade', similarly appealed to the ghost of Charles Stewart Parnell to return to his grave and sleep through the stormy present: 'And gather the Glasnevin coverlet / About your head till the dust stops your ear'.[8] In an earlier Sigerson Shorter poem, 'Dark is the Tomb' from *Love of Ireland* (1916), she outlined her preferred site of burial, Glasnevin Cemetery in her native Dublin, 'near where O'Leary lies'.[9]

Beyond the threaded and embedded allusions to Yeats in 'The Patchwork Quilt', several of Sigerson Shorter's more explicit political elegies for the Easter Rising appeared in tandem with, or even preceding, Yeats' 1916 poems. Sigerson Shorter's 'Sixteen Dead Men' was published two years before Yeats' poem of the same name and both poems end, as Campbell has noted, by naming a longer litany of executed Irish patriots in similarly patterned rhymes: Patrick Sarsfield, Theobald Wolfe Tone and Robert Emmet in Sigerson Shorter's closing quatrain; Lord Edward Fitzgerald and Wolfe Tone in Yeats' final stanza.[10] In a six-stanza poem, 'The Choice', Sigerson Shorter reflected on Roger Casement through his many, seemingly contradictory, facets in life: 'Consul Casement', 'Sir Roger Casement', 'Irish Casement', 'doomèd Casement'.[11] These later collections, and even individual poems, waver between elegy and self-elegy. The final poems in *The Sad Years*, for example, cross the threshold into death. 'The Black Horseman' begins with the speaker lifted from her 'bed of sickness' by the eponymous black horseman. The horseman asks if she fears him or the journey they will embark upon, to which she replies, 'Why should I fear when there are friends before me?'[12] Thomas MacDonagh and Roger Casement might be numbered among those departed friends.

If *The Sad Years* reflects a grief-stricken and chronically ill Sigerson Shorter in the aftermath of the Easter Rising, the poet nevertheless remained an enigmatic voice in modern Irish poetry. According to her husband Clement Shorter, one of Sigerson Shorter's favourite phrases was that '[t]he writers of books should be heard and not seen' – a witty inversion of the oppressive proverb that women or children should be seen, but not heard.[13] Sigerson Shorter seemed to emphasise the speaking voice over the persona or personality of the author. She instructed her husband to destroy all her letters before her death in January 1918. But her ear for poetry and crafting of a distinctive Irish voice was heard, acclaimed and recited in public by her contemporaries. John Masefield recalled that Yeats recited Sigerson Shorter's 'Cean Duv Deelish' to a rapt London audience in Woburn Buildings on 5 November 1900:

> Cean duv deelish, I cry to thee
> Beyond the world, beneath the sea,
> > Thou being dead.
> Where hast thou hidden from the beat
> Of crushing hoofs and tearing feet
> > Thy dear black head?[14]

According to Masefield: 'His reading was unlike that of any other man. He stressed the rhythm until it almost became a chant; he went with speed, marking every beat and dwelling on his vowels. That wavering ecstatic song, then heard by me for the first time, was to remain with me for years.'[15] Yeats included 'Can Doov Deelish' in his anthology *A Book of Irish Verse*, remarking that Sigerson Shorter had 'put old Irish stories into vigorous modern rhyme'.[16]

Thomas MacDonagh similarly described her wavering, chant-like music in verse as exemplary of the 'Irish mode' in poetry. MacDonagh dedicated his seminal study *Literature in Ireland* (1916) to her father George Sigerson and named Dora Sigerson in a list of modern poets writing English-language poetry in an Irish mode, which included Seumas O'Sullivan, James Stephens, Emily Lawless and Alice Furlong.[17] According to MacDonagh, Sigerson Shorter had already 'written some of the best modern ballads, poems very distinctively Irish. Her work has a breath of romance all its own, that "breath of flowers" that she feared to leave behind in Ireland. Beautiful lyrics of hers, such as *Ireland* and *Can Doov Deelish*, may be read in the anthologies.'[18] The 'breath of flowers' features in the final stanza of Sigerson Shorter's wistful apostrophe to 'Ireland', in which the distant and deracinated speaker reflects:

> I have left you behind
> In the path of the past,
> With the white breath of flowers
> With the best of God's hours,
> I have left you at last.[19]

Her poem constructs alliterative and assonantal rhythms that depart from sense, in keeping with MacDonagh's Irish mode. That romance of Ireland is still heard in the cadences of her later poems, and indeed, in a short eight-line poem, 'Nora', the speaker is transported back to Ireland when she hears the lyrical brogue of a young Irish girl in an English village: 'The pretty notes, the accent ever dear, / Shy as the wind soft singing from the South! / I, hungry, kissed the brogue upon her mouth.'[20]

Sigerson Shorter's poem in memory of Thomas MacDonagh from *The Tricolour*, 'They Did Not See Thy Face', invokes the *Róisín Dubh* tradition, connecting MacDonagh's death to a history of heroic sacrifice in order to see the face of Kathleen.[21] In 1917, a version of Sigerson Shorter's poem was illustrated by Constance Markievicz with a watercolour drawing while she was incarcerated in Aylesbury Prison. Below the calligraphed poem, Markievicz depicted an angelic Kathleen Ni Houlihan bending over a dead volunteer and placing a hand upon his heart, in a pose that was visually similar to a *pietà*.[22] The illustration reflected the recurring image of Kathleen at the end of each quatrain: 'They left for thee their earthly loves, these heroes of thy race, / And died, as all must die, Kathleen, who once have seen thy face.'[23] The profits from Sigerson Shorter's last collection of poems, *The Tricolour*, were donated by Clement Shorter to pay for a *pietà*-style memorial to the 'sixteen dead men' of the 1916 Rising. The memorial in Glasnevin depicts a dying volunteer, modelled on Patrick Pearse, held by Kathleen Ni Houlihan. The Sigerson Shorter memorial was an appropriate tribute to the poet, and not just the 1916 leaders, as her friend Katharine Tynan recalled some of Sigerson Shorter's happiest early years were spent living in Clare Street, Dublin, where she experimented with painting and sculpture as well as poetry: 'She was always "making" in one way or another. When I arrived at Clare Street I sometimes met her coming upstairs from a mysterious atelier in the underground regions, wearing an overall from head to foot, the clay of her sculpture sticking to her fingers, her eyes with vision in them.'[24]

Lola Ridge (1873–1941)

Tara McEvoy

from **The Ghetto**

Nights, she reads
Those books that have most unset thought,
New-poured and malleable,
To which her thought
Leaps fusing at white heat,
Or spits her fire out in some dim manger of a hall,
Or at a protest meeting on the Square,
Her lit eyes kindling the mob …
Or dances madly at a festival.
Each dawn finds her a little whiter,
Though up and keyed to the long day,
Alert, yet weary … like a bird
That all night long has beat about a light.[1]

As a poet, painter, editor and activist, Lola Ridge (née Rose Emily Ridge) was a figure of great cultural significance during the early decades of the twentieth century. Born in Dublin in 1873, Ridge immigrated to Australia with her mother four years later, and spent her adolescence in New Zealand in the wake of the country's gold rush, before returning to Sydney in 1903 to take classes in painting at the Académie Julienne, and music at Trinity College (New South Wales). In 1907, she set sail for the United States of America, where she lived briefly in San Francisco before relocating to New York. She would remain resident in the city until her death in 1941. The lines excerpted above from perhaps her most well-known poem, 'The Ghetto', describe one of its primary characters (Sadie, the protagonist's roommate), but they also reflect something of Ridge herself: they evoke her irrepressible energy, her intellectual curiosity and her political resolve. Indeed, the books she later produced would themselves have the power to 'unset thought' with their anarchist, feminist agendas.

A caveat: at first glance, Ridge might seem to figure oddly in any narrative about Irish poetry. Can we claim her as an Irish poet, given the peripatetic nature of a life divided between the country of her birth (from which she emigrated as a child), New Zealand, Australia and the United States? Ridge might be more accurately thought of as a transnational writer, and certainly her poetry bears no obvious resemblance to the work being produced by her Irish contemporaries during the country's 'literary revival', with its avowedly nationalist agenda. Instead, Ridge's is a poetry that testifies to the experiences of the immigrant, to the multiculturalism of the United States at the *fin de siècle*, themes addressed most explicitly in her debut full-length collection, *The Ghetto and Other Poems* (1918). Nonetheless, 'Irish literature' is not, and never has been, a monolithic entity; one has only to consider the case of Samuel Beckett, who wrote many of his most influential works in French, to realise the folly of reductive categorisation. Insofar as the story of Ireland is bound up with the stories of its diaspora, to exclude Ridge in considerations of modern Irish poetry is to make a crucial omission.

If Ridge's migrations render problematic the attempt to consider her work in the context of any one national canon, then certain other factors of her biography have compounded her critical erasure, her work having been largely undiscussed and unanthologised until the twenty-first century. In his introduction to the recent *Collected Early Works of Lola Ridge* (To the Many), Daniel Tobin cites among them the onset of 'World War II, the Cold War, the advent of McCarthyism, all [of which] would make a poet of Ridge's staunchly leftist beliefs anathema', along with the turn towards formalism in the American poetry of the 1940s and 1950s as experimental writing fell out of favour.[2] Ridge herself was keenly attuned to the ways in which sexism, too, might inform a poet's reception and reputation; in the seminal essay 'Woman and the Creative Will', first delivered as a lecture in 1919, she poses the question: '[F]or how many centuries of silent women of all the world has Sappho's slender song sufficed?'[3]

Given her strident critique of state apparatuses, as well as the challenges she presented to the culturally dominant masculine construction of the figure of The Poet, Ridge's own silencing might come as little surprise. In her incisive book *Living a Feminist Life*, Sara Ahmed neatly delineates how the act of silencing is inflicted on those who call our attention to societal ills: 'When you expose a problem', she writes, 'you pose a problem'.[4] As suggested by the titles of her collections – *The Ghetto and Other Poems*, *Sun-Up* (1920), *Red Flag* (1927), *Firehead* (1929), *Dance of Fire* (1935) – a thematic dichotomy pervades Ridge's work: between, on one hand, the practical and political; on the other, the spiritual and numinous. I wish to focus here on the political valence of her work as, in large part, her reputation hinges on her more overtly radical poetry, on her project of bearing witness to 'problems'.

Consider this statement, which encapsulates the writer's views on what constitutes subject matter appropriate to her poetry: 'Let anything that burns you come out whether it be propaganda or not ... I write about something that I feel intensely.'[5] As the reference to propaganda suggests, more often than not Ridge felt intensely compelled to write about her political milieu, about the injustices she perceived in her society. She had been born to an aristocratic family in Dublin, but in New Zealand had lived in poverty; in New York, too, she struggled to make a living, and over the course of her lifetime developed an acute class consciousness. In America, the friendship Ridge developed with anarchist writer and campaigner Emma Goldman was to prove critical in the development of her politics. They collaborated artistically; Ridge illustrated, for example, the cover of Goldman's *Patriotism: A menace to liberty* (1908). As Ridge's biographer, Terese Svoboda notes, 'Ridge had arrived in America with hope, then measured it against the strictures of class and money ... The poor – and Ridge was one of them – lived poorly, often in situations worse than those they left behind ... Ridge was ripe for Goldman's influence.'[6]

In her seminal essay, 'Anarchism: What it really stands for', Goldman characterises the philosophy as:

> the great liberator of man from the phantoms that have held him captive; ... the arbiter and pacifier of the two forces for individual

and social harmony ... That being the ideal of Anarchism, its economic arrangements must consist of voluntary productive and distributive associations, gradually developing into free communism, as the best means of producing with the least waste of human energy.[7]

A belief in the brand of anarchism advocated by Goldman underpins Ridge's work in the period after her relocation to New York, much of which focuses on individual experience under capitalism; the relationship between a state and its citizens; the figure of the worker. Hers is a campaigning art: one that does not seek to obscure its politics, which is conscious of the conditions of its production. To return to 'The Ghetto', here is a poem peopled with New Yorkers, 'Striving with infinite effort, / Frustrate yet ever pursuing / The great white Liberty, / Trailing her dissolving glory over each hard-won barricade – / Only to fade anew ...', against the backdrop of a landscape dominated by the 'stark trunks of the factories', the rhythm of 'Wars, arts, discoveries, rebellions, travails, immolations, cataclysms, hates'.[8] The aforementioned character Sadie, with whom the poem's protagonist boards, might be read as the hero of the piece: a modern, working-class woman who must endure shambolic working conditions, like the 'biting steel –that twice / Has nipped her to the bone', and seeks to build solidarity between her fellow workers ('She – who stabs the piece-work with her bitter eye / And bids the girls: "Slow down – / You'll have him cutting us again!"').[9]

Elsewhere, too, Ridge confronts readers with depictions of the toll manual work takes on labourers. In 'Spires', Ridge addresses Grace Church (a French Gothic Revival Church constructed in the mid-nineteenth century in Manhattan): 'For you the workers of the world / Travailed with the mountains ... / Aborting their own dreams'; the finished building 'Scorn[s] their hands'.[10] The body of 'An Old Workman' is 'Well-used as some cracked paving stone', instrumentalised then discarded.[11] Iron becomes a recurrent symbol of the industrial revolution, of the unstoppable tide of capitalism, in, for example, 'The Song of Iron', 'The Legion of Iron', 'Fuel' – which lambasts 'foolish dreams of making things ... / (Ten million men are called to die[)]' – and the impressionistic 'Wall Street at Night', in which we find 'down among iron guts / Piled silver / Throwing gray spatter of light ... pale without heat ... / Like the pallor of dead bodies.'[12] 'Reveille' (an invocation for workers to 'wake up') forms an appeal to the working class:

> They think they have tamed you, workers –
> Beaten you to a tool
> [...]
> Let the fires grow cold,
> Let the iron spill out of the troughs
> Let the iron run wild
> Like a red bramble on the floors ...[13]

Alongside generalised indictments of capitalism, Ridge presents poems written in response to current events, often addressed to or profiling well-known leftist activists. These include 'Emma Goldman' ('How should they appraise you, / who walk up close to you / as to a mountain'); 'To Alexander Berkman', written for another leading member of the anarchist movement; 'To Larkin', for the trade union leader Jim Larkin, and 'Kelvin Barry', which reacts to the hanging of the Irish rebel Kevin Barry ('Did your red young mouth / Suck in the wind as a lover sucks in a kiss that is one of the last').[14] Collectives, as well as individuals, are celebrated, whether the Irish Volunteers of 1916 in 'The Tidings' ('*They are fighting to-night in Sackville Street, / And I am not there!*' [italics original]), or the Russian revolutionaries of 1917, who provide the inspiration for numerous poems in *Red Flag*: from 'Moscow Bells, 1917' to 'Czar's Watch' and 'Libation'.[15]

As Nathaniel Cadle argues convincingly, 'By demanding readers' compassion for a variety of persecuted anarchists and revolutionaries from both the United States and Europe ... Ridge constructs a radical counter-history built around bonds of sympathy for political dissidents that stretch across national borders.'[16] 'Electrocution' is a striking example of a work that performs such a demand for compassion. Although Ridge does not supply specific details, the poem addresses the executions of Nicola Sacco and Bartolomeo Vanzetti, two anarchists who were sentenced to death after being found guilty of murder and armed robbery. Their sentencing provoked worldwide outrage, and spurred hundreds of thousands of people to join protests on their behalf; their supporters suspected the verdict was motivated by anti-immigrant and anti-leftist bias.[17] The sonnet reads as a deliberate attempt to inspire sympathy for the pair, here represented in martyr-like terms:

> He shudders ... feeling on the shaven spot
> The probing wind that stabs him to a thought
> Of storm-drenched fields in a white foam of light,
> And roads of his hill-town that leap to sight
> Like threads of tortured silver ... while the guards –
> Monstrous deft dolls that move as on a string,
> In wonted haste to finish with this thing,
> Turn faces blanker than asphalted yards.
> They heard the shriek that tore out of its sheath
> But as a feeble moan ... yet dared not breathe,
> Who stared there at him, arching – like a tree
> When the winds wrench it and the earth holds tight –
> Whose soul, expanding in white agony,
> Had fused in flaming circuit with the night.[18]

By decontextualising Sacco and Vanzetti from the details of their lives, their locations in time and space, Ridge pushes readers away from the particular and towards the universal; the text becomes a rumination on injustice that is irreducible to one particular instance of injustice. The executed men are conflated into a single, symbolic personage, 'He' (an address, incidentally, imbued with biblical resonances), while the 'flaming circuit' of the last line gestures outwards to the legacy a 'sacrifice' such as theirs might have. But the poem is not only sensitive to the repercussions of personal suffering; Ridge also attends to structural violence. The guards might be 'monstrous', but there is a kind of ambivalence in how they 'Turn [their] faces blanker than asphalted yards'; they, too, might be read as victims of the state's deadly, and deadening, machinery.

The poet's critiques are at once of their era and germane to our present moment, as pertinent for readers today as they were for Ridge's contemporaries in the early twentieth century. Evan Mauro characterises the conventional narrative of twentieth-century avant-gardes, among whom we might count Ridge, as 'a story of decline, from revolutionary movements to simulacra, from *épater le bourgeois* to advertising technique, from torching museums to being featured exhibitions in them', but troubles this reading with 'an alternative genealogy of avant-gardism … that might avoid nostalgia', arguing for the persisting relevance of the philosophies underpinning the project, and tracing their influence on subsequent artistic movements.[19] Reading Ridge in these terms, we might begin to better understand how her work has acted as a poetic springboard for writers of subsequent generations. Anne Stevenson contends that Ridge 'should be recognised as a forerunner of Muriel Rukeyser and Denise Levertov, a strong figure anticipating Adrienne Rich'; Robert Pinsky hears in Ridge's writing a 'premonitory echo' of Hart Crane, and to this list we might add countless other names: Allen Ginsberg, Bernadette Mayer and Eileen Myles spring to mind.[20]

I have gestured towards the reasons why Ridge's influence was obscured in the critical discourse of the twentieth century; we are left with the question of why her legacy is being resuscitated *now* – with, over the past decade, a renewed critical interest in her work, the publication of Svoboda's biography and the republication of her poetry. To contextualise Ridge's critical revival, it is useful to return our attention, briefly, to Ahmed, who theorises how sexism influences canon formation, and how feminist practice might challenge this dynamic:

> Sexism is justified as what is received because it is assumed as in what is received. Sexism becomes a received wisdom. Sexism, in other words, by being accepted as in the pattern or in the traditions is rendered not only acceptable but inevitable. Sexism: the elimination of a gap between inheritance and reproduction … Things tend to fall how they have tended to fall unless we try to stop things from falling that way. An intending is required given this tending, given this tendency.[21]

Undoubtedly, an 'intending' has arisen to reclaim Ridge's poetry; reviewing *To the Many*, Rio Matchett draws attention to how 'we rewrite history as it suits us to reflect the present', arguing that, 'the resurgence of interest in Lola Ridge has plenty to tell us about how we see ourselves, how we see transnationalism, and how we conceive of our own identities, one hundred years on from her first collection's publication'.[22] For her biographer, Ridge is a cautionary example: 'The truncated branch of poetry that Ridge represents should remind readers that the discourse of today does not have to take the form that it does.'[23] At a moment when borders, globalisation and global nationalisms are the subjects of intense debate (specifically, Britain and Ireland, in the wake of the Brexit vote); when, as Svoboda notes, 'the same neo-fascist threat that Ridge experienced in the earliest years of the [twentieth] century appeals to Americans and Europeans in search of order and conformity', Ridge's poetry – with its ethics of documentation, its conference of dignity onto those marginalised by society – provides us with an instructive model of artistic resistance to prevailing cultural and political forces.[24] As a plethora of aesthetic traditions have emerged and evolved in both Ireland and America, the radical principles underpinning Ridge's work have been seized upon by generations of poets. It is imperative that we recognise and understand her contribution to our current poetic landscape; how a woman born in Dublin made a splash halfway across the world, and how the ripples are still being felt.

Florence Mary Wilson (1874–1946)

Carol Baraniuk

The Sea-Folk

I saw the sea-folk ride
Roun Rachra in the Dawn;
On their white leppin horses
Thunderin' on.
I wisht they hadn't looked my way
So be I might forget,
For they tried to stove the boat on me,
An' they tore my trawlin'-net.

Each wan wi' a whippin'-weed
Lashed at his foamin' horse;
An' him who drove the hardest
Carried a drownded corse.
I closed my eyes as it went by,
Swingin' through the brine,
But off the swirl o' old Ceann Ban
I saw its wet hair shine.

I heard their piper play
The Black North Win'
An' when you hear thon skirlin'
Quare dreams come to your min'.
There's not a tune in Ulster,
I'd put before the wan

> That led the sea-folk leppin',
> Roun Rachra in the dawn.
>
> Now I've seen them ridin',
> The sea must be my bed;
> I'd liefer have the green sods
> An' roses sweet an' red;
> But wanst there'll be a callin',
> When I be to rise an' stir –
> Nor all the sea-folk in the sea
> Will keep me back from her![1]

Florence Mary Wilson's brief lyric poem 'The Sea-Folk' is memorable for its evocation of the turbulent seascape off Rathlin Island on Ireland's north coast, its mingling of folklore with lived experience, and for the perfectly rendered voice of its speaker: a county Antrim fisherman who discloses details of a terrifying, supernatural encounter. His swift, fast-paced narrative reveals that while enduring extreme conditions at sea he has had the misfortune to come upon a party of mermen rolling a drowned corpse through the raging water and spume.

In speech typical of this part of Ulster where the Scots influence is strong, the narrator at once draws the reader into the experience he has suffered, conveying his horror through brief, tense comments, such as 'I wisht they hadn't looked my way' and 'I closed my eyes as it went by'. Thus, he indicates his fearful certainty that he has fallen under a curse due to what he has seen, and because he too has now attracted the malign attention of the sea folk, having ventured into their element. Though the account is of necessity terse, Wilson's stimulation of the senses is potent and concentrated. The rhythmical pattern is not smooth, varying sometimes unpredictably between iambic and trochaic, or in length of line, to convey the erratic rocking of the boat and the speaker's disturbed state of mind. Onomatopoeic expressions frequently assault the reader's ears: 'whippin'-weed', 'lashed', 'skirlin'', conveying the seaweed's flailing, the rushing foam and the howling wind of the storm. Visual detail is used to maximum effect. The speaker conveys the grand prospect of the seas between Kinbane Head and

Rathlin, effectively employing place names in the local forms, 'Ceann Ban' and 'Rachra'; then in a particularly chilling moment he recalls, near at hand, the 'wet hair shin[ing]' on the corpse, all the more eerie for being glimpsed in the uncertain half-light of dawn.

In the final stanza the speaker contrasts the peaceful death and quiet grave he wishes for with the violent drowning to which he now feels he is fated at the whim of the pitiless sea folk. It is a compelling piece to read, and conveys to the rational reader not only superstitious fear, but also the genuinely petrifying, ruthless environment of the wild Atlantic, with which the fisherman in his tiny boat must engage.

Though today 'The Sea-Folk' is virtually unknown, Florence Wilson's stirring dramatic monologue, 'The man from God knows where', about the hanged United Irish leader Thomas Russell (1767–1803), has not lacked attention over the years. In *The '98 Reader* (1998) the piece is described as the 'Dangerous Dan McGrew' of Irish recitations,[2] particularly associated with Cathal O'Byrne, singer and Irish language enthusiast.[3] The voice within the poem belongs to a County Down farmer who recalls the arrival of a compelling and mysterious figure, on 'his big roan mare' at a rural inn 'on a night of snow'.[4] This was Russell, on a mission to inspire and train for revolt the largely Presbyterian peasantry of the district. The speaker expresses some of the suspicions entertained by the 'dour' tavern clientele concerning the stranger's purpose, nevertheless they treat him hospitably, are careful not to enquire too deeply about whom he intends to meet, and glimpse his furtive departure 'at skreek o' day'. The narrative then in more general terms offers a summation of the tragic course of the 1798 Rebellion – 'the time o' the Hurry', with pikemen's battles; the devastation and the crying of 'weemen' throughout Ulster; Robert Emmet's abortive attempt to revive rebellion in 1803; and the eventual execution at Downpatrick Gaol of the former shadowy visitor to the pub. The narrator, a witness to the public hanging, uncompromisingly adds his own sympathetic 'Amen' to Russell's dying prayer.

Employing many local references, the monologue is expressed in the colloquial diction characteristic of this heavily Scots-settled region in the neighbourhood of Newtownards and Strangford Lough. It is remarkable for conveying the native canniness of the speaker in addition to his romantic commitment to the United Irish ideal of liberty. The execution scene in the final stanza affords Russell heroic martyr status, while the speaker's concluding supplication is 'That the Wrong would cease and the Right prevail' – an ending seemingly calculated to inspire Wilson's contemporaries in the era of sustained lobbying for Home Rule when the poem was composed.

Though the poem is well known, information about Wilson herself has not been widely disseminated. She was born Florence Mary Addy, the daughter of a well-to-do Methodist family – her father was a linen mill manager in Lisburn, County Antrim. In 1898 she married Frederick Wilson, a solicitor.[5] They made their home in Bangor, overlooking Ballyholme Bay, and in the course of the marriage at least eight children were born. In the early twentieth century, Wilson enjoyed a growing reputation as a writer; she contributed to a range of Irish and English journals and newspapers, including Belfast's *Northern Whig* and Dublin's *Irish Review*, which published her brief, softly hypnotic lyric 'A Dreamer' in November 1911.[6] The recognition she achieved throughout Ireland is evident from Padraic Gregory's inclusion of three of her works in his *Modern Anglo-Irish Verse*.[7] There, thanks to the alphabetical presentation of the contributors in the contents, her name sits just before that of W.B. Yeats, with whose early pieces her oeuvre bears comparison. Wilson's networks included the coterie associated with the Belfast antiquarian, F.J. Bigger. Alice Milligan, writer, editor and Home Rule activist, was a close friend and for a time a major influence. Wilson appears to have supported Milligan's ambition 'to counter Dublin's exclusive claim to the [Irish Literary] Revival by promoting a specifically Northern focus'.[8]

The era in which Wilson wrote was especially turbulent. She published during a period of intense, competing agitations when the Home Rule movement and the Easter revolutionaries of 1916 strove to get an independent national parliament established in Dublin, and the Ulster Covenant campaigners committed themselves to preventing the break-up of the Union, 'using all means which may be found necessary'.[9] Meanwhile, in Europe and further afield, a chain of events was unfolding that would culminate in the carnage of the First World War. Wilson, a Methodist who married a Presbyterian, and her literary compatriots such as Bigger and Milligan, the latter also a Methodist, strongly identified with Ireland as a nation and with Gaelic language and culture, though Wilson's archive has not yet disclosed her specific opinions on the issues of independence and partition.

Regarding Wilson's friend Alice Milligan, Catherine Morris argues that her 'work reveals her abiding commitment to a nationalist politique that could accommodate north and south, urban and rural, Protestants and Catholics, men and women, Irish speakers as well as English'.[10] Wilson left a vivid memoir of Milligan, but much of its focus is on the personal interaction between the two women rather than on contemporary politics. They met almost every day while they were near neighbours in Ballyholme, Bangor, for some years before the First World War. It is touching to read of the great warmth with which 'Aunt Milly' was regarded by the Wilson children, but Milligan's purpose in her visits was serious: to get the children's mother to focus on her writing. As she shares such anecdotes, Wilson herself emerges as wry and self-mocking. She reveals a degree of frustration with Milligan, her driven, activist friend. It was apparently useless to point out to Alice that a husband and children required attention, and when Wilson busied herself with gardening, picnics, music and other family pastimes, she admits to feeling 'more or less haunted by Alice's reproachful form'.[11] She adds:

> What Alice did not appear to comprehend in those five years was this … I, too, wanted to live the life she was leading at the time. I would have liked to sit down behind a locked door in an upper room and write from morn to night.[12]

Perusing the memoir's twenty pages, the reader gains a deeper understanding of the sometimes fraught relationship between the two women; about Wilson's political perspective (or her claimed lack of it); and about her experience as a married woman writer in the early twentieth century. She sets out snippets of conversation with Milligan in brief dialogues, like scenes from a play repeating in her head, and as she recalls disputes about culture and politics, the account loses some of its whimsy. Milligan possessed the capacity to anger and hurt her:

> 'I don't believe for one minute,' Alice stated emphatically 'that you really in your inner-most soul consider Cuchulain worth while bothering about.' I regarded her with a wistful smile then slipped

out through the open window. I was cut to the bone by that careless remark ... the wound throbbed and continues to throb like a fresh wound.[13]

In a further scene, Milligan criticises her for sending material to English weeklies, on the grounds of their 'political tendencies'. At this, Wilson claims to have 'no more interest in politics than the dog there had in the Stone Age'. Milligan's response is scathing as she deplores the 'unpatriotic conduct' of 'that Irish man or Irish woman who refuses to think in these times and act for himself or herself'.[14] Wilson bats away the issue of 'patriotism', and by implication Milligan's political activist version of it, insisting on her greater concern about social issues, in particular the physical and spiritual welfare of the population.

Wilson lived in an era when, as a married woman, she had limited personal independence or political influence. She portrays herself as dignified and measured in their dispute. Milligan, on the other hand, appears strident with a taste for directing. This tendency only increased with the years, eliciting a strong response from Wilson when a short collection of her poetry was being prepared for publication. She confided to F.J. Bigger:

> I wanted to tell you that Alice M. is on the war-path with regard to the poems coming out ... She insists she must select and revise the proofs and I say she must not get them in her hand on any account ... What can we do save insist on the publishers refusing to let her handle the MSS?[15]

Milligan may have been an early mentor, but Wilson was not formed in her image. Her sense of her vocation also sometimes put a strain on relations with her husband:

> Fred once said to me I was no better than a Pagan because I worshipped trees, and I told him the trees grew heavenwards and were the green churches of the praising birds ... I wonder, now, has he found out that my poetry was more pleasing to God than his lengthy discourses.[16]

The resentment Wilson voices is striking, but it offers further evidence that opposition served only to hone further her determination to be true to her personal vision. She believed explicitly that her northern location and its hybrid history gave her work a special edge. As she remarked to Bigger:

> ... why shouldn't the Co. Down peasant be as dramatic and as emotional as Yeats's Sligo people and Synge's Wicklow tinkers? As a matter of fact the Co. Down countryman is an extraordinary individual. He has the Scott [sic] and the Gael mingled in him, and, in consequence, when relating a story, he draws upon both with astounding results ...[17]

Wilson counted nationalists, both cultural and political, among her friends. Bigger's circle included Bulmer Hobson, with whom she was on familiar, first-name terms. He was a member of the IRB and the Irish Volunteers, actively involved in the gun running through Howth. However, during the First World War Wilson was also a mother whose eldest son Niall[18] served on the Western Front. There he endured months under fire and was gassed at Vimy Ridge. She wrote of her anxiety for him in a 'world that has gone mad for blood'.[19] She was aware that some of her poetry that expressed sympathy, at a personal level, for Irishmen fighting in the crown forces in Europe, would 'not please some friends of mine in Ireland'.[20]

The Bigger correspondence reveals the extent to which 'F.J.B.' gave practical support to her, as well as literary advice. The incidental information she includes about 'flu in the household, money problems and scraping together school uniforms for her children offers further insights into a woman writer's life, and into the powerful, creative drive that, despite distractions, kept her pen in her hand until the small hours.

Wilson's published work demonstrates her mastery over the production of lyric verse. The forms may appear simple, but the scansion is smooth, with the rhymes occurring so naturally as to appear effortless. In the anthologised 'Ballad of Lost Lochlann', the speaker speculates about a missing lover, a free spirit dwelling in the 'old woods of Faughan'. He has the potential to be portrayed as a mythical figure, a wildly passionate type of 'wandering Aengus', but the speaker's depiction of him combines no-nonsense practicality with wistful longing:

> But Lochlann, lonesome Lochlann!
> Did you ever have a dream
> Of barefoot children, amber-eyed?
> Of ducks on a rushy stream ...
> And someone watching you
> Behind the gable pane?
> Oh, many's the man has dreamt the like,
> And will do so again.
> Trees warm and green nigh Lammas
> By Holl'ave are dour and black;
> But I think that the barefoot childer
> Will bring you wanderin' back.[21]

The poem is vintage Wilson, with characteristically deft touches: imagery both homely and sensuous, colours painted in with an artist's skill, an underlying melancholy in the reference to the year's decline from Lammas to 'Holl'ave',[22] and an adroit sprinkling of local words to strengthen the authenticity of the voice.

In addition to her journal publications, Wilson produced one slim book of poems which ran through two editions in 1918. It was named *The Coming of the Earls* after the first piece in the collection, which imagines the return of the Gaelic earls who had fled Ulster in 1607 prior to the Stuart Plantation of Ulster.[23] Ireland is presented as rejuvenated, and some readers have interpreted this as encoding aspirations for the flourishing of the island under Home Rule. But Wilson's printed works retain an elusive quality that may have been deliberate. The final poem in the volume, 'The Northern Dead', invokes the ancient saints of the Celtic church in Ulster who, the speaker asserts, will rise again one day, not for 'Ulster's need', but to welcome 'Eirinn's Lord'.[24] Here, she appears to reject the mentality that assumes God favours one side or another in the nation's contemporary religious and political conflicts, choosing instead to imagine the country unified spiritually under God Himself, at the Second Coming of 'Eirinn's Lord'. She prefaced the collection with a poem dedicated to her son Niall, who survived the horrors of the Western Front.

Many of her poems employ a lexis originating in the Ulster-Scots vernacular with which Wilson was familiar, having lived throughout her life in Antrim or Down, where many Scots migrants had settled. The following extract is typical in its appreciation of the tough, prickly yellow whin bushes so prevalent in the Ulster countryside:

> The whin is out afore the short day's turnin';
> Och but the whin is brave!
> It sets a ring o' fairy candles turnin'
> Roun' dour Winter's grave.[25]

Two poems in particular demonstrate Wilson's power to evoke the uncanny, and her sense of an 'other world' hovering near our own, with which her protagonists both long and fear to interact. The first is 'All Souls Eve', in which a speaker bereaved seven years previously undertakes an eerie ritual to bring about an encounter with a lost, dead loved one. At first, the atmosphere is comfortable and charming:

> I have decked my fireside with the haws glinting red,
> Left the half-door open, set the table spread
> With brown bread 'of my baking, and cups of gold and blue;
> We two will sit together as once we used to do.

But the mood changes and chills. A key word is 'dayli'gone' – an Ulster variant of the Scots 'daylicht-gaun', meaning 'daylight going', or dusk creeping over the landscape:

> I have said three prayers for you since dayli'gone;
> That the moon be your lantern, and the stars glimmer on
> The dark ways you wander, and no cold mists there
> Draw their clinging fingers through your yellow hair.
>
> I will hear your footsteps seven miles away,
> Feet the mould has fettered in a house of clay;

The conclusion replicates the cosiness of the opening, abruptly rising to a prayer that mingles anger, terror and a desperate hope. It is a work that lingers in the memory, retaining the power to unsettle:

> I have made the place gay with brown leaves and red,
> Here the turf is flaring; here the board is spread.
> *God who took you from me, show you to my sight!*
> *Lest I turn away from you, you who walk tonight.*[26]

Equally disturbing is 'The Sea-Folk', discussed above, in which a North Antrim fisherman relives a shocking doppelganger experience. Overwhelmed by the sight of a corpse rolling amid tempestuous seas and noisy winds, he takes it as a portent of his own death. The poem superbly conveys how the wild currents and wailing storms of this unforgiving seascape can possess the imagination and quell the human spirit. As the speaker remarks: 'when you hear thon skirlin' / Quare dreams come to your min'.'

'Quare dreams' indeed came to the mind of Florence Mary Wilson, one of the most intriguing and evocative writers from the north of Ireland in the early twentieth century. She died in 1946 and is buried in Bangor, County Down. This essay is offered in the hope that her mission, her creative output and her experience may become better known and understood.

May Morton (c.1880–1957)

Stephen O'Neill

from **Spindle and Shuttle**

>Last night I darned a damask tablecloth.
>>Back and forth
>>Warp and woof:
>The cloth was old; a hundred years and more
>Had come and gone since, master of his loom,
>Some skilful weaver set the hare and hounds
>Careering through the woodland of its edge
>In incandescent pattern, white on white.
>It was my mother's cloth, her mother's too
>(Some things wear better than their owners do)
>And linen lasts: a stuff for shirts and shrouds
>Since Egypt's kings first built their gorgeous tombs
>And wrapped their dead in linen, it may be
>They held it symbol of a latent hope
>Of immortality.[1]

Although she was one of the central figures in various Irish literary societies during the mid-twentieth century, May Morton's work has received little attention since. This is despite the relative popularity that she enjoyed in her lifetime, as well as her importance across a range of local and national literary institutions in Ireland in her later years. Born in Limerick into a Church of Ireland background, Morton became a national teacher in Sligo before moving to family near Strabane, County Tyrone, at the age of twenty-two.[2] From there, she moved to Newington Avenue in north Belfast, where she boarded with her sister, Millicent (Milly), teaching in Belfast Model School for Girls. She was eventually made vice-principal before her retirement in the 1930s, by which time she and her sister had moved to the nearby suburbs at 19 Waterloo Gardens. There, Morton began writing poetry in earnest, with three collections following: *Dawn and Afterglow* (1936), *Masque in Maytime* (1948) and *Sung to the Spinning Wheel* (1952). In her role as secretary and later chairperson of the Belfast Centre of P.E.N. International from the 1930s, her Waterloo Gardens home would be visited by practically every major writer who lived in or travelled to the city. It was also a site of frequent correspondence with figures such as John Hewitt, Roy McFadden, Austin Clarke, Sean O'Casey, Kate O'Brien and many others throughout Morton's productive retirement, which also included occasional broadcasts for RTÉ and the BBC in Belfast.

Morton's most prominent commercial and critical success came late in life. This was at the Festival of Britain, held during the summer of 1951, where she won the north of Ireland's poetry prize at the arts festival in Castlereagh. Tasked with writing a poem on the subject of 'Northern Ireland', Morton entered 'Spindle and Shuttle', which was chosen by the judges, W.R. Rodgers and H.O. White, over a hundred other entries, including John Hewitt's 'The Colony'.[3] Unlike Hewitt's regionalist and essentially masculine apologia for the Ulster Plantation, the 200-line 'Spindle and Shuttle' was focused on the receding traditions of domestic work undertaken by women in the countryside, making a clear break from the neo-revivalist lyric poems in her earlier collections. In 'Spindle and Shuttle', Morton's opening lines – which preface this essay – transform the domestic labour of linen repair to a form of remembrance of tradition and history. Here, as in other stanzas, the narrative pentameter is interrupted by the refrain, a metapoetic device that emulates the delicate needlework undertaken by the speaker while also alerting the reader to the 'skilful weave' of the poem itself. But there are two separate narrative strains running through the poem: one of a matrilineal tradition – 'It was my mother's cloth, her mother's too' – and another contrasting this with the patriarchal rituals of the Egyptian dynasty. Although it is essentially about one of the major industries adorning the six-county government's 'Farm and Factory' display at the Festival of Britain, the skilful weave of 'Spindle and Shuttle' subtly voices a marginalised history as set against the metanarratives of ancient history – Egypt and Rome – as a metaphor for the state, the failing linen industry recast as an Ulster Ozymandias.

Sharing much in common with Sam Hanna Bell's contemporaneous novel *December Bride* (1951), the poem blends visions of a turn-of-the-century farm with the coterminous growth of an urban industrial enclave – her adopted homeplace Belfast – to lament the loss of history and community in the metropolis. What is preserved by Morton here is not simply a valorisation of linen as a resource for tourists and merchants, but also her own personal memories of the years she spent on her uncle's flax farm in Liscurry in North Tyrone at the turn of the century, so that the growth of the linen industry in the north-east is essentially her *bildungsroman*. In the second stanza, the damask tablecloth is transformed into 'A field of blossomed flax in North Tyrone / [...] As shy and secret as an Ulster maid / Who saves her smiles like shillings, unaware / Life pays no dividends on thrifty love'. If these lines stake her claim for lived experience with the work of harvesting and weaving linen, they also taint the nostalgic reflection with a more wistful sense of regret for her emotional austerity. This isolation and enervation is cast into focus by the march of time, as represented by the relentless 'Darning, learning, / Yarning, yearning, / Spinning, weaving, / Joying, grieving' of the flax-spinner, essentially manipulating 'the coiling rope / We label time'. The speaker wistfully reflects upon these early years from a sense of nostalgic sentiment. This is underlined in the next stanza's contrasting depictions of an 'old blind woman with / Her spinning-wheel' as a representation of rural tradition, which is obliterated by an image of 'millies' in Belfast city:

> The hand-loom turns to lumber and the wheel
> Becomes a thing to win a tourist's glance
> When far from field and bird the factories rise,
> A myriad spindles and a maze of looms
> Cradled within four walls. On every side
> Thin streets of small brick houses spawn and sprawl
> Though none could give its neighbour elbow-room.
> Sleep flies each morning at the siren's shout

And women hurry, shapeless in their shawls,
In multitudes made nameless, to the mill,
Some young, some old, and many great with child:
All wage slaves of the new industrial age,
All temple vestals of the linen god.

Where 'the old woman' is an easily identified icon within Irish culture, and heavily associated with the rural scene that frames the opening of the poem, this symbol of continuity and tradition is ruptured by the urbanisation and mechanisation of the nineteenth century. With the wheel rendered merely a symbol of cultural capital in the face of these dark satanic mills, the image of the 'multitudes' offers a standard modernist depiction of alienation in the city, something where women are hurried, 'shapeless', and 'nameless [...] slaves'.[4]

The bleak image of 'community' offered by these descriptions of the city is then set against the construction of the city centre by men, a place where

linen prospers and the linen lords
Build fine town mansions for their families
And plan a city hall whose splendid dome
Will soar above the long lean streets and look
Beyond them to the green encircling hills.

Again, the influence of the Festival of Britain is clear – sharing much in common with commissioned artworks that celebrated the foundation of Belfast such as John Luke's Belfast City Hall mural – but this image of Belfast's construction is in contrast to the lived experience of labour in the linen mills. And as a line in the penultimate stanza re-emphasises, 'we still are country-folk at heart / Deep-rooted in the fields our fathers tilled'. This then gives way to the wistfulness of the earlier stanzas being transformed into a *carpe diem*:

Hear the crying of the fiddle:
Hands across and up the middle
Choose your partners for the dance
Weave your webs or take your chance!

> Hear the clatter of the loom:
> Atom bomb and day of doom!
> Will the clatter never cease?
> Work for war and hope for peace.
> Hear the spindle's gentler hum:
> Work for peace and peace may come.

The reference here to the 'Atom bomb' firmly places the poem within the milieu of post-war Europe, which still remembered the devastation of the previous decade – particularly in a Belfast that was still reconstructing itself after the 1941 Blitz. Morton transforms the sound and image of the 'spindle's gentler hum' into a sign of peace, with the last lines reverting to the pastoral setting of the first stanza: 'In fields of North Tyrone the bright flax grows, / The blackbird sings / And past the farm a quiet river flows'.[5]

Morton's work, and 'Spindle and Shuttle' in particular, have enjoyed something of a minor renaissance since the 1990s, with critics such as Lucy Collins, Katie Donovan and Ailbhe Smyth recovering her somewhat beguiling voice in various analyses and anthologies.[6] In quoting the refrain of 'Spindle and Shuttle', Smyth recast the stanza in 1991 as representative of the 'dual struggle with the imprint of colonially induced dependence and patriarchally imposed otherness', the weaving not just a representation of mass labour but also symbolic of 'the altogether simultaneous web that binds us into the pattern of dual non entity'.[7] Though this seems to be a departure from the central purpose of the 1951 poem, it does serve as a perfect description of Morton's own struggles with the political and institutional exigencies of cultural activity in Ireland during the mid-century. That she was published in outputs as diverse as the aforementioned Festival of Britain pamphlet and pamphlets for P.E.N.; the 'Ulster' regionalist titles *Lagan* and *Rann*; Seán O'Faoláin's anti-revivalist organ *The Bell*; Denis Ireland's anti-partition pamphlet *The North* (1945); and the journal of Thomas Carnduff's Young Ulster Society, *Young Ulster* suggests the many competing frames in which her work was consumed in mid-century Ireland. Indeed, as a retiree Morton was heavily involved in many of these organisations and journals, serving as a founding member of the Young Ulster Society, chairperson of the Belfast Centre of P.E.N.

and delegate to many P.E.N. International conferences. Remembered somewhat disparagingly in 1979 by Roy McFadden as a woman whose presence was felt at P.E.N. meetings – 'whose gentle gloves sheathed knuckle dusters and for whom young poets were slight challenges in plasticine' – Morton seemed to cut an often-frustrated figure at these events. In the same piece, McFadden also memorably described her as 'Maud Gonne of the Ulster Union Club, Lady Gregory of P.E.N.', suggesting at once her importance in these organisations but also her incongruity within the social and political confines of each organisation.[8]

This frustration is certainly evinced by her awkward correspondences with John and Roberta Hewitt, as well as her various missives to other members of P.E.N. For example, in a letter to the Dublin-based Kathleen O'Brennan in 1945 as secretary of the Belfast group, Morton complained to her friend about the impossibility of meetings between the northern and southern centres, while ending on a note of thanks for the Dublin president Maurice Walsh's 'most kindly interest and sympathetic understanding of our wish for a "united Ireland P.E.N."'.[9] Morton's oscillation between these male-dominated literary scenes was a particularly troublesome activity in her adopted city, which she described as a place in which 'it was not easy to keep a liberal non-sectarian society alive'.[10] For all these frustrations, she persisted in organising P.E.N. activities in Belfast until the end of her life, and this activity clearly informed her poetry. Lucy Collins describes how 'May Morton's work emphasises its regional identity', and this emphasis can be traced back to the poet's connections with these burgeoning regionalist movements in the north during her lifetime.[11] But Morton, like many others in this period, was also anxious to codify what that regionalism might mean. In her contribution to the first ever publication of the Belfast Centre of P.E.N. in 1942, Morton outlined what the task of the 'Ulster' writer should be. Appearing alongside D.A. Chart, Michael McLaverty and Jeanne Foster Cooper, Morton's opening contribution explicitly stated that a writer had 'no power to adjust frontiers or to reform economic systems'. This was a somewhat unconvincing protest against the efficacy of literature, since her prescription of the ideal 'Ulster' writer instead fastened upon concepts of truth and sincerity above objectivity:

> Let him paint the Ulster background with fidelity, whether it be farm or factory, the glory of a gorse-crowned hillside or the squalor of a city slum. Complete objectivity may not be attainable, it may not even be desirable; every work of art should bear the imprint of its creator's personality. But it should also bear the hallmark of truth. Sincerity is all.[12]

Such a description resounded with the many regionalist manifestos that appeared in the north after the partitioning of Ireland, and suggested, like many other writers in the pamphlet, that 'Ulster' literature should focus upon a truthful depiction of the landscape and people of the area.

While her work largely focused on an 'Ulster' setting, Morton's fullest realisation of her writerly ideal came late in life, but it did so by inverting the themes of her poetry in the 1930s and 1940s, as well as including far more references to the political and economic history of the north of Ireland. The earlier lyric efforts *Dawn and Afterglow* and *Masque in Maytime* resembled much of the then-dominant neo-revivalist strain in Irish poetry, but this was geared towards a romanticisation of the idea of 'Ulster' in common with her fellow Belfast poet Richard Rowley. In these, the northern setting is simply a blank canvas for standard romantic lyric poems, where there is more than an element of what Eamonn Hughes describes of Forrest Reid's use of the 'Ulster' landscape, in his 'dehistoricising it … much like the unionist myth of nurture from the land without guilt'.[13] Her 1936 poem 'Mountain Mist' forms a case in point:

> Maiden of the mountain mist,
> Stooping boldly to be kissed
> When the young and ardent sun
> First pursues you – half in fun,
> Wherefore snatch your robe of grey
> From his grasp, and haste away
> When his passion's hot desire
> Follows you with lips of fire?[14]

Richard Kirkland describes these lines as encapsulating an 'erotically charged delight in the Ulster countryside'.[15] They also evoke how the later 'Spindle and Shuttle' contrasts such pastoral delights with an ascetic meditation on youth from the perspective of the speaker's old age and the wider history of 'Ulster'. This thematic development reflects that of Morton's craft. If the theme of love remains constant throughout Morton's work, 'Spindle and Shuttle' also marks a distinct break from these *ex nihilo* depictions of a pastoral north, a skilful weave of past and present that bears much of the personal and political frustrations of its author's life.

Blanaid Salkeld (1880–1959)

Michelle O'Sullivan

Leave us religion.
We have all been given
Saints' names. Whether you call Bernadette,
Philomena, or Margaret,
And the rest –
Some pure unpressed
String echoes, under her palm,
Through an Angel's psalm,
In that still, calm,
Illumined Region –
So we are linked up with Heaven.

Man, less significant
Than the ant
With its plan of campaign –
Thinks to sting Heaven with his pain.
'Pity!' we cry, and think to rive and raid
Its golden forests with our pestilent storms:
Adulteries and deceits, the shifting forms
Of fear and hope – our follies, legion.
Yet we are starred from baptism though the taints
Of infidelities divert us,
Patrons shall convert us.
We are all called after the saints;
We shall find, having left the years,
That untouched of tiredness, tears,
And flesh, Region.

Blanaid Salkeld (1880–1959)

A spoiled child's insurrection –
Kept from the wild flutes of our lips' election,
Dumbed like a brute,
We would refute
Authority, and bite the mother's hands,
However, she understands.
Ignorant above day's indecision
And night's derision –
Leave us religion.
Trivial flower lifts sunward chin.
Higher than tree-tip, over dust and din.
The stony finger gold-thorned for sun-polish –
If hordes demolish,
Rebuild more loftily what signals higher
Than poplar spire,
To sun-superior, light-surviving Region.
Leave us religion.

An escape? Why not. The Church is gay.
Escape, from pleasure – to nurse lepers.
The face shines plain:
Can you explain?
Successful seekers have found pleasure out;
And the escape from love, of lechers
Is a lame rout;
Dead their gaze, no inner ray.
The warring proud borne off in stretchers;
All fugitives, we should be wary steppers.

Through leafless trees, this dreary day,
Blooms at the monastery steps,
Blue and unfading, the Virgin's dress –
In every weather, clear and gay.
For no new-fangledness
Will I turn away.

> We have drunk fire and eaten dirt.
> Given candid beauty much hurt;
> Scrawled blasphemies on city walls;
> Drawn coarse jests out with bitter drawls;
> Our charity was curt.
>
> In naked celerity, remorse
> Plunges out of its course,
> Like a white frightened horse;
> Our sins are legion.
> Leave us religion.[1]

Known and respected in her time as an accomplished poet, dramatist, translator, reviewer and publisher, Blanaid Salkeld's literary contributions span the first half of the twentieth century. My first introduction to her work came through A.A. Kelly's *Pillars of the House: An anthology of verse by Irish women* (1997).[2] In that faraway place known as adolescence, I cannot say exactly what my thoughts were on the poet or the poems. Pencil marks next to a title: 'MOSTLY SUPERSONIC'; an asterisk marking the phrase 'muffled jungle howl' and further exclamation marks indicate some sense of surprise. However, like the fate of other poets in that anthology and the sufferance of being under-read or not read at all, this remained my only experience of Salkeld's poetry for a number of years. Any further reading would have been limited to the possibility of a library's rare book collection, if that. There's an irony in finding and reading Russian poet Anna Akhmatova in and around the same time: would it have made a difference to my psyche to have known that Akhmatova's translations were on my doorstep, that Salkeld had translated her too?

Born in Chittagong, India, Blanaid Salkeld spent her childhood in Dublin. She later married an Englishman in the Indian civil service and returned to India with him until his death in 1909. Coming back to Dublin, she settled at 43 Morehampton Road, where she lived with her artist son Cecil. Over the next five decades, they transformed their unassuming residential home into a locus of literary and artistic activity. An avid hostess of literary salons, Salkeld founded the

Women's Writers' Club with Dorothy Macardle in 1933, which, as Moynagh Sullivan describes, 'served as a fulcrum for much creative life in Ireland at the time'.[3] Number 43 Morehampton Road would remain significant not only for the gatherings Salkeld held there, but also as the production site for her main literary venture of the 1930s and 1940s: the Gayfield Press. Salkeld launched the press with Cecil in 1937, when they designed and printed her third published poetry collection *...the engine is left running*. Looking at the arc of her career from this centre illustrates not only her inclusive approach to poetry to provide a modern experimental voice, but also provides context for the political and cultural limitations she was writing against. Nationally, 1937 was an important year, significant for what Salkeld had already produced and for what she would be producing. The decisions made between 1922 and 1937 regarding Ireland's constitution were overwhelmingly a story of men discussing the rights of women, whose subordinated social role was successively conceived within the confines of domesticity. Lucy Collins observes that 'women were virtually invisible in the public structures of the Free State', a condition that was successively enshrined in the legislative landmarks of the post-Independence decades. 'The 1937 Constitution directly expressed the aim that Irish women eschew public life in favour of their duties in the home', Collins continues, 'and in this it reflected not only de Valera's social conservatism, but also the views of most Irish people at the time.'[4]

In setting up the Gayfield Press, Salkeld challenged the restrictions placed on the Irish woman at the mid-century point, refashioning the domestic space as a site of independent cultural production, by which she assumed agency in a male-dominated publishing sphere. Though she had achieved notable publishing success in London with her first two poetry collections, *Hello Eternity!* (1933) and *The Fox's Covert* (1935), the move to set up a private printing press in Dublin was motivated by Salkeld's subsequent frustrations in finding publishers for her experimental work.[5] Given the overall climate of the time, the tenacity of her decision says as much about her character as it does about the work she produced; from behind her front door she could challenge the conventions of the literary publishing industry and maintain financial independence. Deirdre Brady remarks that the Gayfield Press 'has received little attention and its history has been lost or forgotten. Furthermore, the role of Blanaid Salkeld as a publisher has been virtually erased from literary studies of the period.'[6] Promoted in newspapers as a publisher of deluxe editions of Irish writing, a small piece in the *Irish Press* stated in 1937 that the press 'intends specialising in limited editions, fine-art productions, handwritten MSS, and many things for the connoisseur, as well as ordinary publications'.[7] Working on a small wooden Adana hand press in the garden shed of 43 Morehampton Road, Gayfield Press succeeded in producing eight books along with a variety of pamphlets and broadsheets in the following nine years.[8] Throughout this period the press cultivated a reputation for exclusivity and unconventionality, as the publisher's note printed in Ewart Milne's *Forty North, Fifty West* emphasised: 'The Gayfield Press publishes entirely at its own discretions – uninfluenced by fashionable tastes, cliques or coteries. It will continue to bring out limited and illustrated editions of special interest.'[9]

The digital exhibition *The Poetics of Print: The private press tradition and Irish poetry* chronicles the private press tradition in Ireland and its role in the development of modern Irish poetry, digitising a range of Gayfield Press material including the cover of Salkeld's *...the engine is left running*.[10] The digitised cover foregrounds the experimental typography of the title with its ellipsis and irregular-spaced lowercase black type. The cover illustration depicts a locomotive billowing steam in a telephone-poled landscape. Implied movement or maybe a metaphorical stall, aesthetically speaking, the visual aspect of the book belies its content and perhaps it was a point that Salkeld was keen to make. Beyond the brown board covers and with no contents page, there is a hint of disorientation, as the title suggests, with the reader beginning in *medias res* on opening to the first poem: 'ATTEMPT AT COMMENCING'. Partly presented as a mosaic of rhythm, sound and image, and partly presented as oblique social commentary, the poem signals the 'rogue energy' of Salkeld's experimental voice, stimulating a fragmented poetics that operates in a 'consistent tension between confinement and release'.[11] Immediately confronting the reader with its capitalised title, 'ATTEMPT AT COMMENCING' begins abruptly with the line 'DAWN, The title, *Dead Centre.* Stubborn, / Approach at a slant'.[12] The reader pieces together the disjointed typography in capitals and italics; the staccato punctuation and syntax so abrupt it could almost be mistaken for stage direction, as if to place the reader in the centre of where the poet begins. Agents of constraint and their social impact on the individual begin to clarify as the stanza progresses:

> They sermoned thus:
> There is a beast you have to govern –
> Although no such beast endures in us.
> Out of the auto-toxined brain, sin
> Spawns into our thin blood-stream, the yeast
> Heredity, festering within:
> Mind-sin is slyer than the old beast.

The poem quickly shifts emphasis and focus is placed on the female mind and body. Salkeld's successive references to 'sin', 'shame' and 'mind-sin' carry biblical overtones and register the oppressive influence of religious doctrine, but as the stanza continues it strives to divest the physical of such moral and symbolic significance. 'Does not flesh / Make a fool of the bones – what else?' the speaker challenges, before presenting a starkly dispassionate view of the body and its inevitable decay:

> The bag, the incalculable mesh –
> Plumping, scabbing, shrivelling, in spells –
> Outside the will's control, weak, untame,
> Staleing, from the very first try-on
> Proving the root of our pride to be shame,
> Ourselves—nothing, once the flesh is gone?[13]

By use of contrast and rhetoric, Salkeld's interweaving both underscores and warns of destructive realities, literally and metaphorically, of the body or bodies oppressed. Though near hopeless, there is a resolute belief in the power of art to transform; the abrasion of voice against the idealised submissive, asexual and pure form inverts the argument for a liberal, progressive point of view.

The collection ...*the engine is left running* is arranged in two sections that divide it into eight titled poems and twenty-four untitled poems, which are each identified by Roman numerals. The opening poem of the second section begins with the line 'Leave us religion' and expands upon the themes, images and critique of the preceding section. The speaker calls for a spiritualism based on individual experience, open to the immediacy and variety of life unbound by institutional strictures. As Margaret MacCurtain writes, Salkeld's 'robust' verse style propels the poem's sensual and philosophical discourse: 'theological in its argument, nostalgic in its mood, catching in its images the shadings of women's religious experience, and, like Paula Meehan's statue at Granard, speaks of the reality of many women's desire to give a human face to a harsh church'.[14] 'Leave us religion' highlights abuses of power but also allows for the contrast of what women have inherited from religious institutions. By claiming this inheritance, even by the very act of the poetic voice alone, Salkeld complexly navigates 'the shifting forms / of fears and hope'.[15] Strong reverberating end-rhymes ('dumbed like a brute, / We would refute) are contrasted with looser melodic sections ('Blue and unfading, the Virgin's dress—/ In every weather, clear and gay'), but throughout there is a transparency to the poem that places further emphasis on the content. For Sullivan, Salkeld's style 'defies categorization, operating as it does between a powerful attraction to both embroidered symbolism and abstraction', revelling in an eclectic and unruly approach to form that can be both 'metrical and unmetered, patterned and free'.[16] This heterogenous style allows not only for introspection beyond the poem's confines but can also call for multiple readings and, indeed, meanings. The slant rhyme and repetition of region / religion / legion are fused in a way that embodies the tethered 'we' of the poem. But, elsewhere, the buoyant alliterative energy and natural imagery of 'Trivial flower lifts sunward chin. / Higher than tree-tip, over dust and din' contrastingly effect an untethering, encouraging aspirations of regeneration to 'Rebuild more loftily what signals higher / Than poplar spire'. Such expressiveness and idealism occasion the possibility of transcendence towards a 'sun-superior, light-surviving region'; though the repetition of the thrice-used 'escape' at the same time underscores the unescapable attachments to religious institutions. The 'we' in 'Leave us religion' is noted with something hopeful, even if only in the openness of expression, and, like the speaker in the poem 'A PROPOS TO RADIO':

> Through the fog our progress is slow:
> We know but cannot see the snow
> That puts liveliness in the blood
> Against this muffled evening's mood.

Justin Quinn's dismissal of Salkeld as 'an anomaly, and an unsuccessful one at that' fails to consider the significance of a collection such as ...*the engine is left running*.[17] In a chapter dedicated to male poets (Padraic Colum, Austin Clarke, Patrick Kavanagh and Louis MacNeice), Quinn's passing reduction of Salkeld's 'hectic futurism' is generalising, though perhaps not surprising.[18] It is after all one of the contributing factors that has limited her visibility in the Irish literary canon and perhaps strengthens Sullivan's assertion that 'Salkeld's leap has been a step too far for a tradition that needs her loss to do its own work.'[19] While nearly two decades passed before Salkeld published another collection after ...*the engine is left running*, she remained an influential figure among her contemporaries. From the helm of the Gayfield Press she published a further seven books (five of which were authored by women) and commissioned several artists for a series of broadsheets, *Dublin Poets & Artists*, which included Sheila Wingfield, Austin Clarke and Jack Butler Yeats. Yet, despite Salkeld's many accomplishments and her commitments to Irish cultural life, her posthumous reception has until recently been resigned to what Anne Fogarty described as 'the mute status of texts that remain outside literary history because they were not seen as part of the doctrinaire, patriarchal narratives that often inform the way in which cultural archives were constructed'.[20] In redressing past exclusions, the last two decades have yielded much reconsideration with regard to Salkeld's role and significance in mid-twentieth-century Irish culture. As Collins affirms, it has stimulated an exciting conversation that promises to establish her within a transformed conception of Irish poetry and tradition:

> The fluidity of Salkeld's treatment of poetic subjectivity is itself an interrogation of her role as poet, and of the creative challenges that exist for women on both an individual and a national level. Her work provides a lifeline for later women poets seeking to explore questions of intellectual independence and new modes of subjectivity.[21]

Ethna MacCarthy (1903–59)

Maria Johnston

Viaticum

The sluice gates of sleep are open wide
and through the House its soothing silver tide
from ward to ward flows grave and deep;
now flood, now fretful trickle,
and some it leaves marooned
who cannot sleep.
The nurses chart its course all night
and those who drowse and those who tell their beads
and those who coma vigil keep.
Sunken beyond the lure of light
some watch the shadows with unfocused eyes,
dull and indifferent, ears attuned
to soundless music of the Boatman's oar
and rhythmic singing of the rowlocks' strain
as the dark ferry swings to shore.
An old old woman and a little child
soon will meet each other there
but who knows what gay roisterer
before this dawn will pay their fare.[1]

It is thrilling to think that this darkly hypnotic poem, composed by Ethna MacCarthy in February 1942 and published in *The Irish Times* two months later, might have been in the mind of her lifelong friend Samuel Beckett when he was writing (and later translating) *Malone Meurt / Malone Dies* in the late 1940s. In Beckett's

1951 novel we find similar imagery of a boat's rowlocks ('No sound save the oars, the rowlocks, the blue sea against the keel'), there is the same persistent sense of sleep as death, as the final nothingness ('In my head I suppose all was streaming and emptying away as through a sluice, to my great joy, until finally nothing remained'), and most of all, perhaps, that weighty word 'viaticum':

> The horror-worn eyes linger abject on all they have beseeched so long, in a last prayer, the true prayer at last, the one that asks for nothing. And it is then a little breath of fulfilment revives the dead longings and a murmur is born in the silent world, reproaching you affectionately with having despaired too late. The last word in the way of viaticum.[2]

In MacCarthy's poem there is a play on the word 'viaticum' which, as well as meaning the Eucharist given to a person before death, etymologically means 'travelling-money': 'A supply of money or other necessaries for a journey; a sum given or taken to cover travelling expenses' (*OED*, 2, a). The poem takes place in the shadowy zone between sleep and wakefulness, between life and death, wherein time becomes elongated for those who find themselves on the cusp, restless and unslumbering. The orchestration of language on display in MacCarthy's poem is breathtaking in its precision, and a sinuous poetic control is evident from the start; the enjambed lines that carry the words over the line breaks are mimetic of the flow of 'sleep' as four long sentences are drawn out over nineteen poetic lines. Listen to how the sonic pattern of end-rhyme ebbs and flows over the lines, to how the opening couplet (its rhyme on 'wide' and 'tide') then gives way to the delayed end-rhymes of 'deep' and 'sleep' (and later 'keep'), to how 'night' at line-end finds its echo in 'light' just as the 'oar' at the end of line thirteen travels over the lines to 'shore'.

The way MacCarthy manipulates a compelling verbal music is mesmeric as the long *oo* sounds ('sluice', 'through', 'soothing', 'marooned', 'attuned') prolong the rhythmic pulse to stretch out time. The nightly rhythms of the hospital ward are thereby evoked as the nurses go about their work attending to and observing their patients' rituals, and our ears are similarly attuned and attentive to the musical pull of language, its haunting repetitions ('and those …', 'and those…', 'and those…'; 'an old old woman') and the way that the 'singing' of the rowlocks' propulsive strain is answered by the 'swing' of the ferry to shore. The effect is entrancing as the workaday reality of a hospital ward at night slides into the dark territory of the underworld, the closing images of the boatman and ferry taking us back across the centuries to the underworld of Virgil and Dante. With its shifting, shimmering texture, 'Viaticum' might put one in mind of a nocturne by the impressionist composer Claude Debussy. Throughout, the economy of death (literally, the coin that must be paid to Charon to ferry the newly dead across the River Styx) is balanced by the economy of both the poet's exact artistry and the nurses' meticulous measuring and mapping. In the line 'now flood, now fretful trickle', there may be an echo of Alfred Lord Tennyson's effects: one thinks of that famous opening line of the sonnet in *The Princess*, 'Now sleeps the crimson petal, now the white' and its own soothing, soporific atmospherics.[3] MacCarthy's literary and artistic hinterland is as extensive as it is suggestive. Richly layered and endlessly resonant, 'Viaticum' is undoubtedly one of MacCarthy's finest poems and a superb example of her ability to transport the reader from one reality to another and to render the familiar strange and otherworldly. Indeed, the surrealist, even apocalyptic, strain in MacCarthy's work has recently been highlighted by the inclusion of her poem 'Insomnia' in a 2020 anthology of British and Irish Apocalyptic poetry.[4]

MacCarthy's dark poetic journeying and deep awareness of life as a process of ebb and flow, of rise and fall, may have influenced Beckett more than even he was conscious of: when we read the opening line of her poem 'Exile': 'Beloved, my life has ebbed again' (composed in 1930 but published in *The Irish Times* in September 1940), we might find ourselves in the terrain of Beckett's Molloy: 'Much of my life has ebbed away before this shivering expanse',[5] or that of Beckett's 1937 poem 'Dieppe' which opens, 'again the last ebb'.[6] An undated draft of a short story titled 'Kaimak' discovered among the papers of the late A.J. (Con) Leventhal (whom MacCarthy married in 1956), and which is almost certainly by MacCarthy, features similar imagery: 'We sat like very old people who draw dreams and comfort from a fire … It was so tranquil there that I became aware of the minutes' ebb … The ebb tide began to drag at my heart.'[7] Indeed, the symbolic 'bruised bunch of violets' that wither in a glass on the mantelpiece at the end of the story may look forward to the same violets that Beckett will send to MacCarthy from Ussy in March 1959 as she lies dying of terminal cancer: 'This is just my heart to you and my hand in yours and a few wood violets I'd take from their haunt for no one else.'[8] Key words and motifs that resonate across MacCarthy's work appear to have been picked up by Beckett and developed across his own oeuvre. In MacCarthy's startling poem 'December 1948' (broadcast on Radio Éireann in 1949), the memorable closing image of Saint Francis who, 'weary of it all / counts the sparrows as they fall', must surely have found its way into Beckett's 1956 radio play *All That Fall* at the point where the character Mrs Rooney contemplates the meaning of the biblical sparrows: 'It's like the sparrows, than many of which we are of more value, they weren't sparrows at all.'[9] The echoes are unmistakable.

'It is, however, probably as a physician that Ethna MacCarthy will be remembered in times to come', a contributor to *The Irish Times*' 'Irishman's Diary' decreed after her death in 1959.[10] Born in Londonderry in 1903, the daughter of medical inspector Dr Brendan MacCarthy and the granddaughter of the famous nineteenth-century poet Denis Florence MacCarthy, Ethna MacCarthy was a writer, academic and linguist of formidable intellect. Brought up in south Dublin – the family moved to a house on Sandymount Avenue in Ballsbridge some time after 1911 – she was a student at the Royal Academy of Music for a period and then studied French and Spanish as part of a Modern Languages degree at Trinity College Dublin. Perhaps influenced by the death of her renowned father in 1934, she went on to study medicine (graduating in 1941) and practised as a paediatrician in hospitals in both Dublin and London's East End after having lectured in French and Provençal Literature at Trinity College Dublin for a number of years. Her career as a doctor and public health expert suffered a blow in 1953 when she was successfully appointed Medical Leader of the World Health Organisation's Maternal and Child Health Project in Baghdad only to then fail the required physical examination. 'Irish Poetess Heads Health Project', the *Irish Examiner* newspaper reported at the time – prematurely, as it turned out.[11] As we know from a number of letters written at the time by her very concerned friend Samuel Beckett, the devastated MacCarthy spent some months in Paris trying to undo the decision. However, the post, which would have taken her beyond Ireland on to the international stage, was not to be.

It was in 1923, as an undergraduate at Trinity College Dublin, that MacCarthy met fellow student Samuel Beckett, who immediately fell in love with her; 'her beauty and wit threw a vivid light over the front square of Trinity College and over the lectures', a contemporary would later recall her luminous presence.[12] Beckett's romantic love for her was unrequited but she would remain his dear friend and one of the trusted first readers of his work until her death from throat cancer in 1959. Although she never published a collection of poetry during her lifetime, MacCarthy's poems, stories and a play were published in outlets such as *Hermathena*, *Dublin Magazine*, *Ireland To-Day* and *The Irish Times*, as well as in a number of contemporary anthologies, including *Poems from Ireland* (edited by Donagh MacDonagh in 1944) and *New Irish Poets* (1948), in which three of her poems appeared alongside work by contemporaries including Freda Laughton, Robert Greacen, Valentin Iremonger and John Hewitt.[13] In many ways, her life as a writer and as a medical practitioner cannot be separated; so, too, she is both a poet of Dublin city (the poem 'Advent' features 'screaming seagulls [...] flashing their storm stained shadows on the glass / of shops in Grafton Street') and a truly outward-looking, cosmopolitan writer.[14] Her poetic output contains translations from Spanish and from German, many of which were praised by reviewers of the day. As Gerald Dawe has observed of her work across languages and literature: 'This web of allusion, intertext and connection between various European artists across different languages underlines the cultural awareness MacCarthy shared with her European contemporaries.'[15]

Although biographical details are scant, we may get some sense of the texture of MacCarthy's life by tracing her living presence across the newspapers and magazines of the day. MacCarthy's life as a writer in the pages of *The Irish Times* is fascinatingly diverse and it confirms her place in the literary culture of the time. Many of her own poems (including 'Viaticum', 'Evergreen', 'Exile' and 'Advent') were published in *The Irish Times* soon after composition and were often placed in the middle of or alongside articles by Patrick Kavanagh, Austin Clarke, Padraic Colum and others. The poem 'Evergreen', for instance, appears in the centre of a 1944 piece by Clarke remembering his 'First Visit to the Abbey', while her 'Advent' appears in the middle of a piece by Clarke titled 'Nature Poetry in England'.[16] Reviewing a new study of the French dramatist Jean Racine in 1948, MacCarthy's authority as a scholar of the French language and of European literature is clear: 'The appreciation of Racine has always been difficult for English-speaking people. They find his Alexandrines wearying, his restraint cumbersome, his characters' speeches long-winded, and his simplicity infantile.'[17] Her lively 1957 review of Honor Tracy's *Silk Hats and No Breakfast: Notes on a Spanish journey* takes us from La Coruña back to Dublin as MacCarthy draws on her own experience travelling in Spain before the Civil War with her trademark compassionate insight and keen social awareness: 'Those who visited Spain before the Civil War will remember only too well the procession of diseased and crippled beggars in front of the great cafes of Madrid and Barcelona – a hideous pageant of human suffering and degradation.'[18] A crucial record of her own development as a poet and sense of her own literary identity, MacCarthy's notebook contains, as well as her own poems (both in handwritten form and in published format), a number of newspaper cuttings of poems by other poets of the day that would have been published in *The Irish Times:* writers such as Austin Clarke ('Fashion' and 'Marriage'), J.H. Orwell ('Winter-Piece') and her close friend and later husband, A.J. Leventhal ('The Misery of Remembered Speech') were clearly of interest to her as she worked at honing her own craft. MacCarthy also assembles an anthology of her own honourable mentions: an *Irish Times* review by Austin Clarke of David Marcus and Terence Smith's *Irish Writing No. III* praises her 'fine translation' of an anonymous Spanish poem, the 'Ballad of St. Simon's', which had been adapted by F.R. Higgins into 'At Flock Mass',[19] while an unsigned review of the latest issue of the *Dublin Magazine* takes her poem 'Lullaby' to task for being too 'modern'.[20] More interesting in terms of MacCarthy's double life as writer and physician, the 'Books of the Week' section of *The Irish Times* in 1943 places Clarke and MacCarthy alongside each other – he as poetry critic, she in her capacity as paediatric doctor – as his article on 'Popular Poetry' flanks her much lengthier review of a new study titled *Tuberculosis in Childhood* in which she lays out a strong case for the treatment of tuberculosis in Ireland. 'It will take the full force of strong enlightened public opinion to break this evil chain of disease and death', MacCarthy warns, writing with the good of both the individual patient's wellbeing and the larger public health standpoint in mind as she makes a case for reform and urgent response: 'The immediate need of adequate accommodation cannot be over-emphasised.'[21]

In the same way, a 1951 essay for the *Irish Journal of Medical Science* has MacCarthy educating the medical profession on the disease entity oxyuriasis (thread worms), which, though widespread in Dublin (as part of the 'silent triad' comprising headlice, thread worms and nosebleeds) at the time, was constantly misdiagnosed and mistreated, owing in part to public shame around the condition: 'It is *not* a disease of dirt, being equally prevalent in all social grades', she stresses. Thus, 'The harassed doctor is not justified in reassuring the mother that "the child will grow out of it" and thus turn loose another potential lifelong carrier', she concludes firmly.[22] MacCarthy's delicate uncoverings of the silence and evasiveness around these widespread diseases are lively and accurate, and in this article and others (such as her more detailed 1948 research paper on 'Public Health Problems Created by Louse Infestation') she humanises a potentially dry, medical topic into something lived and real, showing its deleterious effects from first-hand accounts and observations. Might it be from here that the 'louse' or *pou* in Beckett's *Waiting for Godot* originates? In *Eh, Joe* (written in 1965) a woman's voice asks: 'Why don't you put out that light? ... There might be a louse watching you ...'[23] MacCarthy's own first-hand accounts of infestation make for compelling reading:

> One of our own cases gave us the answer to unsuccessful disinfestation. This was a young girl who had not combed her head for three years, and who was heavily infested with body lice. When the knots in her hair were opened up the lice, as the chronicler said of Thomas à Becket, 'boiled up'. Lice were recovered from her in thousands ... It is hard to imagine how any sane person could tolerate them, but this girl did, and it explains 'spontaneous generation' in asylums.[24]

Readers of MacCarthy's poetry will be reminded of her poem 'Nell Gwynn', in which 'ecstatic lice rejoice in carefully curled and uncombed hair'.[25] In this way, the medical experience finds its way into the art of poetic expression to make for a poetry of persuasive originality and a humane, unflinching vision that refuses to look away and is committed to searching out the life that goes on in the shadows. Singled out by a reviewer for its 'beauty and dramatic quality', MacCarthy's 'poetic drama' *The Uninvited* takes the reader into macabre territory as the world of fairy story and the Shakespearean supernatural collides with the world of human genetics.[26] That our human fates are determined by forces beyond our control is one of the themes of MacCarthy's savagely subversive modern fairy tale; marriage and the prince's kiss do not make for a happy ending and the unborn are doomed to inhabit limbo.

Such depth and richness of experience also crossed over into her prose fiction. In MacCarthy's 1937 short story 'Flight' – described by a reviewer of the day as 'remarkable' for its 'mixture of brilliance and over-sophistication' – we inhabit the confused inner reality of a hospitalised, unnamed 'nervous lady' who appears to be in some form of a sodium bromide delirium, as her sense of the world around her is diminished.[27] That she is, despite her compromised psychological state, sharply intelligent, fluent in French, and well educated is clear, and when she wryly declares on 'The Trauma of Birth', we are reminded of Beckett's interest in psychoanalysis and his annotation of Otto Rank's *The Trauma of Birth* in the 1930s. Beckett's favourite composer, Claude Debussy, is also mentioned in a way that speaks of an intimate relation between the inner life of words and music:

> if only he would go on talking like the plain chant from Debussy's 'Cathedrale Engloutie' sounding through the twilight surge of her bromidian sea, but alas! alas! she had forgotten the crashing dominant sevenths.[28]

It is an accomplished, intelligently crafted and, at times, terrifying story, which may well have been partly inspired by MacCarthy's own hospitalisation in December 1931 following a single-vehicle car crash on Dublin's Victoria Bridge; Beckett, unharmed, was the driver of the car, and MacCarthy's serious injuries left him deeply traumatised.[29]

In 'Flight' it is the charming Count Banjax who tempts the lady up into his aeroplane, which he attempts to fly solo: 'It was never very clear what happened and still less why they were not both killed, but they crashed almost as soon as they started' (p. 57). When the narrator at one point professes that, 'Life [...] is largely a problem of orifices' (p. 56), MacCarthy's wit and humour is unmistakable and when she has her narrator order 'a huge slab of gorgonzola' (p. 57) one cannot help but think she is flaunting her modernist credentials and following in the footsteps of both Belacqua in *More Pricks than Kicks* (MacCarthy is considered the inspiration for the Alba in Beckett's *Dream of Fair to Middling Women*, written in 1932, which also centres on Belacqua) and James Joyce's Leopold Bloom. There is a twist, however. For this nervous lady, the gorgonzola ('sour, sickening and overpowering') induces nausea and becomes 'a sweating abomination of corrupt lactation where foul mites teemed' (p. 57). MacCarthy's real gift is to create a world in fiction that is entirely its own and that manages to keep the reader not merely at bay but in a state of high alert, if not alarm. At a heightened moment that is cinematic in its execution, the lift shaft grows into a 'sheer and sickening abyss', inducing vertigo in the narrator and a similar sensation in the reader: 'in her terror of that nauseating drop, the floor on which she stood seemed to be giving way crumbling into the vortex of its fearful attraction' (p. 55). Added to this, there is something utterly and lastingly unique about how the story operates as a female-centred and female-voiced circular experience that negotiates a troubling relation to language itself: 'The lady wanted to say "perfectly" [...] but found she could not articulate the word without a hitch [...] It was strange how since the accident she could *think* words so clearly but how thickened and unmanageable they became unless she spoke slowly' (p. 54). The troubled speaker of MacCarthy's poem 'Barcelona' articulates a similar moment of linguistic breakdown, as she listens to the foreign language spoken by her sailor companion, who 'laughed and talked in a tongue I knew / but could not understand / for the blankness in my head'.[30]

'There are bits that will murmur to you', Samuel Beckett wrote to the dying MacCarthy in April 1959, referring to his newly finished radio play *Embers*, which had been provisionally titled 'Ebb'.[31] Previously, in a letter to his 'Dearest Ethna' dated 4 February 1959, he had alluded to his struggle to find a title for the radio piece, commenting: 'You'd find me a title for it, but I can't.'[32] MacCarthy died a month later. Visiting the terminally ill MacCarthy at her home in Dublin in December

1958, Beckett would find her 'sat for most of the day crouching, silent, over the fire'[33] and the word 'embers', redolent as it is of death and diminishing life, recurs in poems by MacCarthy such as 'Requiem' and 'Old Toys'. Published in *The Irish Times* in October 1942, 'Requiem' is articulated by a speaker who yearns for restful death: 'rest like shadow needs an ardent noon / and in disuse its pallid embers fall'.[34] In 'Old Toys', broadcast on Radio Éireann on 31 January 1949, the dolls, cast off, become eerie half-living symbols of the inescapable fact of death. Here, again, MacCarthy's surreal poetic vision and keen musical ear are to the fore, as the proximity of life and death is amplified by the sonic similarity of the linked words 'embers' and 'embryo':

> the embers crumble,
> the room grows chill,
> [...]
> Stiff effigies, eyes gummed, but still they live.
> Do not rouse them. Do not weep
> these embryos of eternal sleep.[35]

MacCarthy wrote as a poet who was intimately familiar with the colourless fact of death, with the grim and unspeakable nature of human suffering, and as one who witnessed time and again the degradations of the body and spirit as it descends towards its last breath. One of the last pieces MacCarthy wrote before her death in May 1959 was an account of her own experience undergoing radiotherapy treatment for cancer and the debilitating effect of losing one's sense of taste (what she termed 'mouth blindness'), published posthumously in the medical journal *The Lancet*.[36]

For decades after her death, she would be remembered primarily for her role in Beckett's personal life as his 'first crush' and as the real-life figure behind the 'Alba' and the girl on the punt in *Krapp's Last Tape* – as James Knowlson summed it up, 'a powerful inspiration for his work and, in later years, a dear friend'[37] – but, as the recent publication of her *Poems* (Lilliput Press, 2019) has now confirmed, MacCarthy was an accomplished poet in her own right. Far from being merely a Beckettian muse, her words haunted his, and her legacy opens up Irish modernism to the sound of other voices, reanimates the conversations that go on among writers and across their work, and forces us to listen to, and to regard, life in the shadows. Her writing across genres is persuasive, perceptive and quietly powerful, lit with a compelling attentiveness to life and to languages. 'She is an exceptional woman, and a very modern one … is well-educated, speaks fluent French and Spanish ("hijo de la puta blanca" as she calls for a drink) and can recognise most of Belacqua's erudite or literary allusions and return them in kind. She has fiercely independent views, a scathing wit, and a talent for not pulling any punches with her criticisms.'[38] So James Knowlson enumerates the formidable talents of Beckett's Alba and their source in Ethna MacCarthy, and the self-same traits mark MacCarthy out as a literary figure of lasting importance, whose poetry and literary output exudes intellectual vivacity, philosophical depth and musical sensitivity. Praising MacCarthy's 'tantalising' poems for their 'tight memorable phrases' and 'talent for jumping right into a subject', Eiléan Ní Chuilleanáin has observed of MacCarthy's 'restless' poetics: 'These are poems of exploration, of questioning … They really do address the mysteries of life.'[39] There is much exploration still to be done by readers into the multi-faceted and immensely varied work of this most questing and arresting of poets.

Freda Laughton (1907–95)

Jaclyn Allen

While to the Sun the Swan

While to the sun the swan
Pledges the homage of serenity,
Mirroring with the music of her form
The cadence of the sliding river,

I on my nest, that labyrinth
Beneath the skin of thought,
Built of the straws of circumstance and time,
Warm with my heart a bird

Lying encircled in the expectant shell,
That moon-seed echo of the lovely sun
That sometimes lays its face upon the river,
Cheek against cheek, the bright upon the darkness.[1]

Born in Bristol in 1907, Freda Laughton moved to Ireland in 1932 and settled in County Down. The scant surviving details of her life have determined her enigmatic presence in mid-twentieth-century Irish poetry. Though a notable female presence in the male-dominated literary periodicals and anthologies of her time, Laughton would publish only one volume of poetry, *A Transitory House*, in 1945. Initially praised as 'one of the few poets to-day who are worth watching, who have a strong individual talent, and a distinct flavour of their own', she nonetheless quickly vanished from view in the decades following her first collection.[2] The impact of Laughton's poetry among her contemporaries speaks to its distinctive qualities of subject, style and image. For Lucy Collins, the brevity of her publishing career belies its unique and radical import. '[Laughton] was ground-breaking in her representation of women's lived experience', she affirms, 'her exploration of dynamics of human connection and alienation revealed the extent to which women's cultural marginalization could be productive of unique explorations in poetry'.[3]

'While to the Sun the Swan' opens *A Transitory House* and foregrounds the avian imagery and metaphor of maternity that features throughout Laughton's work. A succession of sensual images of the natural world coalesce in the poem's fluid form, creating a surrealistic and dream-like effect. Laughton's relaxed syntax, minimal punctuation and enjambment encourage the free association of subject and symbol. The poem flows in one unbroken sentence across three stanzas, mirroring '[the] cadence of the sliding river'. The swan observed in the first stanza becomes personified as the speaker in the second stanza, culminating in a metaphoric pregnancy as the speaker blurs the distinction between bird and human. The speaker's nest becomes the unconscious mind at the centre / heart of which lies an unhatched bird. As the 'moon-seed echo of the lovely sun', this bird reflects the outside world, but the image of mother bird and egg in the second stanza indicates that this bird is her own creation born of the mind in reaction to the external world. In essence, it is her created object born of female experience. By allying imagery of maternity with her poetic praxis, Laughton exemplifies Gerardine Meaney's claim that her work 'insists her gender is part of her poetic identity, but this is regarded as a strength'.[4]

The creative process is expanded upon in 'In a Transitory Beauty', where Laughton again deploys the metaphoric association of pregnancy and egg to construct a model of creativity that is self-perpetuating:

> Maternal the shell
> Cradling the embryo bird,
> A transitory house
> Fashioned for a brief security,
> Of purposeful fragility,
> A beauty built to be broken.[5]

The poem opens with a 'maternal shell' that houses a bird, but only its destruction allows for it to be free. Creative production is implied in the second stanza when the speaker asks how the shell can 'Petition for immortality' when it must be destroyed to free the bird, while the bird itself is defined as an 'ephemeral' object which will eventually be erased. This calls into question how an author can live beyond their lifetime when all eventually fades away. The response is implied by the phrase 'Perpetual genesis', as the third stanza states that the 'maternal shell' will re-form to hold the bird once again in a perpetual cycle of creation–destruction–recreation. This process and the repeated reference to the maternal affirm Laughton's construction of creativity grounded in the female body.

Laughton's preoccupation with femininity and female creativity informs her darker subjective poetry and she frames her call for a regeneration of the feminine creative self with Jungian psychoanalysis. Reviewing Jungian psychoanalyst John Layard's case study *The Lady of the Hare* in *The Bell* in 1945, she expresses her interest in 'the Jungian method of analytical psychology and belief in the healing power of dreams', whose method of analysis 'lays great emphasis on the intuitional function, which latterly we have come to distrust'.[6] Laughton discusses Jung's belief in intuition and the claim that 'modern man is sick precisely because he no longer gives proper attention to this redemptive process'. By repressing our instinctive feelings and desires, we deny their potential transformative psychological effects:

> Outwardly ignored it sinks into the Unconscious, and there giving rise to dreams whose symbols refer back thousands of years, it endeavours again to attract the attention of Consciousness and restore the balance, for it appears that until the contents of the Unconscious can be recognised, their immense power for good remains latent, and may even work in a detrimental fashion.[7]

In 'Portrait of a Woman' and 'Nightly Slim Adventures Slide', Laughton suggests the process of the dream 'cure' to diagnose conventional femininity as creatively sterile and then calls for alternative models to restore balance within the female psyche and allow for creative expression. First published in *The Irish Times* in September 1945, 'Portrait of a Woman' opens by figuring its female subject in the stereotypical terms of the cultivated garden:[8]

> She is a garden with a careful face
> Tended and drilled and every grass-blade combed
> Neatly in place. She wears the usual flowers,
> Hydrangeas' rose and sapphire sponges, gowns
> Of fuchsias wardrobed in their leaves, stone urns
> Of rouged geraniums. The cordyline
> Is sharp with all her comments, worldly-wise;

The floral profusion generates an expressive form that is at once beautifying and limiting for the female subject. The manicured beauty of the garden is the product of external control and containment, where the landscape is 'tended and drilled' and every individual grass blade is 'combed / Neatly in place'. The garden furniture is similarly figured in constraining, even coercive, terms with its 'chairs of iron discomfort' and empty 'tables of arrested growth' creating an atmosphere of enforced stasis and consequent enervation.[9] If the garden is emblematic of the repressive influence of literary conventions and tropes, then the third and final stanza provides a potentially transfiguring response to this condition. Rising from the unconscious in resistance is the free-growing ash tree, a recurring image of the female autonomous self in Laughton's work, which indicates that a return to the psychological origins of masculine *animus* and feminine *anima* is necessary in order to restore balance within the female subject:

> There grows in spite of her, a weeping ash,
> Wilfully obedient to the wind
> Against all orders; baldaquin of green
> And gracious canopy for some crowned head
> Who, passing and the gate inviting him,
> Might some day stride across the short-fleeced lawn
> And set up court beneath the trembling boughs.

In 'Nightly Slim Adventures Slide', the speaker ventures into the subconscious dreamworld to unearth a new kind of woman poet. This woman wears 'a wreath of words / Transposed, beheaded, biting their own tails' in a cycle of perpetual creation–destruction–recreation seen in 'In a Transitory Beauty'.[10] The figure causes fear in the speaker, however, as she must carry 'unknown corpses', slain by her, to the graveyard where this archetype waits. This mirrors the anxiety apparent in 'In a Transitory Beauty', where destruction and sacrifice are inextricably and painfully linked to the creative and generative process. The poem ends with the speaker seizing power with the statement 'I hold the mirror up to life and death'. Both poems end with the speaker suggesting that a new form of the creative feminine is necessary, although the exact nature of that form is undefined. In 'Portrait of a Woman', the revolution lies in the future rather than the present, and while the speaker in 'Nightly Slim Adventures Slide' states that she could take the form of 'bride or serpent, bird or tree' to seize power, she does not ultimately choose. Laughton may critique conventions of femininity and womanhood, but alternative models of redefinition remain difficult to conceive.

Laughton's contemporary reception in Irish periodical culture registers the radical complexities of her poetry. Anne Mulhall has identified 'the profoundly masculinist … literary bias' in Irish literary magazines during the 1940s and 1950s, which helped to maintain the conditions by which women were 'overwhelmingly absent' in the published literary discourse of the period.[11] Laughton is remarkable however in that she featured regularly in *The Bell*, so much so that a disgruntled Austin Clarke could remark in 1946 that she 'has been sponsored by that magazine'.[12] Laughton in many ways fits in with *The Bell*'s agenda to reimagine the expressive forms by which Irish life and culture could be captured. As the magazine's editor Seán O'Faoláin declared in his opening editorial:

> All our symbols have to be created afresh, and the only way to create a living symbol is to take a naked thing and clothe it with new life, new association, new meaning, with all the vigour of the life we live in the Here and Now.[13]

Laughton aligns with this ambition in the intense sensory and psychological qualities of her poetry, where the immediacy of experience merges with a radical symbolism. *The Bell* cultivated an aesthetic based on personal insight, observation and feeling. It was these qualities that Valentin Iremonger consequently emphasised in his reviews of Laughton's work for the magazine. Iremonger saw her as representative of the younger generation of poets in that she drew 'her inspiration from the depths of her experience'.[14] Iremonger saw more than just realism in her, however, and praised her verse for its 'sensuous and imaginative quality' which raised it to 'a Spinoza-like identification of God and Nature producing a world, absolute in itself yet rooted in life, in which the mind, advancing step by step in observation of nature in relation to any event, finally, by intuitive insight, catches a glimpse of God'.[15] As Mulhall has observed, however, Iremonger also restricted Laughton's vision to the traditionally feminine realm of house and garden, thereby subduing the proto-feminist energies in her work.[16] For Meaney, '*The Bell's* championship of Laughton's work indicates it understood feminine self-representation as part of its modernizing project', although this could at times mean reducing that representation to traditional gender models.[17]

The Bell provided a major outlet and supportive network for Laughton's work in the 1940s. Not everyone shared the magazine's esteem for the poet, however, and she suffered criticism for her perceived failure to conform both to the nationalist narrative of Irish poetry and to the expectations of the Irish woman poet. Austin Clarke took specific issue with Laughton's Irishness, writing 'it would be pleasant to welcome her as a new Irish poet, but, with the exception of one poem, there is nothing in this collection which has the slightest relation to this country'.[18] Because of the lack of explicitly Irish references or themes and what he viewed as 'the horrible ingenuities of the contemporary English poetic mind' in her work, Clarke places her instead in the context of a British poetic milieu and tradition.[19] He prefaces his review of her collection by remarking that the younger poets draw inspiration primarily from contemporary English verse and that *The Bell* itself is an example of this trend, so that 'many of the poems might have been selected from *Horizon* or any other English modernist compilation'.

Laughton also became a subject in the debate over the nature and expectations of the woman poet. Writing into *The Bell* in August 1945, Patricia Harrison broadly criticised Laughton's poetry but found particular fault with 'The Woman with Child'.[20] This poem celebrates pregnancy as well as the woman's developing identity as a mother by comparing the pregnant female body to unfurling flower buds, growing apples and the waxing moon. Harrison takes issue with the 'treatment' of the pregnant female body about to give birth at the end of the poem:[21]

> The apple waxes at the blossom's root,
> And like the moon I mellow to the round
> Full circle of my being, till I too
>
> Am ripe with living and my fruit is grown.
> Then break the shell of life. We shall be born,
> My child and I, together, to the sun.[22]

Meaney has discussed the extent to which the public, visibly pregnant female body remained a taboo in Irish society at this time and efforts were made to obscure the reality of pregnancy and childbirth in popular representation.[23] It is unsurprising, therefore, that Harrison's objection to this depiction of the pregnant body centres on its perceived excessive sensuality, declaring that '[in] these poems there is sensuousness for the sake of sensuousness, and not real imagination'.[24] Laughton's physical, sensual woman is deemed morally repugnant, with Harrison concluding that her representation of maternity is 'ugly and forced'.[25] The fundamental issue lies in Laughton's lack of conformity to Harrison's conception of female self-representation and of the woman poet.

This 'storm among the teacups of Irish literature's back pages' demonstrates the challenges faced by Irish women poets during the mid-twentieth century.[26] Though Laughton was a notable female presence in the patriarchal domain of Irish periodical culture in the 1940s, and published her first collection with the major London firm Jonathan Cape, her curtailed literary career ultimately speaks to the difficulties in maintaining such success. Her dramatic falling away into obscurity in the decades following her first collection more broadly reflects the institutionalised patterns of forgetting and loss that have occluded the tradition of Irish women's literature. Yet, to return to Laughton's poetry is to encounter a radical expression of femininity and female creativity, where 'the sensuality of her work is a testament to its resistance to the norms of female representation of the mid-century years, and is evidence of its untapped potential as a liberating model for later generations of poets'.[27]

Madge Herron (1915–2002)

Jane Robinson

Frog

Look at me,
Look what they have done.
I was torn.
I think about the rains
And where they fell,
Where once I had four hands
And now have none.[1]

Madge Herron was a performance poet before that label had been invented: a spoken word poet before her time. A vivid, fleeting presence on the stage, at reading groups, and across the airwaves in Dublin and London during the difficult decades of the mid-twentieth century, Herron infused her poetry with the force and musicality of her speaking voice. Brazenly anti-authoritarian in her life and art, her claim that 'I hated being told what to do' propelled a transgressive poetics that crossed linguistic, spatial and temporal borders.[2] Herron's bilingualism channelled the verbal energies of her native Irish and adopted English, while her poetry reached out to the threatened natural world of her childhood and the losses suffered by wild animals and wildness in modern society. As Patricia Herron, her niece, writes, Herron's unique poetic gift was that 'she was a visionary, she could see the unity of the past, present and future, but she could not always reconcile what she saw there with the material world in which she also lived'.[3]

Madge Herron (1915–2002)

Madge Herron was born in 1915 in the remote townland of Glenamohill, Fintown, in the Gaeltacht area of south-west County Donegal, and she grew up speaking Irish and running over the wild landscape. 'In Donegal, Gaelic is our language, / With its humps, its shadows, it is like ourselves', Herron affirms in the poem 'A Prayer to St Theresa', describing how 'You go up a mountain and down the other side / To find out who you are'.[4] The poem then continues with the Irish-language interjection:

> Theresa – go Dé mar a tá tú?
> (In English that means, how do you do?)
> Theresa, they said last night you were all love,
> Tossing rose bushes out of the sky.

The casual-seeming repetitions, the alliteration and the playful rhyming of the Irish 'tú' and English 'do' are deployed in a way that does not distract from the conversational tone. That the saint should toss 'rose bushes' rather than individual flowers from the sky is an example of the unconventional phrasing and imagery that animates Herron's poetry. 'A Prayer to St Theresa' begins by describing an unspecified familial affliction: 'This thing we have they call "mental" / in no way restricts us', and continues with an address to St Theresa, patron saint of the sick. Although the poem bears the italicised epigraph '*(on behalf of my father who is mad)*', the opening two stanzas relate more to the speaker, empowered by a communal voice that celebrates the people of the Donegal Gaeltacht region: 'Socially, we are tremendous'. Later, the poem narrows its focus to the personal relationship between the speaker and the father. 'The clothes line in his head's gone bust', the speaker bluntly describes, before opening the final stanza with the startling invocation, 'Theresa, take him by camera – and you kill the light', which is tempting to read as the expression of some kind of atavistic taboo against being photographed or specified, but more likely reflects the speaker's desire to shield her vulnerable father from public exposure or criticism.[5] Herron's expressiveness is evident in the closing stanza, the suddenness of the father's step is caught with the compound phrase 'ink-quick splash of his heel', which is jarringly followed by the stark surreal image of him 'full of holes / With scores of dead sheep popping out of him'. The culminating wish to 'Put him seated between two mountains / And at his ease' adds scale, grandeur and a sense of deep time to the portrait.[6] Although the poem is ostensibly a prayer addressed to St Theresa, it is also addressed to Herron's English-speaking audience by way of the rhyming translation, and, in spite of the epigraph, the poem embodies its speaker to such an extent that the prayer seems as much on behalf of herself as on behalf of her father, who died when she was only five years old. For Patricia Herron, 'A Prayer to St Theresa' speaks to the essential 'timelessness' in Herron's poetry whereby 'the present, past and future merge into one state of consciousness', emboldening the poet who 'talks about her dead father, and asks for help for him, as if he were still alive and still affecting her life'.[7]

In the small portion of her poems that has survived, Herron frequently stretches time and space, imagining herself, for example, a thousand years in the future or in the past:

> Do you remember me now?
> Can you place me – say –
> A thousand years before
> On that same hill?[8]

Madge Herron's early traumatic loss of her father was followed by the death of her mother when she was nineteen, spurring her departure from the wilds of Donegal to Dublin in 1935. There, she soon met Micheál Mac Liammóir, co-founder of the Gate Theatre, who encouraged her budding interests in acting and stage writing. Herron also gave her first national radio broadcasting performance in October 1935. The Irish-language poem 'Áilleacht Tír Chonaill', the only poem to have been published from that performance, is much more formally composed (with a stately pace, alliterative patterns and regular rhythm) than Herron's later English-language poems. Rooted in the landscape of Donegal, we see the deep identification with native animals, habitats and landscapes in the poem. The complex interweaving of assonance and alliterative 'l' sounds give a sense of the musicality of Herron's original performance, and the voice that writer Gerry Moriarty described as 'resonant, mellifluous and beautiful when reciting her own poetry':[9]

Is glas iad na coillte faoi láthair
Fíor bheo le síor chantain na néan
Tá cúmhra na nóinín ins na bóithre
Ag gealladh dúinn sonas agus séan.
Fan trá tá an faoileog ar eiteoig
Ag seoladh anonn is anall,
Ní mian léithe scaradh a choíche
Le cuanta Thír Chonaill na dtonn.[10]

They are green, these days, the woods
and alive in sweet songs of birds,
with a scent of daisies by the road
to promise us joy and good fortune.
Stay while a seagull lifts off from shore
and soars back, ranging here and there,
unable to separate herself, ever,
from Thír Chonaill's harbours and swells.
[Author's translation]

Herron's natural flair for drama was recognised with the award of a scholarship to the Abbey Theatre School of Acting in 1936. She performed in her first production, George Shiel's comedy of small-town business life, *Quin's Secret*, in 1937.[11] Having made a name for herself in Dublin, Herron moved to London where she spent a brief period training at the prestigious Royal Academy of Dramatic Art and writing her own stage work. She returned to Donegal, however, following the outbreak of the Second World War. Arriving home alone, exhausted and with an unnamed illness, as reported in the *Irish Press*, 'her nerves were breaking after the strain of these trying years; real war had come; and one night she set out to return to the heather and the crags that she knows and loves so well'.[12] In a later poem, 'Londonderry Air', the following image is striking in that it appears to describe some lived truth from this time: 'If war should shatter you to fishes / Who is to accompany you onto the ocean floor?' The somewhat mysterious lines

> The wallpaper is blasted through the ceiling.
> Look! Overturned, forests of dead caterpillars.
> Come, and we'll make brooches of them.

seem to carry more than a hint of Armageddon, perhaps in reaction to the later threat of nuclear warfare and nuclear arms testing, against which Herron participated in protests.[13]

The post-war years brought new opportunities for broadcasting in London and Herron renewed her diverse literary contacts of the late 1930s by returning to the city. In 1947 she featured in Frank O'Connor's translated version of Brian Merriman's eighteenth-century play *The Midnight Court* for the BBC Third Programme. The radio play brought together a prominent group of Herron's literary contemporaries, including poets Louis MacNeice and W.R. Rodgers, who were involved as producers, while O'Connor also performed along with renowned Abbey Theatre actor Máire Brennan.[14] Over the following two decades Herron continued to utilise the airwaves as a medium for transmitting her voice. Writing in the *PN Review* in 2004, Canadian-born poet Marius Kociejowski attempted to capture the distinctive power of Herron in performance as he experienced it in London during the 1970s:

> When it came her turn to read, she did so with her whole body, her eyes closed, the words driven by sheer physical force. She could hold the stage with an intensity rarely seen in literary circles. Always she read from memory or perhaps from somewhere even deeper than that, from the soul's furnace where poetry is made. A poem was rendered as if for the first time. She would constantly surprise.[15]

Herron's performances at weekly readings and workshops such as the *Poetry Round* sessions, held at the Poetry Society in Earls Court Square, proved popular and in 1971 she was invited on two separate occasions to read on George MacBeth's *Poetry Now* programme on BBC Radio 3. I found these recordings at the British Library in London and heard Madge Herron's voice released from the vault as fresh and direct as the day it was recorded.[16] This was no self-conscious performance; it had an unusual purity of sound and intent. Listening to her read 'The Bull', it felt as though she were singing out the words to please the mountains a thousand years from now:

> I tell you
> He bugles
> And is akin to birds.
> He pipes streams
> From fine thin fluting.
> Angered, he cracks
> Mountains.
> Sensational is his
> Arithmetic.[17]

Herron's melodious poetics aspire to birdsong with the spry repetition and exchange of vowel sounds and consonants in 'fine thin fluting'. While the opening lines are apparently addressed to an audience or reader (or perhaps to a deity, so confidently but gently does she proclaim them), the address then shifts to the bull, or the earth-based mystery represented here by a bull. Herron credited the sublime experience of seeing a bronze bull sculpture by Pablo Picasso at the Tate Gallery in London in 1967 as an inspiration for the poem. 'I went in and saw this massive thing you know, I don't know, I just went into tears over him.'[18] The bull is initially described in ominous terms as a 'Bell-bugling brute', who threatens the 'identity' of the speaker. But it quickly transfigures from a physically imposing presence into a sacred symbolic creature capable of crying 'black / Tears' to 'Redeem the earth'. This coincides with the speaker's own intensifying passion and lyricism as the bull turns from a potentially threatening to a liberating influence. The speaker invests her subject with an artistry and beauty of its own, urging the bull to 'Sing then, / Split me with your / Bugling', and culminating with the affirmation that 'The music comes / From you'.

The 1970s in London cannot have been an easy time for Herron and she became more eccentric in appearance, walking around Kentish town with bags of shopping, piles of books gleaned from jumble sales and a retinue of stray dogs. Some contemporaries assumed she was homeless but her biographer has gathered evidence that this was not the case.[19] Herron's deteriorating relationship with her remaining family was compounded by her brother's selling of the family farm in Donegal, confining her to a life in London. This loss of home may also have been particularly difficult because she had no pathway back to what her fellow Donegal poet Annemarie Ní Churreáin describes as 'the language of intimacy and community', encoding the ancient heart-knowledge with its links to the landscape.[20] Yet, despite her own troubles, Herron continued to encourage younger writers. 'This detail – you said you would like to do a poem as simple as a flower – Jesus, a flower is not simple, it's gigantic', she wrote to poet Francis Harvey in 1984, 'Get around the other side of it. Relax with it. And you will get there … And don't pity things, a weed is equal to any flower, a small bird is as cruel as a tiger.'[21] Herron admired the work of Romantic poet John Clare but also cultivated a 'starkness and simplicity' that critics have associated with modernist influences such as Imagism.[22] She was well versed, from a young age, in Irish-language poetry and understood her native landscape and its other worlds through the language. In her frequent invocations of flora and fauna Herron worked from that tradition and, amalgamating it with what she learnt from the English-language poetry scene of London in the 1970s, created some startlingly memorable work.

'Give me the Lark' opens in seemingly angry address to someone or something that threatens the lark: possibly referring to the barbaric practice of trapping and eating songbirds; or to the decline of larks due to modern farming methods; or perhaps in conversation with Emily Dickinson's poem (861) 'Split the Lark – and you'll find the Music'.[23] But then, Herron's speaker offers an alternative approach ('I wouldn't do a thing like that / To get the music out') where enticing the lark could be read as a metaphor for the arrival at spiritual enlightenment. While Dickinson questions her puritanical Christian heritage and 'exclusively human-centered or science-centered views of nature' or *logos* (in this instance with her riddling but undeniably graphic examination of the split lark), in 'Give me the Lark', Herron steps out of a more ancient pre-Christian Irish nature poetry tradition or *mythos* and dives into her customary 'thousand years' mythological time scales with unquestioning assurance.[24] The poem's concluding lines are, paradoxically, both mysterious and satisfying, opaque like a metaphysical puzzle:

> Give me the lark
> Before you cut it up.
> I wouldn't do a thing like that
> To get the music out
> I'd rather be a scarecrow
> For a thousand years instead,
> Until a time
> When she is trusting
> And comes to me herself.
> Then scarce I'd pull
> The summer in
> To hear the singing
> In her head.[25]

Unfortunately, what remains of Herron's work is fragmentary and erratic. Madge Herron ran out of time; she did not have a thousand years. There was a falling away, perhaps the beginnings of the dementia of her later years when she retreated first into whisperings in Irish, and then into silence.[26] Patricia Herron has noted her 'lifelong reluctance to publish any of her poetry in written form' and, lacking the support of a sympathetic editor or publisher to convince her otherwise, Herron never developed a career from book to book like her contemporaries.[27] Only two of her poems were anthologised during her lifetime.[28] It is, perhaps fittingly, in performance that we find her in 1979, at a poetry reading in the Peacock Theatre, marking her return to Dublin after decades of exile in London. Taking the stage, she rummages through a plastic bag for crumpled pieces of paper while the audience titters anxiously. When she suddenly finds the scrap she is looking for, she is away. 'Not long did the indulgent tittering greet her extraordinary breathless images', journalist Elgy Gillespie describes, 'as Madge strode back and forth on the Peacock stage with the roll of a merchant seaman, she declaimed her poems by heart'.[29] Clearly moved by the performance, Gillespie recounts Herron's Irish-language poems that have now been lost, but through which she '[assumed] the resonance and some of the occasional brutality as well as the beauty'. Herron was an ambitious poet, and perhaps a seer. Her extraordinary voice can be felt in her few surviving poems and recordings, representing the remains of an oeuvre that has been scattered to the winds:

> He who mans the drawbridge of the night
> His mane, a wet blue ink,
> Confronts time and the beat of his own heart,
> Spits stars out through his teeth.[30]

Patricia Avis (1928–77)

Conor Linnie

Le Deuxième Sexe

Not one haystack
But a whole field of haystacks,
Firm, plump, conical,
Sun soaked, wind scarred,
By moonlight monumental.
It's not as if one feared
To make a move, commiserate
With another across the way;
It's just that each has its own knack
Of living with a shadow.
What was grass once,
Tickled and swayed,
Now broods in the middle distance,
Saved for whatever fork
Is destined to gather it.
Not stiff, nor bowed,
Nor yet by any means importunate,
Each shape describes itself
A little too roundly on its own behalf,
And not too steadily
Being at a standstill.[1]

On the morning of 15 September 1977, readers of *The Irish Times* might have easily passed over the short article on page nine titled 'Patricia Murphy: An appreciation'.[2] Written by Brian

Inglis, the piece provided a belated and all too brief account of a literary life. 'Hearing of Patricia Murphy's death in Dublin earlier this month sent me rummaging among a store of old magazines, looking for a copy of *nonplus*', Inglis opens, referring to the short-lived but influential Dublin literary magazine Avis funded and edited from her home at 1 Wilton Place between 1959 and 1960. Inglis hails *nonplus* as 'just the sort of literary magazine which we used to tell each other Dublin ought to have, and how monstrous it was that Dublin did not have', and attributes its failure to survive beyond a mere four issues to a lack of appreciation for its editor and her independent literary endeavours. 'Did Patricia win kudos for her spirited – and public spirited effort? I doubt it. But perhaps we can recall it with gratitude now.' Though well intentioned, the brevity of the article does little to encompass its subject, who variously assumed the roles of poet, patron, editor and novelist during the 1950s and 1960s. Inglis' closing admission that he has 'read little of Patricia's own work as a writer' in fact heralds her fading presence from the literary field of the mid-twentieth century in the decades following her death. While her tragic death and tumultuous intimate relationships with poets including Philip Larkin and Richard Murphy have remained popular sources of interest, her own literary significance has receded from view.

Patricia Avis was born in Johannesburg, South Africa, in 1928 to an Irish mother and a wealthy Dutch father.[3] 'Her brilliance was scary', Richard Murphy has recalled, and she moved to England at the age of seventeen to study medicine at Somerville College, Oxford. Though she completed her degree and qualified to be a doctor in 1951, Avis refrained from taking up a formal practice.[4] Instead, she drifted away from the medical world into the vagrant post-war literary circles of Belfast, Dublin, London and Paris that would shape the course of her life over the next two decades. Avis first arrived in Belfast in 1952 with her newly married husband, Colin Strang, who had taken up a position as lecturer in philosophy at Queen's University. There, she met and began a two-year affair with Philip Larkin, who was then employed as a sub-librarian at the university. Larkin exerted a vital early influence on her writing and was himself on the brink of becoming recognised as a central figure in a revitalised British post-war literary scene. Avis eventually settled in the Republic of Ireland with Irish poet Richard

Murphy and officially became an Irish citizen in 1955. From there and on various trips across the Irish Sea, she cultivated her position within a widening transnational network of writers, editors and publishers including novelists and poets Kingsley Amis, John Wain and Patrick Kavanagh, and Faber publisher Charles Monteith. Most importantly, she developed a keen friendship with J.R. Ackerley, influential literary editor of the BBC's weekly magazine, *The Listener*, who published her first poems from 1955 onwards and enthusiastically proclaimed her as 'one of us'.[5]

'Le Deuxième Sexe' opens a window on Avis' developing craft and the literary networks that supported her in the 1950s. The poem first appeared in *The Listener* in July 1957, one of three poems that she published in quick succession in the magazine between July and August of that year.[6] 'Le Deuxième Sexe' signals the cosmopolitan affiliations that defined her writing and publishing in these years. The title, taken from Simone de Beauvoir's landmark study of the treatment of women throughout history, published to instant acclaim in 1949, registers the influence of Avis' time spent living in post-war Paris. While at Oxford she had developed a love of French literature and culture under the influence of renowned professor of French Enid Starkie, and Avis eventually moved to Paris in 1954 for a brief period following the break-up of her first marriage. Howard M. Parshley's first abridged and edited English translation of de Beauvoir's treatise was published in 1953 as *The Second Sex*, but Avis' use of the French title for her poem suggests an affinity with the original French version and the Parisian intellectual world she encountered.[7] De Beauvoir's famous assertion that 'One is not born, but rather becomes woman' establishes *The Second Sex*'s central challenge to the social, cultural and economic structures by which women have been figured and determined in a secondary role to men throughout history.[8] De Beauvoir interrogates the myriad ways that women have been represented with fixed and restricting ideals of femininity, against which 'the [male] subject posits itself only in opposition; it asserts itself as the essential and sets up the other as inessential, as the object'.[9]

In her responding poem, Avis playfully pairs de Beauvoir's sprawling polemic prose study with a modest lyric form, immediately subverting the expectations of the title with her humble subject matter: a field of haystacks. 'Le Deuxième Sexe' wryly enacts the personification of woman in nature by feminising the haystacks, characterising them with a shifting series of features and qualities that trigger subtle modulations in tone and effect as the poem progresses. Avis delights in bringing her sophisticated cosmopolitan title quite literally down to earth in the poem's rural setting. The haystacks are first described in shapely terms that tease with feminine fertility tropes: 'firm, plump, conical'. The tone shifts in the following two lines, however, to the more sensitive consideration of the haystacks' suffering endurance of the elements ('Sun soaked, wind scarred') and their contrasting grandeur in more benign conditions ('By moonlight monumental'). Though 'Le Deuxième Sexe' may have opened with the comic deflation of its title, Avis now begins to personify her subject with greater imagination and to more evocative effect. The stacks are imagined as isolated beings in a crowd:

> It's not as if one feared
> To make a move, commiserate
> With another across the way;
> It's just that each has its own knack
> Of living with a shadow.

The image and motif of the shadow features throughout *The Second Sex*, variously symbolising the subordinated female consciousness and man's clouding presence. Avis' judgement of her subjects as having developed a 'knack / Of living with a shadow' defines their lonely isolation and even suggests a meek complicity in their sorry fate, while also more implicitly evoking de Beauvoir's omnipresent 'shadow of the male' that impedes female communion and solidarity.[10] For de Beauvoir, the pressures of patriarchal conventions and expectations create the conditions by which women remain 'turned toward the masculine world' rather than looking instead to 'transcend toward each other'.[11] Avis' verbal economy and muted lyricism ensure that the poem does not swell rhetorically or rhythmically in its latter section to the kind of declarative polemic statement or expression anticipated by its title. Rather, it continues by implication, playing off the suggestiveness of the haystacks' carefully observed features and the surrounding fields, where a marshalling phallic 'fork' gathers the hay and tames what was once a more lively landscape ('what was grass once, / Tickled and swayed'). The poem concludes enigmatically, finding fleeting postures of defiance in the haystacks' varied forms ('Not stiff, / nor bowed') before returning to the affectionately comic characterisation of its opening with each shape describing itself 'A little too roundly on its own behalf'.

Following the publication of 'Le Deuxième Sexe' in *The Listener*, Avis sent it in a letter to Philip Larkin, who 'liked' the poem so much that he asked to include it in the upcoming anthology *New Poems* he was then editing with Louis MacNeice and Bonamy Dobrée.[12] Avis had previously featured in the 1956 anthology *Poetry Now* edited by G.S. Fraser.[13] 'Are *you* ever going to produce a book?', Larkin implored, 'Of course, I don't want you to – hate & abhor competition – but you must be adding them up slowly.'[14] Avis' relationship with Larkin has dominated the posthumous narrative of her life and work, where she is exclusively viewed in the romantic context of their tumultuous two-year affair in Belfast between 1952 and 1953. This has been exacerbated by the biographical revelations that have transformed Larkin studies in recent decades. Anthony Thwaite's selected letters and Andrew Motion's biography of the poet in the early 1990s exposed the maltreatment of women, flagrant sexism and racism regularly voiced in Larkin's private correspondence, revealing what Tom Paulin emphatically declared as 'the sewer under the national monument'.[15]

Yet, these publications addressing Larkin's abhorrent private attitudes have also at times reinforced a misogyny of their own. This is particularly the case with Avis, who features in literary studies most often in association with the poet. Their relationship is typically evaluated in the sensationalised terms of their affair and in the broader context of Larkin's sexual awakening. Avis is consequently reduced to the superficial object of male desire, cast as the alluring but ill-fated figure left in the wake of a brilliant literary man. For Motion, Avis is simply the 'promiscuous' lover who 'dissolved [Larkin's] worries about sex' and provided him with 'the most happily erotic of all his affairs'.[16] James Booth follows a similar angle in his most recent biography, characterising Avis in overly emotionalised terms as 'vigorously acting out her own very different poetic myth, as the helpless victim of a doomed passion'.[17] In this reading she is seductive but volatile, a manipulative but unstable presence, with the 'melodramatic rhetoric' of her love letters reflecting the unravelling mental state of a woman 'driven to anguish by Larkin's cold artistic detachment'.[18]

Avis' affair with Larkin was undoubtedly for her an emotionally exhausting experience.[19] Her deep insecurities and anxieties were compounded by Larkin's oscillating attitudes of infatuation and ambivalence, and a brief traumatic pregnancy that ended in miscarriage in 1952. However, the biographical characterisation of Avis merely as troubled erotic foil for the timid male poet fails to note the extent to which their friendship continued and matured long after the affair had ended. As Larkin's enthusiastic letter responding to 'Le Deuxième Sexe' in 1957 indicates, they in fact developed a respectful and mutually productive literary relationship, their lively correspondence orbiting the concerns and activities of a familiar group of poets, authors, patrons and publishers. Larkin regularly opened up to Avis about his doubts and frustrations and even revised some of his poems based on her suggestions, backing up the later assertion by Richard Murphy that she 'improved my writing with her sensitive criticism'.[20] Avis, meanwhile, looked to Larkin for advice and instruction on her own developing craft.

The measured lyric voice of 'Le Deuxième Sexe' affirms the poetics of restraint continually insisted upon by Larkin in their correspondence; he was quick to challenge any excessive lyricism or rhetoric that threatened clarity of expression. Writing to Avis in February 1954, Larkin emphasised the importance of achieving 'a direct effect or a unified effect' in the poem, and how this could be fatally compromised by 'talking too much in metaphors'.[21] Referencing their mutual friend, the novelist and poet Kingsley Amis, he continued:

> I sometimes read a poem over with a tiny Kingsley crying *How d'you mean?* in my mind at every unclear image, and it's a wonderful aid to improvement, though perhaps you wouldn't care to try the experiment. Forgive me if I sound dogmatic: it must be the influence of this frightful *talk*.[22]

The pared poetics of 'Le Deuxième Sexe' emerge from what Larkin and his co-editors in the *New Poems* anthology of 1958 characterised as the 'stern days' of the post-war years.[23] This chastened period found its voice in Britain with the loosely grouped 'Movement' poets, of whom Larkin was central, and who were defined in the *New Lines* anthology of 1956 as renouncing 'diffuse and sentimental verbiage' for a more intellectual, rational and comprehensible poetry 'empirical in attitude to all that comes'.[24] Avis represents an important Irish link to this primarily British network of writers and publishers. 'Le Deuxième Sexe' also affirms her unique female perspective in a male-dominated literary scene, achieving a deft verse style that moves between irony and earnestness in the feminisation of its subject, subtly eliciting the sympathies of the reader without ever straining for effect.

Avis settled permanently in the Republic of Ireland in 1955 with her second husband Richard Murphy. They first lived together in a remote lodge in rural Wicklow, formerly owned by Ernest Gébler and Edna O'Brien, where Avis gave birth to their daughter Emily in 1956. The marriage would be short-lived, however, ending in divorce in 1959, at which time Avis moved into the top two floors of 1 Wilton Place, near Baggot Street Bridge in Dublin. She quickly established Wilton Place as an 'open house for Dublin poets and writers', with Patrick Kavanagh and Brian O'Nolan among her regular visitors.[25] From there Avis set up the cultural review *nonplus*, an ambitious 'essayists quarterly' that ran for four issues between 1959 and 1960.[26] As Tom Clyde has remarked, *nonplus* was distinguished for its 'very attractive' production standards and wide-ranging purview 'that took in everything from Sarajevo, to Heidegger and the GAA in four short issues'.[27] The magazine testified to Avis' central presence among the Dublin literary milieu of the mid-century. Printed at Liam Miller's hugely influential Dolmen Press, *nonplus* featured a series of prose and poetry contributions from Kavanagh; extracts from Myles na gCopaleen's popular 'Cruiskeen Lawn' column in *The Irish Times*; and extended essays from Hubert Butler and Brian Inglis. The glossy covers of the first two numbers were adorned with high-quality black and white photographs of Dublin city scenes from Elinor Vere Wiltshire's Green Studio on St Stephen's Green. The second two covers were designed with prints provided and arranged by Miller himself. The advertisements that filled each issue testified to Avis' business acumen and impressive commercial contacts. Pan American Airlines, Shell Oil, Dunlop Tyres, Guinness and Gold

Flake are all represented. *Nonplus*' contributions from Patrick Kavanagh in poetry and prose marked the magazine's most significant creative achievement, with Avis becoming a close friend and source of support for the ailing poet at this time. Kavanagh's biographer Antoinette Quinn has noted his 'extraordinarily generous' contributions to each issue, observing that the 'lengthy sequence of prose and poetry' was 'a remarkable coup for a new journal'.[28] Kavanagh's inclusion of the sonnet 'Canal Bank Walk' in *nonplus*' first issue linked his own self-celebrated late period of poetic rebirth with the launching of the new magazine, where he praised the vitality of ordinary experience in enabling him 'to pray unselfconsciously with overflowing speech'.[29]

It is surprising that *nonplus* only lasted for four quarterly issues, given its impressive literary contributions and commercial connections. Avis' dynamic role as publisher and editor concluded with the last issue of the magazine, but she continued to publish her poetry in both Irish and British periodicals into the 1960s. One particularly fruitful outlet in Dublin was the *University Review*, the magazine of the graduates association of the National University of Ireland, which regularly published her work alongside a range of established and emerging contemporaries including Kate O'Brien, Brian Coffey and John Jordan. Avis' poetry in the *University Review* marks a turn towards a more emotionally forceful and uncompromising lyric voice, shedding the playful ironies of 'Le Deuxième Sexe' to foreground directly unnerving and even shocking subject matter.[30] The short poem 'Played Out', one of three poems published in the 1963 edition of the periodical, confronts the reader with a diary-like shorthand account of a traumatic personal experience:

> So you were up all night
> And at the impossible break
> Of day you rang ... couldn't get through.
> Blood, more blood, bandages, police,
> Or drink, why not just drink.
> You sat on mustering fantasies,
> Alone, always alone,
> Never quite facing it.
> One and one made two or none
> Somewhere without you.

This first stanza is at once immediate and elliptical, the conversational idiom is clipped and disjointed by irregular line breaks and internal punctuation that together effect a dramatic abbreviation of expression. The narrated transition from a sleepless night of physical and psychological trauma into the 'impossible break / Of day' is itself fractured by a line break, with the speaker recounting the experience in a cold and almost accusative second-person. Though left unspecified, the reference to 'Blood, more blood' suggests an act of extreme self-harm. Even allowing for the ambiguity of the action, this is stark subject matter to have been published in an Irish periodical in the mid-twentieth century. The second and final stanza provides little relief as it concludes with a sceptical and embittered reflection on the nature of human relationships and personal happiness:

> Should a ball roll
> Off the pavement, gutter drunk
> Down the drain – all hug me there
> Hop skip and jumping joy –
> It might admittedly have bounced for ever
> In the right hands. But balls go wrong
> And having is only holding long
> Enough to cry. Don't thank
> The drain. It serves more purposes
> Than you'd imagine.

The poet of 'Le Deuxième Sexe', who had earlier contemplated her lonely subjects 'living with a shadow', now, six years later, presents a more brutally despairing admission of isolation and loss with the statement 'And having is only holding long / Enough to cry'.

Avis never succeeded in publishing a first poetry collection that could have established her among her contemporaries, a fate that has subsequently resigned her to the margins of literary histories of the mid-twentieth century in Britain and Ireland. Though she received notable early support from prominent literary men of the era, the challenges faced by aspiring women poets in the male-dominated publishing world of the 1950s and 1960s were formidable. Avis' turn towards fiction unfortunately proved unpropitious; her first novel

Playing the Harlot; or, Mostly Coffee was rejected by Charles Monteith at Faber & Faber in 1963. In their introduction to the posthumously published novel, George H. Gilpin and Hermione de Almeida chart Avis' spiralling descent into depression in these later years, exacerbated by alcoholism and substance abuse, leading to her sudden death on 2 September 1977.[31] Avis' tragic death and turbulent romantic relationships have unfairly determined her posthumous image and legacy, their high drama clouding her less sensational literary story of the 1950s and 1960s. But this story can begin to be recovered by attending to the poems that she has left scattered across the British and Irish magazines of her time. When we resituate Avis as writer, editor and patron in the transnational literary networks and publishing contexts of the mid-twentieth century, she becomes a dynamic and challenging presence among her contemporaries. Nuala O'Faolain reasserts Avis' lost literary identity in her uncompromising memoir *Are You Somebody?*, reflecting on how she may well have thrived in more supportive conditions:

> Yet by all accounts, she was as clever as the clever men – Kingsley Amis, Conor Cruise O'Brien, Larkin – she knew. I see articles about her that imply that she was a doomed soul. That's an argument often used to cover up indefensible circumstances. She was nearly in time for the break-out – for getting support from other women, getting published by women's presses and so forth. But when she was in her prime, writing and publishing was a man's world.[32]

Angela Greene (1936–97)

Susan Connolly

Enniskillen

This town is always morning
inside my skull: with slant light
on the slant roofs; the people
coiling into the streets. And
something always just about
to happen. I am caught forever
in the cold ache of it.

I see a long, black car
enter the town with flowers
on its roof glinting like frost.
As if from far away it comes,
out of the morning light, edging
through the hushed crowd to
the war memorial where it stands,
throbbing in the silent air. Then
slowly, purposefully, in the grey light,
it moves on towards our church.

As in a dream I gaze
till my eyes grow dim from watching it.
Then suddenly, into the zone
of hearing comes a fierce cracking sound,
and the pain in a young girl's scream.
And all about is noise
and confusion and everywhere
is stained with poppies.

> Motionless, I feel
> a weight like stone crush my heart,
> and hear a voice that is sure
> with love. Each time I make
> to raise my body to investigate
> a soft, warm hand clutches mine ...[1]

Angela Greene and I first met at the Barbican Writers' Group in Drogheda, County Louth, in September 1983. This group was facilitated by poet and novelist John F. Deane, meeting every second Thursday evening in a room in Clarke's Pub, Fair Street. Barbican had a core of about seven poets and short story writers, with others attending less frequently. Each writer brought a new piece of writing, a poem or short story, to these meetings and would read them to the group. The act of reading a new poem for the first time was always exciting. It seemed to fly on its own wings after being read aloud. Readings were followed by a discussion of the poem or story, usually initiated by Deane, who was by far the most experienced writer involved with Barbican at that time. Most people in the group had something useful to contribute to the discussion during which the fate of the newly minted piece of writing was decided. Successful poems were typically sent in batches of five to editor David Marcus' 'New Irish Writing' page of the *Irish Press*, which, since its inception in 1968, had become an important publishing platform for new work. Sharing knowledge of publishing outlets and literary competitions was a useful feature of the group, with a number of its emerging poets achieving early recognition through this supportive network. Barbican also invited more established writers, who had already published a collection of poetry or short stories, to read their work. These included the writer Jack Harte and poets Pádraig J. Daly, Julie O'Callaghan and Dennis O'Driscoll. These readings were usually held separately from the Thursday evening meetings, as there was a huge ferment of writing activity during those couple of years.

It was at the Barbican Writers' Group where I first heard Angela Greene's poetry. Born Angela McCrea in England in 1936, she lived from early childhood in Dublin. Educated at Dominican College,

Eccles Street, and later training as a nurse at Dublin's Mater Hospital, she eventually settled in Drogheda after her marriage to Austin Greene, where they raised their family together and where she wrote much of her poetry. Many of the poems in her collection *Silence and the Blue Night*, published in 1993 by Salmon Poetry, date from these fortnightly meetings held between 1983 and 1985. Poems such as 'Chain', 'A Life' and 'No Man's Land' were typical of the poetry she was writing then. They were published in the pamphlets *Barbican 1* and *Barbican 2*.[2] Gradually, her poems appeared in journals and newspapers like *Poetry Ireland Review*, *The Honest Ulsterman*, the *Sunday Tribune* and the 'New Irish Writing' page of the *Irish Press*. In 1987 Greene was a prize-winner in the Bloodaxe Books national poetry competition and the following year she won the Patrick Kavanagh Award. In 1990 a selection of her poems was published in the Bloodaxe anthology *New Women Poets*, edited by Carol Rumens.[3] In the same year Blackstaff Press published a more substantial selection of her poems in *Trio Poetry 6*.[4] When *Silence and the Blue Night* appeared in November 1993, almost every poem in the collection had already been published in journals at home and abroad.

At the time Greene began to write poetry, she was emerging from long years spent raising her four children. Those years and the house where she lived set the scene for many of her poems. Her poetry began with portraits of her birth family, her mother ('Wasteland') and her father ('The Path'), and continued with poems about the children she was rearing: 'I have reached a promised land / with you, gift child' ('Chain'). Greene was, at the same time, an intensely private person. If those moving in poetry circles knew anything about her, it was through her poetry. Though ambitious to see her poems into print, she rarely attended poetry readings and knew few poets personally. This was not through a lack of interest; rather it was because her home life absorbed her. But her eyes were still focused on what was happening in the public sphere, as can be seen in her poems 'Terrorist's Wife' and 'Enniskillen'. In the latter poem, a casualty of the Enniskillen bombing speaks: 'This town is always morning / inside my skull [...] I am caught forever / in the cold ache of it'.[5] On 8 November 1987 a bomb planted by the Provisional IRA exploded inside a building near the Enniskillen War Memorial as people gathered for the Remembrance Sunday memorial service, held each year to commemorate local people who died in the First and Second World Wars. The bomb was timed to go off at 10:43 a.m., just before the ceremony was due to start. It killed eleven people and injured sixty-three. 'Enniskillen' draws its voice and narrative from the tragic personal experience of Enniskillen resident Gordon Wilson and his daughter Marie, who were buried six feet deep in the rubble of the collapsed building. Unable to move, Gordon held Marie's hand and comforted her as she lay there. She died of her injuries later that day. Marie, aged twenty and a student nurse, was the youngest victim to die in the Enniskillen bombing. A television interview which Gordon gave only hours after Marie's death brought him to prominence. Wilson's response to the bombing – 'I bear no ill will. I bear no grudge'– was reported worldwide.[6] Enniskillen was seen as a turning point in the Troubles. The bombing was condemned internationally after the killing and maiming of so many innocent civilians.

'Enniskillen' begins just before the bomb blast. It is Sunday morning and a crowd has gathered at the war memorial. The tension of the moment conditions the poem's initially taut form and metre. The opening stanza's short lines and internal punctuation rupture its rhythm. The sense of each line is fractured by line breaks so that the poem's first three full sentences reveal themselves obliquely like the 'slant light / on the slant roofs'. Time and space lose their definition as the speaker is gripped by the 'cold ache' of trauma. In the second stanza, the scene suddenly shifts to a funeral procession and the aftermath of the catastrophe. 'A long, black car' pauses at the war memorial before moving on to the church where the service will take place. The scene then rewinds to the moment of the explosion 'and the pain in a young girl's scream'. These three scenes are fused together in the speaker's mind: the moments before the bomb blast, the funeral hearse pausing at the memorial and the blast itself. The heavy weight that the speaker now feels at the loss is balanced by the memory of his daughter's resilient voice 'that is sure / with love'. In his momentous interview after the bombing, Gordon Wilson stated how his daughter 'held my hand tightly, and gripped me as hard as she could. She said, "Daddy, I love you very much." Those were her exact words to me, and those were the last words I ever heard her say.'[7] 'Enniskillen' transmits the harrowing personal cost of the violence of the Troubles.

The poems in *Silence and the Blue Night* move from the public urban concerns of 'Enniskillen' to the domestic and natural surrounds of Greene's home in Drogheda. Following her marriage to Austin Greene, she lived in an old nineteenth-century house on the North Road leading out of the town. Long before the M1 motorway was built and Drogheda bypassed, this was the main road between Dublin and Belfast. Greene's house was unusual in its being placed back to front, with the rear of the house facing the busy North Road. A side gate led to the front of the house and a beautiful garden carefully tended since the 1800s. The history of the house and its surrounds becomes a live presence in her poetry. One early resident of the late 1800s, Sarah W. Davies, ran a music and drawing school at 6–7 West Street, Drogheda's main street. Greene was fascinated by Sarah's personal belongings that remained in the house ('her polished mahogany knee-desk', 'psalms in her delicate, deliberate hand'). In 'Written Because of Sarah W. Davies, 1882', Greene affirms that 'She lives all round me':

> When, at bedtime, round my doorway,
> her restive, long skirts bring their whisperings,
> I would stop my heart, let her enter into me.[8]

'She Winds the Clock' begins with the description of an unoccupied house in winter, in reality the way her house looked before Greene and her family lived there:

> All year the dated calendar
> hung above the empty shelves;
> naked and brown-boned, winter
> stretched there, a lone robin
> on guard.[9]

The reader is given a view of the house and its garden month by month and season by season: 'March gusted, turned / paths to lakes. [...] Summer slipped by, bursts / of colour and fragrances ignored'. Within a year of the arrival of 'the young woman' at Advent, the calendar is updated and the house has been transformed:

> They heave with goodness now, the shelves –
> dark puddings brim in chalk bowls,
> citrus rind ambers in glossy jars,
> chutney traps tangs and spices;

But more importantly there is the promise of new life to come:

> Under her heart
> a chrysalis of hope moves
> on the breath of butterfly wings.
> She winds the clock.

Writing for *Poetry Ireland Review*, Isabelle Cartwright describes how Greene's poetry 'delves the nature of things through time by delving nature itself':

> Her discovery of self and loss is constantly tempered by a real and vibrant engagement with the natural world. That world is essentially feminine although men as historical figures are present ... This is a poetry which observes the indelible though changing patterns of living things with an achieved and promising style.[10]

Greene's engagement with the natural world transforms the seclusion of the private garden into a restorative site for poetry. To push open the side gate of her house and step away from the dusty, noisy North Road into the sanctuary of her garden was a memorable experience. Cartwright refers to 'The Lost Garden' as 'a lament for the passing of natural refuges in the face of industrial progress':[11]

> In here time waits.
> Bees trade in the pollened air,
> drugging the scented levels.
>
>   a thrush springs
> to crack the seal on a snail's brown box.
>
> And out there, beyond that wall,
> in the high-rise, the plastic world,

> the great earth-eaters rear
> with monstrous jaws, poised
> to consume, consume.[12]

The poem begins with four slow beats ('In here time waits') but the seemingly quiet garden is a place of unfolding activity. Bees industriously 'trade' in pollination among the flowers, while the agile intensity of hunting birds is captured with onomatopoeic verve ('a thrush springs / to crack the seal on a snail's brown box'). Though bustling with life, the poem admits the precarity of such environments where, 'out there, beyond that wall', construction vehicles with 'monstrous jaws' prepare to devour the earth. Behind Greene's own house and garden was an even older building, Laburnum Turret, the grounds of which had once been an extensive garden nursery. Demolished in 1984, it was replaced by seven bungalows, also called Laburnum Turret. For now, this garden is a haven of thriving plants and wildlife, but Greene is aware that eventually everything falls prey to time.

Of the fifty poems gathered in *Silence and the Blue Night*, twenty-one are set either in the house or in the garden. The collection's domestic perspectives encompass the maternal observation of children at different points in their young lives ('Stirrings', 'Aubade for a Schoolboy'); the drudgery of domesticity tempered by contentment with family life ('Monday's Mother'); and the discovery of an ancient doorstep during some building work 'cut / and hefted by P. and J. / 1784', which is re-set and branded 'hauled by P. and J. / 1984' ('Stone Doorstep'). In 'Garden Epitaphs', Greene compares her mother and father, older and younger brothers and her infant son to the different trees growing in her garden:

> You were my elder brother
> brave rowan tree [...]
>
> You were my mother
>   winter cherry
> the 60-watt glow in grey weather.
> A grief of opal tints
> disturbs your summer green.[13]

Angela Greene and I spent ten years working on our poems together, culminating in our respective collections being published in the winter of 1993. After that we saw each other less often; she was continually dogged by ill-health and I, taking up that place she had left behind, was busy with small children. In some of her poems an air of tiredness has crept in and an acknowledgement that she has grown older. Writing as the mother of 'young men and women' in 'Letting Go', she thinks back to when they were children and she 'ruled the roost'. But this dynamic inevitably changed over time so that now 'They talk / inches above my head. Their / laughter and their language / leap / beyond me.' The poem concludes with an admission of loss and ageing:

> ... I've weathered
> as I watch them grow. And
> how at last, as I let go
> and slip behind them, I ease
> my bones into the universe.[14]

Following her death on 5 February 1997, I remembered an evening years earlier when I listened to Greene reading the poem 'Ancient Garden':

> To this ancient garden I am
> a future ghost. A pale shape
> in its tiredness that waters and weeds.

In this poem her existence is defined by the changes she makes in the garden, where she is 'a kneeling form bedding in plants / hopefully, like a pilgrim at a shrine'. The garden itself feels 'wearied / by the seasonal round – the prunings, / the mulchings', by the successive generations of gardeners it has seen come and go. She believes that the garden will also be lost, but not in her time; after she is gone, the particular care she lavished on the flower beds will 'evaporate' as the grounds become overgrown:

> A spate of wilderness
> tangling its fragrances and it will know
> that I have passed on.

Even with her presence diminished to 'A warm pressure on the wintry earth', however, she feels compelled to do this gardening while she is alive, because in contrast to the vigorous evergreen yew trees with their long life span, she is 'a frail woman' who 'would petrify if she did not move. / Would whiten among their harled roots'.

Angela Greene's poetic presence has faded in the years following her death, a fate underscored by her perplexing omission from *The Field Day Anthology of Irish Writing: Irish women's writing and traditions*.[15] By returning to her work and recognising the achievement of *Silence and the Blue Night*, however, we reclaim a compelling voice in the recent history of Irish women's poetry. Her significance was best described by Patricia Boyle Haberstroh in her important early study, *Women Creating Women: Contemporary Irish women poets*. Writing in 1996, Haberstroh situated Greene among an exciting new generation of Irish women poets, her poetry representative of 'the emergence of a more self-conscious and self-confident female poet, ready to rewrite the story of Irish women and redefine and explore female identity and the image of women in Irish history, culture, and literature'.[16]

Lynda Moran (1948–2020)

Kenneth Keating

Something Else

Salt in the cut,
Harpsichord in my throat,
Tripe pale in the tentacled brine;
I'm a butcher myself –
Eating the heart
Out of my skeleton.
My caged-organ guts
Strut through male streets –
A smile in a skirt,
Apron left at home.
Look at my purpose, my basket
My ankles, my feet –
Genderless on concrete.
At the head of my carcass
See face, see smile, see mouth;
Won't show you my shopping list –
It's not meat I need.
I'm out of my reach now.
I want to be empty;
I need something else.[1]

'Something Else', a slim twenty-line text in Lynda Moran's *The Truth About Lucy* (1985), includes four dashes to mark where the first four quatrains end; typographical nicks, taking the place of the spaces between these stanzas. This structure foregrounds the piece as a single body, but one composed of distinct component parts. It is a subtle use of punctuation intended to underscore the lyric subject's understanding of their own body, which involves both the acknowledgement of the whole, and the metaphorical dismemberment. As Moran's lyric subject states here, 'I'm a butcher myself', and in this butchery the subject carefully carves their body where the poet could only mark the text. The subject's body is dissected, their throat, heart, skeleton and 'caged-organ guts' all separately brought outside of the body and displayed for the reader to view, while those parts of the body already visible to the world are brutally cut from one another: ankles, feet, 'the head of my carcass', face, smile, mouth. This violence, the poem suggests, is required for the subject to enter the male-dominated public space, to 'Strut through male streets', rendering the body 'Genderless on concrete'. Having carved up the once-female body, its gender implied in the references to the patriarchal signifiers of an apron and a skirt, Moran undermines the stable singularity of the lyric subject, divorcing it from the desires of the corporeal world: 'It's not meat I need'. The figure has lost its appetite for flesh, it transcends the borders and limitations of the body, and in this emptying of the self reveals an alternative, previously unspoken of, desire: 'I need something else'.

Born in Dublin, and having lived much of her life in Navan, Lynda Moran featured in journals and anthologies in Ireland and the United States before publishing *The Truth About Lucy*. Two years after the publication of 'Something Else' in this collection, Paul Muldoon published a poem with the same title in his own collection, *Meeting the British*. Muldoon's much better-known 'Something Else' has become central to representations of this canonical poet's literary modus operandi, in which he is freely and playfully led by rhyme and associative thinking to 'think / of something else, then something else again'.[2] In stark contrast to this casual, easily achieved flight of intellectual curiosity, Moran's subject viscerally deconstructs the female body to escape the constrictions enforced on it in order to finally, climactically, achieve the hard-won freedom of declaring the rather modest desire for 'something else'. The identification of this 'something else' is not made explicit in Moran's text, but it is clear that it represents that which transgresses the patriarchal construction of femininity.

Moran's subject asks for something more than that which is afforded to a woman in 1980s Ireland, and in doing so Moran asks the reader to escape the critical limitations placed on the work of a female poet.

Writing in 2008 on the work of Medbh McGuckian, Leontia Flynn convincingly argues that '[i]t is in undermining terms and changing criteria ... that feminism as a reading as well as writing practice continues to have work to do.'[3] Flynn's argument – that it is necessary to break free from the logic and standards of hegemonic patriarchal criticism – seems particularly prescient when examining Moran's 'Something Else'. Reading this text alongside the other poems of *The Truth About Lucy*, it is clear that Moran strains against controlling conservativism. Yet, while a small number of Moran's contemporaries progressed to obtain elevated positions in the canon of modern Irish poetry, one is left to wonder why Moran published only a single full volume of poetry before disappearing, both publicly and critically.

It is perhaps due to the failure of criticism that does not meet Flynn's challenge that this volume was not more successful and that Moran did not publish a second volume. The collection received only one review on publication, a single paragraph in a larger piece by John F. Deane. Despite Deane's overwhelmingly positive description of Moran's work as 'challenging, vital, and highly individual', no other reviews were written.[4] Further, Moran is briefly addressed in only a single critical text: Patricia Boyle Haberstroh's *Women Creating Women: Contemporary Irish women poets* (1996). Her name occasionally appears in certain lists of female poets from the 1980s, but her work has received no significant critical analysis. Even the editors of the fourth and fifth volumes of the *The Field Day Anthology of Irish Writing* (2002), an act of cultural retrieval which sought to preserve and promote the voices of previously marginalised women, did not see fit to include even a single example of Moran's work. The reason for this absence of criticism is difficult to identify, but it may be the result of institutional and structural failings within the industry of Irish poetry publishing. Indeed, Moran's disappearance may represent an exemplary case to underline the conditions of production that facilitated the critical and popular marginalisation of female poets in the latter half of the twentieth century, and, importantly, which remain prevalent today.

Patriarchal wisdom might encourage us to assume that Moran's long poetic silence has been due to the desertion of the muse, or, alternatively, that what she did compose was not of adequate quality to merit publication. The former of these conclusions reductively adheres to the logic of conservative idealism regarding the creation of art, while the poems of Moran's debut collection suggest the latter scenario is not particularly likely. *The Truth About Lucy* presents a strong, distinctive voice, one that foregrounds the female body and sexuality without shame. It is the absence of shame, or the refusal to be cowed by it, that is key in much of Moran's work, underlining both the individuality of her voice and her place alongside her contemporaries. Shame, or what is referred to as the 'shame of existing',[5] that deep-seated, subconscious self-loathing of sorts, was considered by Freud, and others, as foundational to an individual's psychological development, that 'it is desirable literally to shame children into growing up'.[6] This shame has long been 'an enforcer of social conformity', it silences supposedly unorthodox voices, oppressing even the individual's own desire to present themselves in a manner they consider truthful.[7]

A significant part of the revolutionary challenge female poets posed in the latter half of the twentieth century, in Ireland and elsewhere, was found in the embracing of this shame, their refusal to be silenced or to conform, as they opted instead to present defiantly the female experience through the female voice. This is in line with what Marx celebrated when he described shame as 'already a revolution of a kind'.[8] In this revolution, female poets, such as Eavan Boland, Paula Meehan, Nuala Ní Dhomhnaill, along with many other predecessors and successors, challenged the hegemonic, patriarchal, hierarchical canon of Irish poetry which had for so long excluded voices that did not cohere to a singular, reductive, nation-centred, essentialist ideology.

The Truth About Lucy evidences the extent to which Moran was one of these poets. 'The Man-Eater', for example, encapsulates what Haberstroh identified in the poetry of this time as the 'newly discovered freedom, especially sexual freedom, [which] accounts for the more graphic portrayals of female sexuality'.[9] This freedom is identifiable in the poem's final, questioning lines:

> Who would suspect
> When her curtains were closed
> What her appetites hungered for?
>
> Or who would connect
> Such a 'nice' girl
> With the primitive
> Or the taste for trophies?[10]

Moran's explicit depiction of female sexual desire is an act of transgression. In 'Something Else', Moran foregrounds the division of the established norms of the internal and the external: the feminine interior and the masculine exterior. In 'The Man-Eater' the female body is not subjected to violence in order to gain entry to the masculine streets. Instead, the female figure takes possession of the internal space, and in doing so appropriates sexual agency and power.

Moran recognises that the expectation is for this feminine sexuality to remain hidden, foregrounded in the description of the closing of the curtains, or the mask of the 'nice' girl. In these lines, Moran thus gestures towards the limitations placed on female sexuality, and presents, in the poetic lines, an explicit challenge to the control of the female body. The myth of the desexualised 'nice' girl is debunked, the sexual desire of the female body presented as human and natural. The woman rejects objectification and the traditional positioning of the female as a trophy to be won by the male. In this, Moran discards the conventional dynamics of sexual relationships, and in doing this in a poetic text she presents the lived reality of the female body and sexuality as a worthy subject for poetry in Ireland in the 1980s.

Moran was not alone in this move, and a considerable number of peers and successors have gone on to achieve relatively prominent positions in the canon of Irish poetry, albeit such figures often remaining largely relegated to a secondary or marginalised status in relation to the central male-dominated Yeats–Joyce–Kavanagh–Heaney axis of the hierarchical canon. This canon is formed and buttressed by the acts of criticism that continue to privilege the work of male poets over female poets, but it is also perpetuated by other key gatekeepers of Irish poetry, including the publishing industry. While criticism often remains shackled to the restrictions of patriarchal norms and continues to perpetuate the inherited, male-dominated literary histories, this then necessarily feeds into the judgements and decisions of editors, particularly those of the more established print presses. This relationship of influence does not only pass in one direction, however, and the activities of these presses equally informs, shapes and perpetuates the patriarchal practices of acts of criticism. Publishers are not innocent. Rather, publishers of Irish poetry have long been the first line of defence for the male canon, they are the forces that limit the number of female poets whose voices will be heard, and they are the ones who choose what form of female voice is deemed welcome.

Moran's *The Truth About Lucy* was published by a small publishing operation: Beaver Row Press. The precise history of this press is difficult to establish, but it can be confirmed that its operations were directed by the editorial voice of Glenda Cimino. Operating throughout the 1980s, Beaver Row Press published approximately thirty books across a range of genres and tastes authored by figures including Moran, Cimino herself, Anne Le Marquand Hartigan, Brendan Kennelly, Paddy Bushe, John Liddy and Gabriel Fitzmaurice. Beaver Row Press also published Paula Meehan's first two volumes: *Return and No Blame* (1984) and *Reading the Sky* (1986). Here arises an interesting point of comparison. While Meehan subsequently published two collections with the more-established Gallery Press, and others with the Manchester-based Carcanet Press and the Dublin-based Dedalus Press – and has since been elected as the Ireland Professor of Poetry – Moran, in contrast, did not publish a second volume of poetry. Rather, with the closure of Beaver Row Press, Moran's avenue for the dissemination of new work disappeared, as did the distribution network for *The Truth About Lucy*.

Unlike Meehan, Moran did not publish with Gallery Press. Analysis of the history of poetry publishing in Ireland foregrounds the extent to which it was always unlikely for Moran to find another publisher: Meehan's success in this regard was the exception, rather than the rule. Established presses were largely led by male editors, and these male editors primarily published male poets. Beaver Row Press was an outlier at this time, and it did not survive for very long. Salmon Poetry, led by Jessie Lendennie, is another such outlier, one which, remarkably, continues to operate today. Looking at the other, more prominent, presses at this time, however, the absence of female voices from positions of editorial power was clearly the dominant trend when Moran was writing in the 1980s, and such structural bias ensured the continued privileging of male poets over female poets.

The 1980s was not very long ago of course, and it should be noted that this pattern continues today, explicitly condoned by the state in the form of annual funding awarded by The Arts Council / An Chomhairle Ealaíon. A recent report by the organisation Measuring Equality in the Arts Sector (MEAS) – published in 2018 and focusing on publications in Ireland between 2008 and 2017 inclusive – documents the clear link between state funding and the continued marginalisation of female poets.[11] In this ten-year period Gallery Press, edited by Peter Fallon, received by far the most funding of any press in Ireland, totalling €1,681,715; its poetry-related publications were 77 per cent male-authored and only 23 per cent female-authored. Over the same period, the second-most funded poetry press in Ireland, Dedalus Press, edited by Pat Boran, received €838,750, while its poetry-related publications were 75 per cent male-authored and only 25 per cent female-authored. Over the same period, Salmon Poetry received €420,063, a figure approximately one quarter of that received by Gallery Press. In contrast, Salmon Poetry published over two hundred more volumes of poetry than either Gallery Press or Dedalus Press. Yet, even Salmon Poetry published more male poets than female poets, at 60 per cent male-authored and 40 per cent female-authored.[12]

While certain smaller presses, which receive little or no state funding, publish more female authors than male, or operate with gender parity, it is clear that poetry publishing in Ireland demonstrates a considerable bias in favour of male poets. This is particularly evident in the operations of the presses receiving the most funding, and the influence such behaviours have on the operations of newer or smaller presses requires examination. It must be emphasised, however, that this is not a new development. These patterns of behaviour, and the privileging of male poets over female poets, were dominant at the time of Moran's writing and before it. This bias has been allowed to continue up to the present time and, as a barrier to publication and career progress, it played a significant role in the ultimate exclusion of Lynda Moran.

That *The Truth About Lucy* largely disappeared from modern Irish poetry, and that Lynda Moran did not publish a second volume of poetry foregrounds the success of the various branches of Irish poetry operating to perpetuate a hierarchical canon that is inherently patriarchal and that marginalises female poets. This success has long been a failure, limiting the shape of Irish poetry, confining it to a stable entity which can be defined and easily understood, another step in the long-established practice of 'the negation of recalcitrant or inassimilable elements' in Irish literature and society.[13] Moran's voice is one of many to have been excluded, one of many that continue to be marginalised or forgotten. Not all such exclusions are predicated on gender, but it is clearly an informing factor. Structural reform is still required in publishing, funding and acts of criticism, while editors, readers and even poets themselves must reflectively interrogate the manner in which they are silently complicit in perpetuating the long-standing gender imbalance in Irish poetry and the continued disappearance of female poets.

The individual's power in this regard is foregrounded in Moran's 'The Stranger'. It is difficult to read the unnamed male figure in this piece as anything other than an editor or a critic holding sway and influence over the potential trajectory of the female poet's career. The eponymous stranger is an author of words that function to break and reconstruct the female lyric subject. The stranger demands the subject 'change [their] plan', and engages directly with the female body and mind:

> His verbs were hands
> As he remade my mind.
> There was no pain,
> Only the laughter
> Of some old god
> Inventing a woman.[14]

In 'The Stranger', Moran again foregrounds the challenge she poses to those powerful figures controlling the canon, yet unlike other, more defiant texts in the volume, this piece concludes on a note of resignation. The male figure refuses to be a positive force, opting instead to be confrontational, and he is ultimately victorious; the female subject is remade, woman is created, a version that is acceptable to the male. This, Moran suggests, is the fate of female poets when subject to the domination of male figures in positions of power: to be destroyed, reconstructed, controlled. *The Truth About Lucy* often resists this dynamic, striving for independence and female agency. Similar to the conclusion of 'The Stranger', however, the premature end of Moran's poetic career probably means little to the 'laughter / Of some old god', but it leaves the empathetic reader with a sense of sadness and loss for the disappearance of another strong, unique female voice.

Cathleen O'Neill (b. 1949)

Emma Penney

~~~

Off the Wall

The scream started again today
A slow silent scream of frustrated anger.
Today I wailed at the wall of officialdom

Robbed of Independence, dignity in danger
I stood, dead-locked, mind-locked
Helpless in his sightless one-dimension world
I walked away
My mind screamed a long sad caoin for the us
And
Damned their social welfare[1]

Working-class women's poetry is often collective in that you are more likely to encounter an 'us' or a 'we' than an 'I'. The collective aspect of 'Off the Wall', by Cathleen O'Neill, is revealed in the final stanza where the cry is for 'the us'. Written in Dublin in the early 1980s during a time of mass unemployment, the poem reflects the frustrated flow of interaction taking place at a social welfare office: there is a process of tension–release–tension experienced by the speaker. The release only comes from having an outlet, having other listeners, other women who share her experience. In this way the poem maps its own genealogy: from the silence of the welfare office to the space of the writing group where, O'Neill notes, 'we found each other, it was a sharing led process, in the course of conversations you could see other people becoming aware, sharing'.[2]

In 'Off the Wall', the 'caoin' released in the final stanza comes from the Old Irish word *caínid*: to lament, weep or cry, or also *caoinim*, which can mean to deplore and also 'to wail'. However, there is also an Old Irish variation *caín*, which refers to a smooth or polished surface – like a wall.[3] This is significant because the term can encapsulate both the 'wail' and the 'wall of officialdom' from the opening stanza. The 'caoin' is also traditionally a communal cry wherein one woman would lead her community in an expression of loss. Given the loss of voices and the silencing that takes place inside the welfare state, the testimony gathered in this poem places it in the category of community advocacy. Angela Bourke notes how, in Irish folklore, keening reveals an aspect of the lament tradition wherein Irish women used it to 'protest a violence, injustice or indignity in their lives'.[4] She also observes how keening created multiple witnesses: 'the keening woman demanded attention ... calling on other women to join in her crying'. In this way, keening can be understood as akin to testimony in that women used it to document injustices and to create witnesses. This aligns closely with Michael Givoni's notion of how testimony differs from traditions of storytelling, which seek to convey accurate historic reproductions of events, and instead focuses on 'the disclosure of their existential, moral, and psychic repercussions'.[5] For Givoni, testimony 'crosses the threshold of politicization when it is not just an act that realizes a singular instance of witnessing but rather, and primarily, a vehicle for creating witnesses, in the plural'. In O'Neill's poem there is a conscious diminishing of the singular poet-witness, which indicates the corporal presence of multiple witnesses. Older systems of communication among Irish women are drawn on to affirm the social use of O'Neill's poetic praxis.

O'Neill facilitated the Kilbarrack women's writing group in the north Dublin community-based adult education centre KLEAR (Kilbarrack Local Education for Adult Renewal) from the mid-1980s until the early 1990s, before bringing her distinctive feminist practice to the north inner-city community-based educational and rehabilitation centre SAOL (*Seasamhact Abaltacht Obair Leann*), where she still works today. O'Neill recalls how the Kilbarrack women's writing group, based in the north Dublin suburb of Kilbarrack, talked 'about women having a double-burden ... their gender and their poverty'.[6]

Sharing experiences of the class system became a natural extension of their lives and O'Neill notes that women talked often about 'how social-class worked, how you were always made to feel ashamed, how you were always made to feel stigmatised'.[7] Writing or sharing in collective spaces produced new, more positive feelings – echoing the catharsis experienced through keening in Irish folklore. Megan Boler also contends that this kind of critical reflection on emotion is political because 'by expressing and sharing previously hidden and silenced emotions in these collective spaces, women had the opportunity to integrate emotions as knowledge with critical reflection, thereby supporting women's political organization against male-domination'.[8] This praxis, which melds poetry and testimony, was not confined to Dublin but was also present in Cork city; Máire Bradshaw, founder of the Cork Women's Poetry Circle, notes how inequality was a major theme in writing workshops, particularly education inequality:

> A lot of women were being battered you know and being kicked around ... badly. And putting it into poetry, it was hidden. Ya know but coming out nicely ya know and women could talk to each other about it. And so it wasn't just poetry, it was a whole movement.[9]

But, as she also recalls, 'that's how the "real" poets could frown on you: here you are babbling on about your lives and calling it poetry. It was broken down [that stigma], the Kilbarrack women did their bit.'

O'Neill's poem 'Off the Wall' was first published by the Women's Community Press in *Write Up Your Street* (1985) and again by Attic Press and the Combat Poverty Agency in *Women and Poverty* (1989). The second appearance of the poem is interesting because it is in this second context that the poem appears *as* testimony. The author of *Women and Poverty*, Mary Daly, tells us that 'the explanatory framework for this book rests on two key factors: class and gender'.[10] She notes how, up to that point, either 'men' or 'the family' were the subjects of studies of poverty in Ireland with women left out of the frame. Daly argues that this necessitates a sounding out of those experiences and, for this reason, 'women living on low incomes speak for themselves, sometimes through their writings and poems. This kind of information is as important, and in some cases more important.'[11] Each chapter is academically rigorous and explores different aspects of women's lives including education, employment and social welfare. Alongside the research findings are seven poems and a number of personal testimonies. The poems are included as information and as recorded experiences that need a necessary 'sounding out'. The first chapter, 'The Nature and Extent of Poverty Among Women', has nine subsections and Daly consistently reflects on the limitations of the Economic and Social Research Institute (ESRI) findings by providing evidence of the hiddenness of women's poverty in Ireland through poetry and testimony.[12] 'Off the Wall' appears at the conclusion of this chapter.

The practice of including poetry alongside written testimony about working-class women's lives was something initiated by Kilbarrack women themselves in the book project that ran from 1989 to 1992: *Telling It Like It Is* (1992).[13] The book is a social portrait of Kilmount, the large local authority housing area of Kilbarrack where most of the participants lived. O'Neill's poem 'Poverty Is' appears in this text alongside oral testimony and analysis. The poem materialises harm by giving poverty a colour, in the mind: 'Poverty is coloured red / red searing brain pain'.[14] Assigning poverty a colour affirms its affective reality and the prominence of 'shame and fear' – what Jacqueline Rose calls 'the darkest, most discomforting colours of the psyche'.[15] The poem presents us with an affective inequality that emerges at the intersection of gender and class. Women had very few legal entitlements in a welfare system modelled on Article 41.2 of the Irish Constitution, which designated woman's rightful place to be the home. In reality, this meant that women were often expected to fulfil a care-role without the proper resources to carry out that care and this resulted in painful feelings: 'Life hurts / Love tears out my being / as responsibility looms / and dooms me to continue'.[16] The poem appears alongside a series of testimonies about women's experiences of the welfare system in Ireland and the generic boundaries between poetry and testimony become blurred.

The Kilbarrack archive is dominated by poetry and short prose because, as Cathleen O'Neill points out, it was 'cheap, accessible and you didn't necessarily need a typewriter'.[17] These findings are crucial because they allow us to explore the impact of class on creative form and to redraw literary value-systems. In the case of the Kilbarrack archive there is a relationship between poetry and prose that mirrors the story-sharing movement that was taking place in women's groups. Poetry, as with 'Off the Wall' and 'Poverty Is', focuses on how emotional pain can be classed. It tends to be temporally focused in the present and discusses contemporary issues facing the community. Short stories, on the other hand, tend to be more reflective and map affective histories of class. By mapping this affective history, women were giving an intergenerational account of class and this transtemporal building of networks between women helped to depersonalise poverty and to establish the systemic nature of classed affects. O'Neill's story 'Feminist Fatigue' concerns a daughter who must watch her mother 'wearing herself down' with a 'frantic juggling of a miserable weekly finance'.[18] The story describes how:

> The biggest battle of all was centred around her dignity and self-worth. Trying to hang on to it in the face of judges, psychiatrists, social workers etc. All of them male. The shame of standing in line for supplementary welfare. Of proving her poverty week after week. Each hand-out seemed to lessen her value as a woman, a mother.[19]

Bodies queueing or waiting for state assistance is a common theme in writing from Kilbarrack. This writing is about affect because it problematises classed bodies and represents how the body is in space and how the literary imagination responds to these affects. O'Neill's social portrait of Kilbarrack, *Telling It Like It Is* (1992), also traces the affective experience of queueing as women reflect on paying rent in the Gales Office. The Gales Office was situated in the living room of one designated council house and we are told that residents from Kilmount were forced to 'queue out in the open' in order to make their rent payment while residents in private houses, just across the road, could 'conduct the business of paying mortgages in more congenial surroundings'.[20] In telling this story the women's focus is not only on the difference in physical surroundings or material wealth, but on the fact that Kilmount residents were less likely 'to have their privacy respected' and so more likely to experience shame and humiliation. O'Neill's story 'Feminist Fatigue' provides further evidence on how the affective experience of queueing is interpreted by the women themselves as shameful. Queueing 'out in the open' *classes* them in specific ways and in *Telling It Like It Is* we learn how the welfare system 'is characterised by queuing, lack of privacy, and the constant telling and retelling of personal details'. Conversations held in a space like KLEAR produced new affective relations: where women created value or, as Cathleen O'Neill has remarked, where women felt 'held up' by the listener.[21] This writing is a social document and maps a feminist social praxis.

The publishing boom in Kilbarrack happened in the context of deindustrialisation. The state responded to high unemployment in working-class areas by creating state-funded training schemes for women. Working-class women utilised these programmes to write and share their stories. However, having to fit writing and publishing into temporary, state-funded training schemes, which were not intended to support it in its own right, made it difficult for projects and writers to be sustained. Daly notes that in 1987 the Combat Poverty Agency received 220 applications for funding local women's groups, including arts and writing groups. She argues that a lack of appropriate funding from the Arts Council 'forces local groups to align themselves with individuals and organisations whose interests and political perspective may differ from theirs'.[22] Community projects received very little funding from centralised arts or cultural institutions and work completed under the banner of community arts was often narrowly valued as an incentive or pathway towards employment. Gerri Moriarty states that in the 1980s in Ireland 'it was simply inconceivable that work of any kind of quality could be taking place in council estates or in village halls'.[23]

KLEAR was one of these devalued creative spaces. Formed in 1981, the group was made up of local women who first met during a children's summer programme and decided they wanted to stay together. As O'Neill remembers, they 'would talk about inequality, talk about poverty ... They got a school across the bridge, gave them a room – in Scoil Eoghain and ... what did they do there ... I think they did poetry.'[24] KLEAR was the first majorly successful adult education group in the country and it was also the birthplace of the Kilbarrack women's writing group. The early success of the group saw them publish their first book of writing in 1981 and Norrie Gibney recalls their motivation for an independent publishing initiative:

We didn't want something imposed by someone who didn't know what it was like not to have the confidence to get out of the house or the money to pay up front for classes in September because you'd spent everything on your kids for school.[25]

Their first book, *From Wits End to Humble Beginnings* (1981), was printed using a Gestetner machine, an old Victorian printer that the women accessed in the equally Victorian setting of Mountjoy Prison. Such resourcefulness meant that by the time Irish Feminist Information (IFI) commenced grassroots feminist publishing, Kilbarrack offered a crucial strategic alliance.

Founded in 1978 by Mary Doran and Roisín Conroy, the IFI provided training courses for unemployed women in the 1970s and early 1980s, before eventually consolidating its efforts under Attic Press, the first press in Ireland to publish women exclusively. The first community writing anthology to emerge from an IFI training course was a book of writing from the Kilbarrack women's writing group. In fact, the group had already completed the book and were trying to find a publisher. The collaboration with IFI meant that *If You Can Talk ... You Can Write* (1983) came to mark the foundation of the Women's Community Press (WCP), which quickly created the conditions for the development of Attic Press. In *The Oxford History of the Book Volume IV: The Irish book in English*, Siobhán Holland points out that the IFI had been 'frustrated in their efforts to find non-professional women to take part in their community publishing programme but eventually succeeded in establishing a grassroots feminist publishing initiative – with the important inclusion of women from Kilbarrack'.[26] Holland also observes how 'the success of *If You Can Talk ... You Can Write* created confidence in the possibility of creating a viable press'. Rebecca Pelan similarly argues that the Kilbarrack anthology acted as a stepping stone for the viability of Attic Press and for this reason she names it among 'the most important historical and literary works of the period'.[27]

The IFI publishing programme was funded by the Industrial Training Authority and, within that funding framework, the IFI committed to 'develop self-employment motivation among trainees / or encourage skills needed to acquire employment'.[28] Middle-class feminist groups relied on these state training schemes in order to carry out publishing activities. This meant that they also had to establish relationships with working-class communities and with people eligible for state-funded employment schemes. Charlotte McIvor explores how, within these state-funded collaborations, the community is often stigmatised as non-professional – which undervalues the agency and creativity of community members.[29] The historic erasure of working-class women's role in the development of feminist publishing could be due to the funding discourses, which positioned working-class communities as participants, non-professionals or trainees and certainly not active, skilled sources of creative energy. This discourse was reproduced by the Arts Council and by middle-class professionals seeking funding for creative projects. Later, however, when the WCP sought funding for subsequent projects, they leaned heavily on the anthology and were granted funding based on the success of *If You Can Talk*.[30] In their grant application for the publication of a community writing anthology in 1985, the WCP mention the major success of *If You Can Talk* (though this time they neglect to mention KLEAR or Kilbarrack) and point out how 'the unique aspect of this writing is that it is done in groups which are locally based'.[31] The true origins of feminist publishing involved a dialogical exchange of knowledge between middle-class and working-class women and not a top-down training project that imparted skills to working-class women. In fact, most of the trainees in the first publishing course were middle-class women whose learning was facilitated by working-class women.

Archival theorists Kate Shilton and Ramesh Srinivasan point out how 'documents lose elements of their meaning if separated from the context of their creation'.[32] This means that the loss of a working-class feminist history of writing and publishing impairs our understanding of the women's movement more broadly. Shilton and Srinivasan insist that one way to restore lost context is by working directly with the community involved. To this end, I have consulted with record creators in order to restore a context that has been lost to official narratives and to a process of tailoring. Working-class women had to create a narrative to suit the particular training or employment programme in question. These tailored narratives did not always reflect the political or creative programmes taking place, so counter-narratives (which emerge from speaking and consulting with communities and record creators) provide new articulations of this social movement. A collaborative approach to appraising and interpreting the archive has also yielded some exciting analytical tools for critiquing poetry and short prose, illuminating the social use of poetry and foregrounding how form is classed. Literary value systems are closely related to form and are not universal. The non-economic discourse of academic literary criticism conceals a desire to protect the private assets of the middle classes. Working-class poetry reveals the relationship between class and form and opens up avenues for re-examining literary value systems.

Brian Singleton observes how 'the justification for canon formation is determined by the literary quality of the play / text all the while ignoring completely the extent and the significance of the cultural and sometimes political intervention an actual performance might have generated in a particular historical moment'.[33] An examination of the impact of socio-political developments on working-class literary production establishes that local women's groups were a place of counter-testimony and resistance. Women's groups created spaces for oral testimony about working-class life that found their final expression in short literary forms, small pamphlets and self-published anthologies that were funded by state training schemes. However, this writing has never been examined by literary scholars – perhaps because the schemes under which projects took place were not designed to support creative production but to deal with the problem of unemployment. What is troubling is the extent to which middle-class feminist publishing relied on strategic alliances with groups like KLEAR in order to establish an Irish feminist press, but did not maintain these ties. A full history of the Kilbarrack women's writing group could illuminate their importance and foreground the process of knowledge exchange between middle-class and working-class women in the 1980s.[34] Despite the influence that working-class writing groups had on women's publishing in Ireland, they have been excluded from historical accounts of the women's movement. O'Neill's work belongs to an unexamined archive that illuminates the links between class, form and genre. Aesthetically and critically turned towards its conditions of production, this archive challenges the lack of critical attention on class and literature in Ireland by illuminating the social use-value of working-class writing.

AFTERWORD

The Future of Irish Women Poets: A new language

Lucy Collins

a new language
is a kind of scar
and heals after a while
into a passable imitation
of what went before[1]

I

The exclusion of generations of Irish women from a place of equality in Irish history and tradition has inflicted a wound that not only harms individual artists but also damages Irish culture as a whole. Eavan Boland – whose life and work has had such a profound impact on contemporary women poets and readers in Ireland – recorded the debilitating effect of such marginalisation and its power to shape a woman poet's attitude to literary tradition in lasting ways. The image of the scar expresses the enduring nature of suffering, but also its tendency to become indistinguishable from the rest of experience, and virtually invisible to the wider world. It is a trope re-used by newly marginalised writers: Nokukhanya Dlamini, a migrant poet, asks: 'How many more times / do I have to tell the buried scar / for you to believe?'[2] The necessity for repetition speaks of continued rejection, and affirms the importance of bearing witness to the omissions of history. Yet, to be compelled to articulate past distress is to become trapped within that structure of feeling. The slowness with which Irish critical cultures have responded to these demands for inclusivity has not only limited our experience as readers, it has also fundamentally changed how our literature has evolved. When we attempt to broaden the tradition of Irish poetry, we not only bring the work of some extraordinary women poets to light but also transform our understanding of tradition. This should – and must – make us more receptive to diversity of experience and expression in the future.

Significant omissions in the canon of Irish writing have long since been identified, but new generations of scholars are bringing fresh perspectives to forgotten or neglected work, as well as new insights into the political implications of these acts of exclusion. The *Fired!* movement, founded in 2017 to address the continued marginalisation of women poets within Irish cultural institutions, has campaigned for honest reflection by editors and publishers, and sought once again to amplify women's voices. The events organised in the first year of the movement – in Belfast, Cork and Dublin, and as far afield as Barcelona – brought new energy to the debate and drew diverse audiences. Giving space to these issues, festivals and conferences, in their turn, demonstrated that urgent change was needed to restore faith in Ireland's critical culture. Yet, 'the smart thing about exclusion', as Anne Enright has observed, is that it is 'hard to call out, or identify. The real problem with silence, is that it is also silencing. People are, by exclusion, slowly undone.'[3] So, despite the commitment and enthusiasm of informed readers, critics and teachers, few women writers have a secure place within the literary canon. As quickly as contemporary women writers can be added to the university syllabus, their predecessors are lost from sight, or confined to courses exclusively devoted to gender issues. Every teacher who has extended the curriculum by exploring hitherto neglected women writers has given new life to forgotten texts, in the hope of changing how future generations read and understand the Irish poetry tradition as a whole.

With these apparently enduring limitations in mind, what is most striking about this selection of seventeen poets is their diversity of voice and subject matter, as well as of life circumstances. Yet, these are particular, not representative, figures; they are neither contained within an argument, nor subject to any overarching theory. Instead, these are poets who have caught the eye and imagination of readers and critics, and who offer us new ways of reading the Irish literary past. Each woman poet also demonstrates the many pathways that the creative artist may take to literature. Some are caught up in the life of the home or workplace, producing a small number of poems in borrowed time: Olivia Elder wittily itemises the many household tasks that keep her from her literary pursuits, and her frustration resonates across the generations, concluding in this volume with the trenchant class critique of Cathleen O'Neill. Others – such as Dora Sigerson Shorter and Blanaid Salkeld – were professional writers, publishing in multiple genres and playing an active role in the artistic networks of their time. The varying statuses of these women, and their differing levels of engagement with the reading public, reminds us of the dangers of generalising about the 'woman poet', and confirms the individuality of the writing life, and the extent to which each creative artist is driven by different practices and concerns. What these women hold in common, though, across more than two centuries of history, is the demand for time to write, and the desire for creative freedom.

Some of these women were well-established writers in their time, others were barely known outside a small circle of readers, yet all deserve to have their poetry read and remembered. The valuable work of recovery must continue, but it is vitally important that the very many women whose work we are now discovering – or re-discovering – are not forever trapped in that cycle of loss and retrieval. There are always new finds to be celebrated, as the recent publication of Ethna MacCarthy's poetry so clearly demonstrates; but it is essential that we deepen our engagement with some of these figures through sustained critical exploration. Without this attention, women poets come to express only the limitations of tradition, and their creative achievements remain unexamined.[4] While individual poems may be known and appreciated, these are seen as exceptions, rather than as key constituents of Ireland's literary history. It is this pattern that prevents so many women poets from finding a permanent place in the Irish tradition. Good scholarly editions, whether in print or digital form, are an important prerequisite for this process of integration.

Attention to the publishing history of these women not only deepens our engagement with their work, but also sheds valuable light on the larger networks of production and reading that are formative of ideas of literary merit.

II

At the heart of the exclusion of many of these poets is the vexed question of aesthetics, and the domination of modern literary tastes by a circumscribed view of literary value. Moynagh Sullivan has drawn attention to the ways in which particular formal choices have become naturalised; for (male) critics, divergence from these norms signifies bad art.[5] The conservative approach to form that has been the hallmark of Irish poetry criticism is, as Eric Falci has recently pointed out, closely linked to the relatively small body of work under scrutiny.[6] These aesthetic limitations have disproportionately affected the Irish woman poet: it is on the grounds of form that she is so often dismissed, her achievements seen as happy accidents, her experiments evidence of confusion. Yet, many of the poets included here deliberately subverted expectations, an approach that excluded them from the literary mainstream and made them difficult to categorise as writers. Not all of the poets are as formally innovative as Blanaid Salkeld or Madge Herron, but there are other ways in which tradition can be repurposed. Kenneth Keating's essay on Lynda Moran begins by drawing attention to typographical detail as a means to reflect on the dismemberment of the lyric subject, and other women poets too were attentive to the potential of form to rupture authorial stability. Some consciously experimented with new styles, though this exploratory work often appealed less to editors and publishers than more familiar modes. Since these poets are sparingly represented in institutional archives – where work by women is often found among the papers of male poets and editors, rather than in their own named collection – it can be a difficult task to piece together their full creative life. A greater commitment to the preservation of the papers of women poets would shed valuable light on their writing processes, as well as encouraging the sustained textual and biographical work needed to fully recuperate them.

All writing is a repository of texts, and a number of the poets discussed in this collection composed in direct response to earlier poems, while others found their work shaped by the form and language of the literature they loved to read. Everywhere in this volume women's engagement with texts is evident, yet their work has often been critically framed within a context of emotion and experience, rather than as part of an intellectual tradition. Though for some critics authenticity of emotion is a hallmark of valuable work, this space of feeling is often created by a sensibility born of reading and reflection. These women seek new ways of thinking about the world, and we must acknowledge the political and philosophical dimensions of their work, and the sustaining importance of diverse creative affinities, to fully understand their creative aims.

III

All of these women are identified as Irish poets, yet their relationship to Ireland is often a complicated one. Some are Irish by birth, others settled in Ireland as adults; a number spent the larger part of their creative lives abroad. Yet, despite a range of affinities, Ireland has helped to shape their imaginative identity and the poetry they write. For the earlier figures, local and regional affinities are strong – in the topographical detail of the poems, in the communities they invoke and in the use of language itself. By the time of the Irish Revival, mythological and folk materials had become closely linked to the formation of a distinctive Irish identity, one attractive to readers at home and abroad. These sources offered further opportunities, however: a plentiful supply of stories and a sensual language to enrich inherited poetic forms. For a poet such as Sigerson Shorter, these influences deepened her nationalist affinities, but facilitated troubling otherworldly encounters too. Other women poets also used these shared narratives to explore psychological states or the dynamics of personal or familial relationships. Historical materials offered an entry point to an inhospitable tradition, and a way to reflect on issues of continuity and inclusion. The past, whether real or imagined, was a space for serious reflection, and one in which political and social concerns could be obliquely expressed.

The settings these women choose for their poems often has particular resonance, and in many cases their sensitivity to their surroundings gives us unique insights into the Ireland of their time. Though landscape might function as a convention of the pastoral poem, nature was, in the words of Seán Hewitt, 'a way of thinking'. He shows how Emily Lawless combined a historical sensibility with an obsessive interest in biodiversity, and other women also drew on these elements of change and continuity to reflect on the human condition. Freda Laughton's reading of nature links its generative aspect to her own aesthetic freedoms, and Salkeld's poetic sequences manifest organic forms in even more startling ways. For others, though, the natural world was an everyday environment – a space of work and reflection that was more familiar than sublime.

Despite the prevalence of Irish imaginative materials in the oeuvres of these women, the transnational impulse of much of this work is an important dimension of its afterlife. While a figure like Lola Ridge exemplifies the capacity for self-transformation that departure from Ireland might allow – and the impact of a cosmopolitan experience on both her subject matter and form – other women also registered diverse influences, whether through the experience of travel or through textual encounters. We are especially alert now to the mobility of the woman poet, and to the impact of crossing borders of language, culture and religion, but there is also, as Annemarie Ní Churreáin reflects in a recent poem, the need for stillness in order both to survive and to create: 'Your task is simply to hold steady.'[7] Endurance is essential to the marginalised writer, yet is often overlooked in favour of the poem of dramatic immediacy. In the company of these women poets we learn the value of both achievements, and the responsibility to represent them accurately.

The range of work represented in this volume is a testament to the individuality of these poets and of their readers, as well as to the innovations of style and subject matter they adopt. In addition, it raises important questions about diversity within our current conceptions of Irish literature. Much has changed in the past ten years in how this field has been defined, and much remains to be done to represent the differing creative processes, and varying access to power, that women demonstrate in Ireland today. A new generation of migrant writers express with a particular intensity the uneasy relationship that the woman poet has with the Irish state. Eavan Boland was acutely aware of this continuing estrangement, and the currents of feeling stirred by her recent death reflect the solidarity registered by writers and readers all over Ireland for whom the silencing of the woman's voice is part of a larger process of exclusion and repression. Many of the women included in this book offer essential perspectives on these experiences. Out of these insights they have made their art, and we must, in turn, re-make our criticism.

Endnotes

INTRODUCTION: ACTS OF ATTENTION

1. Anne Carson, 'Pronoun Envy', *The New Yorker*, 10 February 2014, pp. 48–9.
2. Lucy Collins, 'Introduction', in Lucy Collins (ed.), *Poetry by Women in Ireland: A critical anthology 1870–1970* (Liverpool University Press, 2012), p. 1.
3. Heather Ingman and Clíona Ó Gallchoir, 'Introduction,' in Heather Ingman and Clíona Ó Gallchoir (eds), *A History of Modern Irish Women's Literature* (Cambridge University Press, 2018), pp. 1–17 (p. 2).
4. 'Preface', in Angela Bourke et al. (eds), *The Field Day Anthology of Irish Writing: Irish women's writing and traditions* (vols IV & V) (Cork University Press, 2002), pp. xxxii–xxxvi (p. xxxii).
5. *Missing Voices: Irish women poets of the 18th–20th centuries* was a one-day seminar held at Poetry Ireland, 11 Parnell Square East, Dublin, on 6 October 2018.
6. Gerald Dawe (ed.), *The Cambridge Companion to Irish Poets* (Cambridge University Press, 2017). For more on the public reaction to the book, see Mary O'Donnell, 'A Prosaic Lack of Women in the Cambridge Companion to Irish Poets', *The Irish Times*, 8 January 2018, p. 10; and in response Gerald Dawe, 'Selected Poets and their Work, Alive and Present to the Reader', *The Irish Times*, 24 February 2018, p. 27. See also Seán Hewitt, 'The Cambridge Companion to Irish Poets: Insightful essays', *The Irish Times*, 30 June 2018, <https://www.irishtimes.com/culture/books/the-cambridge-companion-to-irish-poets-review-insightful-essays-1.3542052>; and Chris Murray, 'Fired! Irish Women Poets and the Canon: Preamble to the Pledge', https://poethead.wordpress.com/2017/12/16/fired-irish-women-poets-and-the-canon-preamble-to-the-pledge/.
7. *Fired! Irish Women Poets and the Canon*, <https://poethead.wordpress.com/fired-irish-women-poets-and-the-canon-preamble-to-the-pledge/>; *Irish Women's Writing (1880–1920) Network*, <https://irishwomenswritingnetwork.com/>.
8. Ingman and Ó Gallchoir, 'Introduction,' *A History of Modern Irish Women's Literature*, pp. 1–17 (p. 1).
9. Collins, 'Introduction', *Poetry by Women in Ireland*, p. 1.
10. Eileen Battersby, 'A Vivid Diary of a Woman Scorned', *The Irish Times*, 13 September 2004, p. 13.
11. David Wheatley, 'Like Bitter Wine', *Times Literary Supplement*, no. 6026, 25 September 2018, p. 33.
12. Ingman and Ó Gallchoir, 'Introduction', *A History of Modern Irish Women's Literature*, p. 9.
13. Anne Mulhall, '"The Well-Known, Old, But Still Unbeaten Track": Women poets and Irish periodical culture in the mid-twentieth century', *Irish University Review*, vol. 42, no. 1, spring/summer 2012, p. 32.

14 Gerardine Meaney, Mary O'Dowd and Bernadette Whelan, 'Introduction', *Reading the Irish Woman: Studies in cultural encounter and exchange, 1714–1960* (Liverpool: Liverpool University Press, 2013), pp. 1–12 (p. 6).
15 Eiléan Ní Chuilleanáin, speaking at the launch of *Ethna MacCarthy: Poems* (by Ethna MacCarthy, eds Eoin O Brien and Gerald Dawe, Dublin: Lilliput Press, 2019), Trinity College Dublin, 3 October 2019.
16 Eoin O'Brien and Gerald Dawe, 'Introduction', in *Ethna MacCarthy: Poems*, p. xxiv.
17 Margaret Kelleher and Philip O'Leary, 'Introduction', in Margaret Kelleher and Philip O'Leary (eds), *The Cambridge History of Irish Literature* (Cambridge: Cambridge University Press, 2006).
18 Kenneth Keating and Ailbhe McDaid, Measuring Equality in the Arts Sector (MEAS) <https://measorg.com>.
19 Nuala Ní Dhomhnaill, in Medbh McGuckian and Nuala Ní Dhomhnaill, 'Cómhra', by Laura O'Connor, *Southern Review*, 31.3 (1995), pp. 581–614 (p. 598).
20 Elizabeth Bishop, in Eileen Farley, 'Pulitzer Prize-Winning Poet Visits UW', *University of Washington Daily*, 28 May 1974, reprinted in George Monteiro (ed.), *Conversations with Elizabeth Bishop* (Jackson: University Press of Mississippi, 1996), p. 54.
21 Fiona McCann, 'Tackling the Poetry Patriarchy', *The Irish Times*, 2 December 2008, p. 16.

OLIVIA ELDER (1735–80)

1 'To Mrs A.C.H., an account of the Authors manner of spending her time', in Andrew Carpenter (ed.), *The Poems of Olivia Elder* (Dublin: Irish Manuscripts Commission, 2017), p. 3. Subsequent page references are to pages in this edition. The extract refers to the third duke of Queensberry, Charles Douglas (1698–1778), and his duchess, Catherine Douglas (1701–77), who were patrons of the poet, and dramatist John Gay (1685–1732); and poet Edward Young (1683–1765). A 'dishclout' is a cloth or rag for washing or drying dishes.
2 'New Light' refers to the more liberal-minded theology, whereas the 'Old Light' clergy were conservative Calvinists and their belief in original sin and predestination particularly riled Olivia Elder.
3 National Library of Ireland MS 23254. See the printed edition of the manuscript, Carpenter (ed.), *The Poems of Olivia Elder*.
4 Authorial footnote, Carpenter (ed.), *The Poems of Olivia Elder*, p. 93.
5 Slightly misquoted from Jonathan Swift, 'Stella at Wood-Park' (1723), ll. 76–80.
6 Elder's previous verse letter to Miss M.B. had included an unflattering portrait of a 'gentleman' called Davy, who clearly played some part in Miss M.B.'s life.
7 Angle brackets denote authorial footnotes in the manuscript. <a Gentleman once so intimate with the Lady as to admit of calling [each] other by their Christian names, but at this time seemd to have forgot her on which she says, "how shoud he [*recte* we?] know great people, but by a shortsightedness yt makes them forget all those yt have ye misfortune neither to be heirs to Cresus nor Helen["]. this the author purposely here perverts for ye sake of ye jest.> In the view of Dr Linde Lunney of the *Dictionary of Irish Biography*, herself a native of the Coleraine area, the surname here is Torrens.
8 <ye Lady was inclined to be fat, but this peice is as much of ye carrikatura as ye other.>

9 <To bar mistakes, take notice friend,
I mean a Barrel set on end,
For even fancy never sprung,
A head and neck up from a Bung.
Altho to lengthen out my song,
I make you broader than your [*recte* you're] long.
Now this I think is the first time
E'er Margin note was put in Rhime.>
10 Reading uncertain. might = fosset, the narrow end of a barrel (*OED*).
11 = faucet, tap.
12 tie.
13 Authorial note in Carpenter (ed.), *The Poems of Olivia Elder*, p. 3.
14 See *A Letter to the Reverend Mr. Robert McBride; Occasion'd by his pretending to defend Mr. Elder's suspension, and by divers reflections cast upon Mr Elder, in his late pamphlet entitled The Overtures transmitted by the general synod, 1725. Set in a fair light &c.* by John Elder A.M. minister of the gospel (Belfast, 1727).
15 'The Near Way to Heaven, an Orthodox Garland (as supposed to be written by ye Revd Mr Mc Dowel or any other Orthodox parson) to ye tune of ye bigbellied bottle' (Carpenter (ed.), *The Poems of Olivia Elder*, pp. 99–102).
16 For the background to this poem, see the *Oxford Dictionary of National Biography* entry for John MacNaghten (1722–61).
17 Carpenter (ed.), *The Poems of Olivia Elder*, p. 79.

ELLEN TAYLOR (years unknown; one extant publication, 1792)

1 Ellen Taylor, 'Written by the BARROW side, where she was sent to wash LINEN', in *Poems by Ellen Taylor, The Irish Cottager* (Dublin: G. Draper, 1972), pp. 8–9. The poem has been anthologised in Roger Lonsdale (ed.), *Eighteenth-Century Women Poets* (Oxford: Oxford University Press, 1990), pp. 455–6, and in Andrew Carpenter (ed.), *Verse in English from Eighteenth-Century Ireland* (Cork: Cork University Press, 1998), pp. 473–4. As Carpenter explains, the 'Barrow side' refers to the River Barrow, which flows through Graiguenamanagh (County Kilkenny) where Taylor was working as a maid at the time of the poem's composition.
2 Introduction, *Poems by Ellen Taylor*, p. 2.
3 Leith Davis, 'Ellen Taylor', in *Irish Women Poets of the Romantic Period* (Alexander Street Press, 2008), <https://lit.alexanderstreet.com/iwrp> [accessed 2 March 2020].
4 Ibid.
5 There are only forty-two subscribers, which is very small for a subscription publication in this period. Interestingly, thirty are women (about 70 per cent), which is again unusual.
6 See Chapter 3 of Amy Prendergast, *Literary Salons across Britain and Ireland in the Long Eighteenth Century* (London: Palgrave Macmillan, 2015).
7 Janet Todd, 'Ascendancy: Lady Mount Cashall, Lady Moira, Mary Wollstonecraft and the Union Pamphlets', *Eighteenth-Century Ireland / Iris an dá chultór*, vol. 18, 2003, pp. 98–117.
8 See Prendergast, Chapter 4, *Literary Salons across Britain and Ireland*; Todd, 'Ascendancy', p. 105.
9 He was a neighbour of the poet Mary Tighe. See Prendergast, *Literary Salons across Britain and Ireland*, p. 170.

10 The Griffiths published an account of their courtship letters, *A Series of Genuine Letters between Henry and Frances*, in 1757 to much contemporary notice and sensation. Elizabeth was also a dramatist and novelist. She died in 1793.

DOROTHEA HERBERT (*c.*1767–1829)

1 Dorothea Herbert, 'Lines to a Friend', in Frances Finnegan, *Introspections: The Poetry & Private World of Dorothea Herbert* (County Kilkenny: Congrave Press, 2011), p. 132.
2 Louis M. Cullen (ed.), *Retrospections of Dorothea Herbert* (Dublin: TownHouse, 2004), p. vi.
3 The manuscript of *Retrospections* is held in the Manuscript Library of Trinity College Dublin: TCD MS 10121. First transcribed by Geoffrey Fortesque Mandeville (GFM), it was published in 1929 as G.F. Mandeville, *Retrospections of Dorothea Herbert 1770–1789* (London: Gerald Howe, 1929), followed by G.F. Mandeville, *Retrospections of Dorothea Herbert 1789–1806* (London: Gerald Howe, 1930). GFM and Howe added an extensive index to both editions and a family tree to the 1930 publication. TownHouse republished *Retrospections* in 1988 and 2004 edited by Louis M. Cullen.
4 Mary Catherine Breen states that 'The text *Introspections: The Poetry & Private World of Dorothea Herbert* was based on an incomplete photocopy of the original manuscripts.' See Breen, 'The Making and Unmaking of an Irish Woman of Letters', D. Phil thesis, Linacre College Oxford, 2012, p. 24. <https://pdfs.semanticscholar.org/d5ce/cba2fa70e20082054c58b678e7b6e61ac70a.pdf> [accessed February 2020]. Frances Finnegan acknowledges that 'some words, unfamiliar or faded, are difficult to decipher'. See Finnegan, *Introspections*, p. 8.
5 Cullen (ed.), *Retrospections*, p. 345.
6 Ibid., p. 311.
7 Herbert, 'The Villa', in Finnegan, *Introspections*, pp. 21–7.
8 Breen, 'The Making and Unmaking of an Irish Woman of Letters', pp. 68–71.
9 Finnegan, *Introspections*, p. 47.
10 Mary Wollstonecraft, *A Vindication of the Rights of Woman*, ed. Miriam Brody (London: Penguin, 2004), p. 83.
11 Cullen (ed.), *Retrospections*, p. 144.
12 Finnegan, *Introspections*, p. 85
13 Ibid., p. 66.
14 Cullen (ed.), *Retrospections*, p. 267. We know this from the various direct and indirect references to Pope. It is interesting to note that he too suffered twice from unrequited love. See Peter Quennell (ed.), *The Pleasures of Pope* (London: Hamish Hamilton, 1949), p. xxiii.
15 Alexander Pope in his 'A Letter to the Publisher' states: 'not only the Author's friends, but even strangers, appear engaged by humanity, to take some care of an orphan of so much genius and spirit, which its parent seems to have abandoned from the very beginning'. See Herbert Davis (ed.), *Pope: Poetical Works* (Oxford: Oxford University Press, 1966), p. 430.
16 Finnegan, *Introspections*, p. 13.
17 Cullen (ed.), *Retrospections*, p. 232.
18 Finnegan, *Introspections*, p. 314.

19 Michael Coady, 'The Troubled Shade of Dorothea Herbert', broadcast 1 December 2013, RTÉ Radio 1, <https://www.rte.ie/radio1/sunday-miscellany/programmes/2013/1201/489918-sunday-miscellany-1-december-2013/> [accessed 2 March 2020].
20 Barbara Hughes, *Between Literature and History: The diaries and memoirs of Mary Leadbeater and Dorothea Herbert* (Oxford, New York: Peter Lang, 2010), p. 17.
21 For example: 'Before I was three, I was well grounded in the Greek myths, and the figures of those stories, together with certain images from the illustrations, became fundamental referents.' Louise Glück, 'The Education of the Poet', in *Proofs and Theories: Essays on Poetry* (New Jersey: Ecco Press, 1994), p. 7. See also Elizabeth Jennings, 'From Homer', *Poetry*, February 1973, p. 258.
22 Specifically, Pope's 1720 translation, which she closely follows. For more on this see Finnegan, *Introspections*, p. 263.
23 Finnegan provides Herbert's index as per her manuscript in addition to Finnegan's index of poems which is presented in a different order and includes poems from *Retrospections*. Herbert's index excludes the poems from *Retrospections*.
24 Quennell (ed.), *The Pleasures of Pope*, p. 219.
25 Finnegan, *Introspections*, p. 297.
26 It is believed the manuscript of poems is still held in the estate of Robert Wyse Jackson.
27 I use the term 'part' here instead of 'volume' to reduce any confusion with the four volumes referenced elsewhere.
28 Cullen (ed.), *Retrospections*, p. 418.
29 See Finnegan, *Introspections*, pp. 145, 156.
30 See Brian Brennan, *Máire Bhuí Ní Laoire: A poet of her people* (Cork: The Collins Press, 2000).
31 Cullen (ed.), *Retrospections*, p. 328.

EMILY LAWLESS (1845–1913)

1 Emily Lawless, 'To that Rare and Deep-Red Burnet-Moth only to be met with in the Burren', in *The Inalienable Heritage, and Other Poems*, with a preface by Edith Sichel (privately printed, 1914), p. 37.
2 A good biographical sketch of Emily Lawless is given in Marie O'Neill, 'Emily Lawless', *Dublin Historical Record*, vol. 48, no. 2, autumn 1995, pp. 125–41.
3 Gerardine Meaney, 'Decadence, Degeneration and Revolting Aesthetics: The fiction of Emily Lawless and Katherine Cecil Thurston', *Colby Quarterly*, vol. 36, no. 2, June 2000, pp. 157–75 (p. 160).
4 Quoted in James M. Cahalan, 'Forging a Tradition: Emily Lawless and the Irish literary canon', *Colby Quarterly*, vol. 27, no. 1, March 1991, pp. 27–39 (p. 28).
5 Emily Lawless, 'To the Winged Psyche, Dying in a Garden', in *The Point of View: Some Talks and Disputations* (London: R. Clay and Sons, 1909), p. 44.
6 Emily Lawless, 'An Entomological Adventure', *Traits and Confidences* (London: Methuen, 1898), pp. 3–35 (p. 9).
7 Emily Lawless, 'On the Pursuit of Marine Zoology as an Incentive to Gossip', *Traits and Confidences*, pp. 36–41 (p. 39).
8 Emily Lawless, 'An Entomological Adventure', *Traits and Confidences*, pp. 3–35 (p. 4).
9 Heidi Hansson, 'Kinship: People and nature in Emily Lawless' poetry', *Nordic Journal of English Studies*, vol. 13, no. 2, pp. 6–22 (p. 8).

10 See E. Charles Nelson, 'Emily Lawless and Charles Darwin: An Irish mystery', *Archives of Natural History*, vol. 43, no. 1, 2016, pp. 148–51.
11 Quoted in Heidi Hansson, *Emily Lawless, 1845–1913: Writing the interspace* (Cork: Cork University Press, 2007), pp. 49–50.
12 Max Horkheimer and Theodor Adorno, *Dialectic of Enlightenment*, trans. John Cumming (New York: Herder & Herder, 1972), p. xv.
13 W.B. Yeats, 'The Autumn of the Flesh', in John Eglinton, W.B. Yeats, A.E. and William Larminie, *Literary Ideals in Ireland* (London: T. Fisher Unwin, 1899), pp. 69–78 (p. 69).
14 Edith Sichel, 'Preface' to Emily Lawless, *The Inalienable Heritage, and Other Poems*, pp. v–vi.
15 Emily Lawless, 'From the Burren', in *The Inalienable Heritage, and Other Poems*, p. 24.
16 Emily Lawless, 'To a Tuft of White Bog-Cotton, Growing in the Tyrol', in *With the Wild Geese*, with an introduction by Stopford A. Brooke (London: Isbister & Co., Ltd: 1902), pp. 75–6.
17 Emily Lawless, 'Dirge of the Munster Forest, 1581', in *With the Wild Geese*, pp. 35–7 (p. 36).

CHARLOTTE GRACE O'BRIEN (1845–1909)

1 Charlotte Grace O'Brien, 'Gladstone (1884)', in *Lyrics* (London: Kegan Paul, Trench & Co., 1886), p. 17.
2 O'Brien, 'Gladstone', in *Lyrics*, p. 31.
3 Charlotte Grace O'Brien, 'Horrors of an Emigrant Ship', *Pall Mall Gazette*, 6 May 1881, p. 6.
4 M.C. Keogh, 'Charlotte Grace O'Brien', *Irish Monthly*, vol. 38, no. 443, May 1910, p. 245.
5 W.B. Yeats, 'Easter 1916', in Peter Allt and Russell K. Alspach (eds), *The Variorum Edition of the Poems of W.B. Yeats* (New York: Macmillan, 1957), p. 11.
6 For more on this, see O'Brien's article 'The Irish "Poor Man"', *Nineteenth Century*, December 1880, pp. 876–87.
7 For context and discussion on this, see Senia Pašeta, *Before the Revolution: Nationalism, social change and Ireland's Catholic elite, 1879–1922* (Cork: Cork University Press, 1999), and Richard English, *Irish Freedom: The history of nationalism in Ireland* (London: Pan Books, 2007).
8 Eugenio F. Biagini, *British Democracy and Irish Nationalism 1876–1906* (Cambridge: Cambridge University Press, 2007), p. 13.
9 Stephen Gwynn, *Charlotte Grace O'Brien: Selections from her writings and correspondence with a memoir* (Dublin: Maunsel & Co., 1909), p. 132.
10 Charlotte Grace O'Brien and Matthew Russell, 'Two Sonnets about Sonnets', *Irish Monthly*, vol. 15, no. 173, November 1887, p. 664.
11 For further discussion of this in the context of Ireland's poor laws, see her article, 'The Irish "Poor Man"'.
12 Matthew Russell, 'Our poets. No. 20: Charlotte Grace O'Brien', *Irish Monthly*, vol. 16, no. 7, December 1888, p. 732.
13 Gwynn, *Charlotte Grace O'Brien*, p. 120.
14 Ibid., p. 101.
15 Sandra Kemp, Charlotte Mitchell and David Trotter (eds), 'Introduction' to *The Oxford Companion to Edwardian Fiction* (Oxford: Oxford University Press, 2002), p. xvii.

16 Matthew Campbell, *Irish Poetry under the Union* (Cambridge: Cambridge University Press, 2013), p. 169.
17 G.K. Chesterton, 'To Them that Mourn', *The Speaker*, 28 May 1898, p. 27.
18 John Wilson Foster, *Irish Novels, 1890–1940: New bearings in culture and fiction* (Oxford: Oxford University Press, 2008), p. 9.
19 M.C. Keogh, 'Charlotte Grace O'Brien', *Irish Monthly*, vol. 38, no. 443, May 1910, p. 245.

DORA SIGERSON SHORTER (1866–1918)

1 Dora Sigerson Shorter, 'The Patchwork Quilt', in *The Sad Years* (London: Constable, 1918), p. 44.
2 Katharine Tynan, 'Dora Sigerson: A tribute and some memories', in Dora Sigerson Shorter, *The Sad Years*, pp. vii–xii (p. xii); Edward Thompson, 'Preface', in *The Augustan Books of Modern Poetry: Dora Sigerson Shorter* (London: Ernest Benn, 1926), p. iii.
3 W.B. Yeats, 'He Wishes for the Cloths of Heaven', in Peter Allt and Russell K. Alspach (eds), *The Variorum Edition of the Poems of W.B. Yeats* (New York: Macmillan, 1957), p. 176.
4 Dora Sigerson Shorter, 'A Vagrant Heart', in *The Collected Poems of Dora Sigerson Shorter* (London: 1907), pp. 249–50.
5 Jahan Ramazani, *Poetry of Mourning: The modern elegy from Hardy to Heaney* (London: University of Chicago Press, 1994), p. 17.
6 Matthew Campbell, '"A bit of shrapnel": The Sigerson Shorters, the Hardys, Yeats, and the Easter Rising', in Alex Houen and Jan-Melissa Schramm (eds), *Sacrifice and Modern War Literature: The Battle of Waterloo to the War on Terror* (Oxford: Oxford University Press, 2018), pp. 124–44 (p. 139).
7 Christina Rossetti, 'A bed of Forget-Me-Nots', in R.W. Crump (ed.), *The Complete Poems* (London: Penguin, 2005), p. 784.
8 Yeats, 'To a Shade', in *Variorum Poems*, p. 292.
9 Dora Sigerson Shorter, *Love of Ireland: Poems and ballads* (Dublin: Mansell, 1916), p. 63.
10 Dora Sigerson Shorter, 'Sixteen Dead Men', in *Sixteen Dead Men and Other Poems of Easter Week* (New York: Mitchell Kennerly, 1919), pp. 15–16; Yeats, 'Sixteen Dead Men', in *Variorum Poems*, p. 395; Campbell, 'The Sigerson Shorters', p. 134.
11 Dora Sigerson Shorter, 'The Choice', in *The Tricolour: Poems of the Revolution* (Dublin: Maunsel and Roberts, 1922), pp. 28–9.
12 Sigerson Shorter, 'The Black Horseman', in *The Sad Years*, pp. 72–3.
13 Clement Shorter, *C.K.S. An Autobiography: A fragment by himself* (London: Constable, 1927), p. 29.
14 Dora Sigerson Shorter, 'Cean Duv Deelish', in Lucy Collins (ed.), *Poetry by Women in Ireland: A critical anthology, 1870–1970* (Liverpool: Liverpool University Press, 2012), p. 109.
15 Quoted in Ronald Schuchard, *The Last Minstrels: Yeats and the revival of the bardic arts* (Oxford: Oxford University Press, 2008), p. 44, n. 25.
16 W.B. Yeats, 'Modern Irish Poetry', in William H. O'Donnell (ed.), *The Collected Works of W.B. Yeats Volume VI: Prefaces and introductions: uncollected prefaces and introductions* (London: Macmillan, 1988), pp. 100–12 (p. 108). Yeats added the paragraph praising the modern lyric poetry of Herbert Trench, Moira O'Neill and Sigerson Shorter for a 1904 reprint of his introduction for *Irish Literature*, published in the United States by John Morris.

17 Thomas MacDonagh, *Literature in Ireland: Studies Irish and Anglo-Irish* (Dublin: Talbot Press, 1916), p. 177.
18 Ibid., p. 238.
19 Dora Sigerson Shorter, 'Ireland', in *The Augustan Books of Modern Poetry: Dora Sigerson Shorter* (London: Ernest Benn, 1926), p. 5.
20 Sigerson Shorter, 'Nora', in *The Sad Years*, p. 42.
21 Sigerson Shorter, 'They Did Not See Thy Face', in *The Tricolour*, pp. 19–20. The poem was previously published in *The Sad Years*; the reprinting in *The Tricolour* included the sub-heading 'In Memory of Thomas MacDonagh'.
22 Constance de Markievicz, 'They did not see thy face', National Library of Ireland, coloured illustration, 36 x 26 cm: <http://catalogue.nli.ie/Record/vtls000516200> [accessed March 2020].
23 Sigerson Shorter, *The Tricolour*, p. 20.
24 Katharine Tynan, *Memories* (London: Eveleigh Nash & Grayson, 1924), pp. 255–71 (p. 260).

LOLA RIDGE (1873–1941)

1 Lola Ridge, 'The Ghetto', in Daniel Tobin (ed.), *Lola Ridge, To the Many: Collected early works* (Stroud: Little Island Press, 2018), pp. 59–61.
2 Tobin, 'Introduction', *Lola Ridge, To the Many*, pp. 29–30.
3 Lola Ridge, 'Woman and the Creative Will', in *Lola Ridge, To the Many*, p. 139.
4 Sara Ahmed, *Living a Feminist Life* (Durham and London: Duke University Press, 2017), p. 37.
5 Lola Ridge, quoted in Teresa Svoboda, *Anything that Burns You: A portrait of Lola Ridge, radical poet* (Tuscon, Arizona: Schaffner Press, 2016), p. i.
6 Svoboda, *Anything that Burns You*, p. 65.
7 Emma Goldman, 'Anarchism: What it really stands for', in *Anarchism and Other Essays*, 2nd rev. ed. (New York: Mother Earth Publishing Association, 1911), pp. 58–62.
8 Ridge, 'The Ghetto', in *Lola Ridge, To the Many*, pp. 59–61.
9 Ibid., pp. 44–5.
10 Ridge, 'Spires', in *Lola Ridge, To the Many*, p. 95.
11 Ridge, 'An Old Workman', in *Lola Ridge, To the Many*, p. 232.
12 Ridge, 'Fuel', in *Lola Ridge, To the Many*, p. 98; 'Wall Street at Night', in *Lola Ridge, To the Many*, p. 210.
13 Ridge, 'Reveille', in *Lola Ridge, To the Many*, p. 228.
14 Ridge, 'Emma Goldman', in *Lola Ridge, To the Many*, p. 231; 'Kelvin Barry', p. 275. A note on the poem clarifies: 'His name is more commonly spelled as Kevin Barry.' Tobin, *Lola Ridge, To the Many*, p. 384.
15 Ridge, 'The Tidings', in *Lola Ridge, To the Many*, p. 134.
16 Nathaniel Cadle, 'Lola Ridge, Modernism, and the Poetics of Radical Sentimentalism', in Jody Cardinal, Deirdre E. Egan-Ryan and Julia Lisella (eds), *Modernist Women Writers and American Social Engagement* (Maryland and London: Lexington Books, 2019), p. 164.
17 For further information on the case, see, for example, Susan Tejada, *In Search of Sacco and Vanzetti: Double lives, troubled times, and the Massachusetts murder case that shook the world* (Boston: Northeastern University Press, 2012).
18 Lola Ridge, 'Electrocution', in *Lola Ridge, To the Many*, p. 272.

19 Evan Mauro, 'The Death and Life of the Avant Garde', *Meditations*, vol. 26, no. 1–2, fall 2012–spring 2013, p. 119.
20 See Anne Stevenson, quoted in 'Praise for Lola Ridge', *Lola Ridge, To the Many*, p. i, and Robert Pinsky, 'Street Poet', *Slate*, 22 March 2011, http://www.slate.com/articles/arts/poem/2011/03/street_poet.html?via=gdpr-consent [accessed March 2020].
21 Ahmed, *Living a Feminist Life*, p. 150.
22 Rio Matchett, 'Anything that Burns: A review of *Lola Ridge, To the Many: Collected Early Works*', *The Poetry Review*, vol. 108, no. 4, winter 2018, p. 111.
23 Svoboda, *Anything that Burns You*, p. 6.
24 Ibid.

FLORENCE MARY WILSON (1874–1946)

1 F.M. Wilson, 'The Sea-Folk', in *The Coming of the Earls* (Dublin: Candle Press, 1918 [2nd edn]), p. 11.
2 Padraic O'Farrell (ed.), *The '98 Reader* (Dublin: Lilliput Press, 1998), p. 106.
3 Guy Beiner, *Forgetful Remembrance: Social forgetting and vernacular historiography of a rebellion in Ulster* (Oxford: Oxford University Press, 2018), pp. 417–18.
4 F.M. Wilson, *The Coming of the Earls* (Dublin: Candle Press, 1918 [2nd edn]), p. 11.
5 These and further biographical details are supplied in A.U. Colman, *A Dictionary of Nineteenth-century Irish Woman Poets* (Galway: Kenny's Bookshop, c.1996), pp. 239–40; D. Armstrong, '"A Lady who has written much admirable verse"', in B.S. Turner (ed.), *'A Man Stepped out for Death': Thomas Russell and County Down* (Newtownards: Colourpoint Books, 2003), pp. 49–56; see also <https://jenjen999.wordpress.com/florence-mary-wilson/> [accessed March 2020].
6 *Irish Review* (Dublin), vol. 1, no. 9, November 1911, p. 435.
7 Padraic Gregory (ed.), *Modern Anglo-Irish Verse: An anthology selected from the work of living Irish poets* (London: D. Nutt, 1914), pp. 101–3, 261–3, 285–6.
8 Catherine Morris, 'Becoming Irish? Alice Milligan and the Revival', *Irish University Review*, Special Issue: New Perspectives on the Irish Literary Revival, vol. 33, no. 1, spring / summer 2003, pp. 79–98 (p. 80).
9 See <https://www.nidirect.gov.uk/articles/about-ulster-covenant> [accessed March 2020].
10 Morris, 'Becoming Irish? Alice Milligan and the Revival', p. 82.
11 These and following quotations from the memoir are taken from *Florence Mary Wilson: The collected writings* in the Florence Mary Wilson Papers, typescripts by Anne Colman, Research Fellow (1996), Institute of Irish Studies, Queen's University Belfast. Quotations from the papers, hereafter 'Colman typescript', are made with the permission of the Irish Linen Centre and Lisburn Museum. With thanks to Dr Ciaran Toal, who made the papers available to me.
12 Colman typescript.
13 Ibid.
14 Ibid.
15 FMW to FJB, undated, 1918. Bigger Correspondence W2 (9) in the FJB Collection, Belfast Central Library, Libraries NI. With thanks to Ms Catherine Morrow of Libraries NI, who advised on presentation of references.
16 FMW to FJB, undated, 1918. Bigger Correspondence W2 (14).
17 FMW to FJB, 16 October 1925. Bigger Correspondence, W2 (22).

18 Spelling as it appears in the dedication to *The Coming of the Earls*. In her correspondence with Bigger, Wilson refers to 'Nial'.
19 FMW to FJB, 1 October 1918. Bigger Correspondence, W2 (5).
20 FMW to FJB, 4 September 1916. Bigger Correspondence, W1 (6).
21 Gregory, *Modern Anglo-Irish Verse*, pp. 262–3.
22 Hallowe'en.
23 Wilson, *The Coming of the Earls*, pp. 5–6.
24 Ibid., p. 22.
25 FMW (1918), p.19.
26 Wilson, *The Coming of the Earls*, p. 18.

MAY MORTON (c.1880–1957)

1 May Morton, 'Spindle and Shuttle', in Festival of Britain Committee, *Northern Ireland Prize Poems: Festival of Britain* (Belfast: His Majesty's Stationery Office, 1951), n.p.
2 *The Field Day Anthology of Irish Writing* (vol. IV) and other recently published sources give Morton's year of birth as 1876, but the Census records for 1901 and 1911 suggest that she was born sometime between 1879 and 1881. May Elizabeth Morton is included in the 1911 Census returns for 25 Newington Avenue (Duncairn, Antrim), where May Elizabeth and her sister Millicent boarded. The 1901 Census states that she was living in Tyrone with her Uncle James Knox, aged twenty-two.
3 Festival of Britain Committee, *Northern Ireland Prize Poems*, n.p.
4 Morton, 'Spindle and Shuttle', n.p.
5 Ibid.
6 One example of this recovery is found in Katie Donovan, A.N. Jeffares and Brendan Kennelly (eds), *Ireland's Women: writings past and present* (Dublin: Gill & Macmillan, 1994). Morton's work is also included in Angela Bourke, Siobhán Kilfeather, Maria Luddy, Margaret Mac Curtain, Gerardine Meaney, Máirín Ni Dhonnchadha, Mary O'Dowd and Clair Wills (eds), *The Field Day Anthology of Irish Writing: Irish women's writing and traditions*, vol. IV (New York: New York University Press, 2002).
7 Ailbhe Smyth, 'The Floozie in the Jacuzzi', *Feminist Studies*, vol. 17, no. 1, spring 1991, p. 24.
8 Roy McFadden, contribution to 'The War Years in Ulster (1939–45): A Symposium', *The Honest Ulsterman*, 64, September 1979 – January 1980, p. 53.
9 May Morton to Kathleen O'Brennan, c.1945, Éamonn Ceannt and Kathleen O'Brennan Papers, National Library Ireland, NLI MS 41,509/6/11.
10 May Morton quoted in Anon., 'Mr. T. Carnduff honoured by Young Ulster Society', *Belfast News Letter*, 14 February 1954, p. 6; cited in Sarah Ferris, *Poet John Hewitt, 1907–1987 and Criticism of Northern Irish Protestant Writing* (New York: Edwin Mellon, 2002), p. 73.
11 Lucy Collins, *Poetry by Women in Ireland: A critical anthology 1870–1970* (Liverpool: Liverpool University Press, 2012), p. 48.
12 May Morton, 'The Writer and the P.E.N.', in *The P.E.N. in Ulster: Contributed by Well-Known Writers of Belfast Centre* (Belfast: Reid & Wright, 1942), p. 2.
13 Eamonn Hughes, 'Ulsters of the Senses', *Fortnight*, no. 306, May 1992, p. 11.
14 May Morton, *Dawn and Afterglow* (Belfast: Quota Press, 1936), p. 27.
15 Richard Kirkland, 'The Poetics of Partition: Poetry and Northern Ireland in the 1940s', in Fran Brearton and Alan Gillis (eds), *The Oxford Handbook of Modern Irish Poetry* (Oxford: Oxford University Press, 2012), p. 222.

BLANAID SALKELD (1880–1959)

1 Blanaid Salkeld, 'Leave us religion', in ...*the engine is left running* (Dublin: Gayfield Press, 1937), pp. 39–42.
2 A.A. Kelly (ed.), *Pillars of the House: An anthology of verse by Irish women* (Dublin: Wolfhound Press, 1997).
3 Moynagh Sullivan, 'The Woman Gardener: Transnationalism, gender, sexuality, and the poetry of Blanaid Salkeld', *Irish University Review*, vol. 42, no. 1, spring / summer 2012, p. 53.
4 Lucy Collins (ed.), *Poetry by Women in Ireland: A critical anthology 1870–1970* (Liverpool University Press, 2012), pp. 37, 40.
5 Blanaid Salkeld, *Hello Eternity!* (London: Elkin Matthews & Marrot, 1933); *The Fox's Covert* (London: J.M. Dent, 1935).
6 Deirdre Brady, 'Modernist Presses and the Gayfield Press', *Bibliologia*, no. 9, 2014, p. 103.
7 'Woman Poet', *Irish Press*, 25 October 1937, p. 5.
8 Liam Miller, *Dolmen XXV: An illustrated bibliography of the Dolmen Press 1951–1976* (Dublin: Dolmen Press, 1976), pp. 7–8.
9 Ewart Milne, *Forty North, Fifty West* (Dublin: The Gayfield Press, 1938).
10 *The Poetics of Print: The private press tradition and Irish poetry*, curated by Dr Conor Linnie, the School of English & the Library of Trinity College Dublin (2019), <http://www.tcd.ie/library/exhibitions/poetics/>.
11 Sulllivan, 'The Woman Gardener', pp. 54, 55.
12 Salkeld, 'ATTEMPT AT COMMENCING', in ...*the engine is left running*, p. 1.
13 Ibid., pp. 1–2.
14 Margaret MacCurtain, 'Poetry of the Spirit, 1900–95', in Angela Bourke et al. (eds), *The Field Day Anthology of Irish Writing*, vol. V (Cork: Cork University Press, 2002), p. 624.
15 Salkeld, 'Leave us Religion', p. 39.
16 Sulllivan, 'The Woman Gardener', p. 61.
17 Justin Quinn, *The Cambridge Introduction to Modern Irish Poetry 1800–2000* (Cambridge University Press, 2008), p. 80.
18 Ibid.
19 Moynagh Sullivan, '"I Am Not Yet Delivered of the Past": The poetry of Blanaid Salkeld', *Irish University Review*, vol. 33, no. 1, spring / summer 2003, p. 197.
20 Anne Fogarty, '"The Influence of Absences": Eavan Boland and the silenced history of Irish women's poetry', *Colby Quarterly*, vol. 35, no. 4, 1999, p. 258.
21 Collins, *Poetry by Women in Ireland*, p. 46.

ETHNA MACCARTHY (1903–59)

1 Ethna MacCarthy, 'Viaticum', in uncatalogued volume of manuscript poetry (hereafter referred to as MacCarthy's notebook), Leventhal MacCarthy papers, TCD MS 11602. First published in *The Irish Times*, 11 April 1942, p. 5. Subsequently published (along with 'Insomnia' and 'Ghosts') in Devin A. Garrity (ed.), *New Irish Poets: Representative selections from the work of 37 contemporaries* (New York: Devin-Adair Co., 1948), pp. 121–2. Also published in Gerald Dawe and Eoin O'Brien (eds), *Ethna MacCarthy: Poems* (Dublin: Lilliput Press, 2019), p. 38. Variants exist between publications. In *Poems*, the first letter of every line of the poem is capitalised. I have chosen here to reproduce the poem as it appears in

MacCarthy's notebook (Leventhal MacCarthy papers, TCD MS 11602) and in Garrity (ed.), *New Irish Poets*, p. 121.
2 Samuel Beckett, *Three Novels: Molloy, Malone Dies, The Unnamable* (New York: Grove Press, 2009), pp. 278, 217, 270. Beckett signed a copy of his novel *Molloy* for Ethna MacCarthy in Paris in 1951 with a quotation from John Ford's seventeenth-century play *The Lover's Melancholy*: 'Sigh out a lamentable tale of things done long ago, and ill done.'
3 Alfred Lord Tennyson, *Selected Poems*, ed. Christopher Ricks (London: Penguin Books, 2007), p. 93.
4 Ethna MacCarthy, 'Insomnia', in James Keery (ed.), *Apocalypse: An anthology* (Manchester: Carcanet, 2020), p. 84.
5 Samuel Beckett, *Three Novels*, p. 63.
6 Samuel Beckett, 'Dieppe', in David Wheatley (ed.), *Selected Poems, 1930–1989* (London: Faber & Faber, 2009), p. 46.
7 Ethna MacCarthy, 'Kaimak', uncatalogued short story, Leventhal MacCarthy papers, TCD MS 11602.
8 See James Knowlson, *Damned to Fame: The life of Samuel Beckett* (London: Bloomsbury, 1996), p. 463.
9 Samuel Beckett, *All That Fall*, in *Collected Shorter Plays* (London: Faber, 1984), p. 37.
10 Quidnunc, 'An Irishman's Diary', *The Irish Times*, 30 May 1959, p. 5.
11 'Irish Poetess Heads Health Project', *Irish Examiner*, 12 September 1953, p. 7. This high-profile appointment was reported in a number of newspapers at the time, including *The Irish Times*, 12 September 1953, and the *Evening Herald*, 11 September 1953.
12 Quidnunc, 'An Irishman's Diary', *The Irish Times*, 30 May 1959, p. 5. It is highly probable that the writer of this anonymous short tribute was none other than Samuel Beckett himself.
13 See Donagh MacDonagh (ed.), *Poems from Ireland* (Dublin: Irish Times, 1944), and Garrity (ed.), *New Irish Poets*.
14 Ethna MacCarthy, 'Advent', in *Poems*, p. 44.
15 Gerald Dawe, 'Introduction', in *Poems*, p. xii.
16 See *The Irish Times*, 19 February 1944, p. 2; *The Irish Times*, 24 April 1943, p. 2.
17 Ethna MacCarthy (signed E MacC), 'Racine', *The Irish Times*, 18 September 1948, p. 6.
18 Ethna MacCarthy, 'Honor Among Spaniards', *The Irish Times*, 27 July 1957, p. 6.
19 Austin Clarke, 'The Day's Work', *The Irish Times*, 6 December 1947, p. 9.
20 Unsigned review, 'Lowbrows Floored', *Evening Herald*, 5 May 1947, p. 4.
21 Ethna MacCarthy (signed 'By a Woman Doctor'), 'Tuberculosis in Éire', *The Irish Times*, 8 May 1943, p. 2.
22 Ethna MacCarthy, 'Oxyuriasis in Public Health', *Irish Journal of Medical Science*, vol. 26, no. 2, February 1951, pp. 74–8.
23 Samuel Beckett, *Collected Shorter Plays* (London: Faber & Faber, 1984), p. 202.
24 Ethna MacCarthy, 'Public Health Problems Created by Louse Infestation', *Irish Journal of Medical Science*, vol. 23, no. 2, February 1948, p. 69.
25 Ethna MacCarthy, 'Nell Gwynn', in *Poems*, p. 31.
26 Unsigned review, 'The Dublin Magazine', *Irish Press*, 24 July 1951, p. 6. The full text of *The Uninvited* can be found in *Poems*, pp. 69–93.
27 Unsigned review titled '*Ireland Today*', dated 6 April 1937, collected in Ethna MacCarthy's notebook, TCD MS 11602.
28 Ethna MacCarthy, 'Flight', *Ireland To-Day*, vol. 2, no. 4, April 1937, p. 53. All subsequent references to this text are given in the body of the essay.

29 An account of this 'appalling episode' and its impact on Beckett's life is given in Knowlson, *Damned to Fame*, p. 143.
30 Ethna MacCarthy, 'Barcelona', in *Poems*, p. 46.
31 Samuel Beckett, letter to Ethna MacCarthy, 22 April 1959, Leventhal Collection, University of Texas, quoted in Lois More Overbeck, 'Letters', in Anthony Uhlmann (ed.), *Samuel Beckett in Context* (Cambridge University Press, 2013), p. 429. Thanks to Elizabeth L. Garver of the Harry Ransom Center, Texas, for providing me with access to a copy of this letter from the Leventhal Collection.
32 Samuel Beckett, letter to Ethna MacCarthy-Leventhal, 4 February 1959, in George Craig, Martha Dow Fehsenfeld, Dan Gunn and Lois More Overbeck (eds), *The Letters of Samuel Beckett: 1957–1965* (Cambridge University Press, 2014), p. 197.
33 Knowlson, *Damned to Fame*, pp. 459–60.
34 MacCarthy, *Poems*, p. 41.
35 Ibid, p. 63.
36 Ethna M. MacCarthy-Leventhal, 'Post-Radiation Mouth Blindness', *The Lancet*, vol. 274, no. 7112, 19 December 1959, pp. 1138–9.
37 Knowlson, *Damned to Fame*, p. 464. Among the Leventhal papers at Trinity College Dublin there is a typed copy of Beckett's 'Alba' with the following manuscript annotation: 'for Ethna MacCarthy who replaces Beatrice as far as Herr Samuel Beckett is concerned. 18/8/31'. TCD MS 11315.
38 Knowlson, *Damned to Fame*, p. 151.
39 Eiléan Ní Chuilleanáin, speaking at the launch of *Ethna MacCarthy: Poems*, Trinity College Dublin, 3 October 2019. Thanks to Eiléan for permission to quote her words here.

FREDA LAUGHTON (1907–95)

1 Freda Laughton, 'While to the Sun the Swan', in *A Transitory House* (London: Jonathan Cape, 1945), p. 9.
2 Valentin Iremonger, 'The Poems of Freda Laughton', *The Bell*, vol. 9, no. 4, January 1945, p. 350.
3 Lucy Collins, 'Poetry, 1920–1970', in Heather Ingman and Clíona Ó Gallchoir (eds), *A History of Modern Irish Women's Literature* (Cambridge: Cambridge University Press, 2018), p. 168.
4 Gerardine Meaney, *Gender, Ireland, and Cultural Change: Race, sex and nation* (London: Routledge, 2010), p. 9.
5 Laughton, 'In a Transitory Beauty', in *A Transitory House*, p. 10.
6 Freda Laughton, 'Review of *The Lady of the Hare* by John Layard', *The Bell*, vol. 9, no. 4, January 1945, p. 354.
7 Ibid., p. 355.
8 Freda Laughton, 'Portrait of a Woman', *The Irish Times*, 22 September 1945, p. 2.
9 Collins has observed the negative effects of stifled energies in Laughton's 'Tombed in Spring', which suggests that the influence of Jung may be wider than the poems discussed here. See 'Poetry 1920–1970', p. 181.
10 Laughton, 'Nightly Slim Adventures Slide', in *A Transitory House*, p. 14.
11 Anne Mulhall, '"The well-known, old, but still unbeaten track": Women poets and Irish periodical culture in the mid-twentieth century', *Irish University Review*, vol. 42, no. 1, 2012, p. 34.
12 Austin Clarke, 'Recent Verse', *The Irish Times*, 19 January 1946, p. 4.

13 Seán O'Faoláin, 'This is Your Magazine', *The Bell: A survey of Irish life*, vol. 1, no. 1, October 1940, pp. 5–6.
14 Valentin Iremonger, 'Aspects of Poetry To-Day', *The Bell*, vol. 12, no. 3, June 1946, p. 247.
15 Iremonger, 'The Poems of Freda Laughton', p. 349.
16 Mulhall, '"The well-known, old, but still unbeaten track"', p. 43.
17 Meaney, *Gender, Ireland, and Cultural Change*, pp. 9–10.
18 Austin Clarke, 'Recent Verse', *The Irish Times*, 19 January 1946, p. 4.
19 Ibid.
20 Patricia K. Harrison, 'Letter to the Editor, with Reply from Geoffrey Taylor', *The Bell*, vol. 10, no. 5, August 1945, p. 448.
21 Ibid., p. 446.
22 Laughton, 'The Woman with Child', in *A Transitory House*, pp. 11–12.
23 Meaney, *Gender, Ireland, and Cultural Change*, pp. 7–9.
24 Harrison, 'Letter to the Editor, with Reply from Geoffrey Taylor', p. 446.
25 Ibid.
26 Meaney, *Gender, Ireland, and Cultural Change*, p. 9.
27 Collins, 'Poetry, 1920–1970', p. 182.

MADGE HERRON (1915–2002)

1 Madge Herron, 'Frog', in Patricia Herron, *Madge: Portrait of Donegal actress and poet, Madge Herron*, 2nd edn (Ballydesmond: Clo Duanaire / Irish and Celtic Publications, 2018; first published 2016), p. 224.
2 Kevin O'Connor, 'Madge Herron', *The Guardian*, 4 October 2002, p. 9.
3 Herron, *Madge*, p. 70.
4 Ibid., p. 201.
5 Ibid., p. 202.
6 Ibid., p. 203.
7 Ibid., p. 70.
8 Ibid., p. 230.
9 Gerry Moriarty, 'The Irish Poet of London's Streets', *The Irish Times*, 12 November 2016, p. 7.
10 Herron, *Madge*, p. 79.
11 Lochlinn MacGlynn, 'The Girl from Donegal', *Irish Press*, 1 July 1940, p. 6.
12 Ibid.
13 Herron, *Madge*, p. 204.
14 Moriarty, 'The Irish Poet of London's Streets', p. 7.
15 Marius Kociejowski, 'The Poetical Remains of Madge Herron', *PN Review 155*, vol. 30, no. 3, January–February 2004, p. 15.
16 Madge Herron reads 'The Bull' on *Poetry Now*, presented by George MacBeth, BBC Radio 3, 30 March 1971 [22:20]. Herron's reading of 'The Bull' is located in the *Poetry Now* Archive, NP1695, The British Library, London.
17 Herron, *Madge*, p. 112.
18 Ibid.
19 Ibid., pp. 182–3.
20 Annemarie Ní Churreáin, email to the author, 2 October 2018.
21 Letter from Madge Herron to Francis Harvey (*c.*1984), in Herron, *Madge*, p. 159.
22 Nessa O'Mahony, 'Writ in Water', *Trumpet*, no. 6, April 2017, p. 32.

23 Thomas H. Johnson, *Final Harvest: Emily Dickinson's poems* (Boston; Toronto: Little Brown & Company, 1961), p. 211.
24 Grace Mei-shu Chen, 'Coda: Natural messages and aesthetic pleasure in Emily Dickinson's nature writing', in Marta Werner & Eliza Richards (eds), *Emily Dickinson's Lyrical Ecologies: Forays into the field* (Dickinson Electronic Archives, 2016) <http://www.emilydickinson.org/emily-dickinson-lyrical-ecologies-forays-into-the-field/coda-natural-messages-and-aesthetic-pleasure-in-emily-dickinson-s-nature-writing> [accessed on 26th April 2021].
25 Herron, *Madge*, p. 220.
26 Ibid., pp. 184–6.
27 Ibid., p. 10.
28 Herron is anthologised in A.A. Kelly (ed.), *Pillars of the House, An anthology of verse by Irish women from 1690 to the present* (Dublin: Wolfhound Press, 1987); W. Mulford et al. (eds), *Love Poems by Women: An anthology of poetry from around the world and through the ages* (New York: Fawcett Columbine, 1990).
29 Elgy Gillespie, 'Madge Herron at the Peacock', *The Irish Times*, 6 March 1979, p. 8.
30 Herron, *Madge*, p. 213.

PATRICIA AVIS (1928–77)

1 Patricia Avis, 'Le Deuxième Sexe', in *The Listener*, 25 July 1957, vol. LVIII, no. 1478, p. 137.
2 B.I., 'Patricia Murphy: An appreciation', *The Irish Times*, 15 September 1977, p. 9. Patricia Avis retained the name of her second husband, Richard Murphy, following their divorce in 1959. Her first poems were published under her maiden name Avis. The editors of her posthumously published novel *Playing the Harlot; or, Mostly Coffee* (London: Virago, 1996), Hermione de Almeida and George H. Gilpin, revert to her maiden name as author. This essay similarly uses Patricia Avis throughout.
3 Avis' family history and early biography are recorded by Richard Murphy in his memoir *The Kick: A life among writers* (London: Granta, 2002), pp. 156–7.
4 Murphy, *The Kick*, p. 156.
5 Ibid., p. 129.
6 Avis, 'Le Deuxième Sexe'. 'Christmas Comet' was published in *The Listener*, 11 July 1957, vol. LVIII, no. 1476, p. 51; 'The Bat' in *The Listener*, 29 August 1957, vol. LVIII, no. 1483, p. 315.
7 Simone de Beauvoir, *The Second Sex*, trans. & ed. by H.M. Parshley (London: Jonathan Cape, 1953); first published as *Le Deuxième Sexe* (Paris: Gallimard, 1949).
8 Simone de Beauvoir, *The Second Sex*, trans. by Constance Borde and Sheila Malovany-Chevallier (London: Jonathan Cape, 2009), p. 293.
9 Ibid., p. 7.
10 Ibid., p. 602.
11 Ibid., p. 601.
12 Philip Larkin to Patsy Murphy (née Avis), 4 August 1957, in Anthony Thwaite (ed.), *Selected Letters of Philip Larkin 1940–1986* (London: Faber, 1992), p. 279.
13 Avis' poem 'Leper Island' featured in G.S. Fraser (ed.), *Poetry Now: An anthology* (London: Faber & Faber, 1956), p. 35.
14 Larkin to Murphy (née Avis), 4 August 1957, in *Selected Letters of Philip Larkin 1940–1986*, p. 279.

15 Tom Paulin, 'The Larkin Letters', *Times Literary Supplement*, 6 November 1992, p. 15.
16 Andrew Motion, *Philip Larkin: A writer's life* (London: Faber & Faber, 1993), pp. 217, 221, 222.
17 James Booth, *Philip Larkin: Life, art and love* (London: Bloomsbury, 2015; first published 2014), p. 173.
18 Ibid., p. 174.
19 George H. Gilpin features extracts from Avis' letters to Larkin in 'Patricia Avis and Philip Larkin', in James Booth (ed.), *New Larkins for Old: Critical essays* (London: Macmillan, 2000), pp. 66–78. Her papers and correspondence are held in the Department of Special Collections and University Archives, McFarlin Library, The University of Tulsa.
20 See, for example, Larkin's letter to Avis on 11 November 1953, where he remarks that 'I altered my poem a bit on the lines you suggested', in *Selected Letters of Philip Larkin 1940–1985*, p. 218; Murphy, *The Kick*, p. 159.
21 Philip Larkin to Patsy Strang, 3 February 1954, in *Selected Letters of Philip Larkin 1940–1985*, p. 223.
22 Ibid.
23 Bonamy Dobrée, Louis MacNeice and Philip Larkin (eds), *New Poems* (London: Michael Joseph, 1958), p. 9.
24 Robert Conquest, 'Introduction', in Robert Conquest (ed.), *New Lines: An anthology* (London: Macmillan, 1967), pp. xii, xv.
25 Antoinette Quinn, *Patrick Kavanagh: A biography* (Dublin: Gill & Macmillan, 2001), p. 386.
26 Avis quoted in 'An Irishman's Diary', *The Irish Times*, 5 September 1959, p. 4.
27 Tom Clyde, *Irish Literary Magazines: An outline history and descriptive bibliography* (Dublin: Irish Academic Press, 2002), pp. 240, 49.
28 Quinn, *Patrick Kavanagh*, p. 386.
29 Patrick Kavanagh, 'Poems and Prose', *nonplus*, no. 1, October 1959, p. 84.
30 Patricia Murphy, 'Played Out', *University Review: Organ of the graduates association of the National University of Ireland*, vol. III, no. 3, 1963, p. 30.
31 Patricia Avis, *Playing the Harlot; or, Mostly Coffee* (London: Virago Press, 1996), pp. 9–10.
32 Nuala O'Faolain, *Are You Somebody?: The life and times of Nuala O'Faolain* (Dublin: New Island Books, 1996), p. 77.

ANGELA GREENE (1936–97)

1 Angela Greene, 'Enniskillen', in *Silence and the Blue Night* (Dublin: Salmon Poetry 1993), p. 45.
2 *Barbican 1* (Drogheda, 1984); *Barbican 2* (Drogheda, 1986).
3 Carol Rumens (ed.), *New Women Poets* (Newcastle: Bloodaxe Books, 1990), pp. 115–19.
4 Angela Greene, O. Marshall and P. Ramsey, *Trio Poetry 6* (Belfast: The Blackstaff Press: 1990), pp. 3–24.
5 Greene, *Silence and the Blue Night*, p. 45.
6 Gordon Wilson to Mike Gaston, quoted in Susan McKay, *Bear in Mind these Dead* (London: Faber, 2008), p. 129.
7 Ibid.

8   Greene, *Silence and the Blue Night*, p. 67.
9   Ibid., pp. 71–2.
10 Isabelle Cartwright, *Poetry Ireland Review*, no. 42, summer 1994, pp. 50–1.
11 Ibid.
12 Greene, *Silence and the Blue Night*, pp. 16–17.
13 Ibid., p. 24.
14 Ibid., pp. 60–1.
15 Angela Bourke et al. (eds), *The Field Day Anthology of Irish Writing: Irish Women's writing and traditions* (Cork: Cork University Press, 2002).
16 Patricia Boyle Haberstroh, *Women Creating Women: Contemporary Irish women poets* (New York: Syracuse University Press, 1996), p. 224.

LYNDA MORAN (1948–2020)

1   Lynda Moran, 'Something Else', in *The Truth About Lucy* (Dublin: Beaver Row Press, 1985), p. 40.
2   Paul Muldoon, 'Something Else', in *Poems: 1968–1998* (London: Faber & Faber, 2001), p. 173.
3   Leontia Flynn, 'On the Sofa: Parody and McGuckian', in Justin Quinn (ed.), *Irish Poetry After Feminism* (Buckinghamshire: Colin Smythe, 2008), pp. 80–8 (p. 85).
4   John F. Deane, 'Blissful Schizophrenia', *Books Ireland*, no. 98, November 1985, p. 198.
5   Robbert Wille, 'The Shame of Existing: An extreme form of shame', *The International Journal of Psychoanalysis*, no. 95, 2014, p. 696.
6   Larry Dossey, 'Shame', in *Explorations*, vol. 1, no. 2, 2005, p. 78.
7   Peter R. Breggin, 'The Biological Evolution of Guilt, Shame and Anxiety: A new theory of negative legacy emotions', *Medical Hypotheses*, no. 85, 2015, p. 22.
8   Karl Marx, 'Letters from the *Deutsch-Französische Jahrbücher*', in Karl Marx and Friedrich Engels, *Collected Works*, vol. 3 (Michigan: International Publishers, 1975), p. 133.
9   Patricia Boyle Haberstroh, *Women Creating Women: Contemporary Irish women poets* (New York: Syracuse University Press, 1996), p. 210.
10 Moran, 'The Man-Eater', in *The Truth About Lucy*, p. 42.
11 Measuring Equality in the Arts Sector (MEAS) is an organisation that monitors and reports on equality in the arts sector in Ireland, founded by Kenneth Keating and Ailbhe McDaid in 2018, <https://measorg.com/>.
12 Kenneth Keating and Ailbhe McDaid, 'Gender in Poetry Publishing in Ireland: 2008–2017', *MEAS: Measuring Equality in the Arts Sector: Literature in Ireland* <https://measorg.com/>, December 2018, pp. 6–10. Although comprehensive statistical analysis of the publishing activities of presses in Ireland in the 1980s, the decade in which Moran worked, has not yet been produced, the marginalisation of female poets during this period is widely accepted. For a detailed overview of this marginalisation in literary magazines, see Laura Loftus, 'The White Blackbird: The marginalisation of Irish women poets from literary magazines during the 1980s', *The Honest Ulsterman* <http://humag.co/features/the-white-blackbird>, nd.
13 David Lloyd, *Anomalous States: Irish writing and the post-colonial moment* (Dublin: Lilliput Press, 1993), p. 5.
14 Moran, 'The Stranger', in *The Truth About Lucy*, p. 30.

CATHLEEN O'NEILL (b. 1949)

1. Cathleen O'Neill, 'Off the Wall', in *Notions* (Dublin: KLEAR, 1987).
2. Cathleen O'Neill, 'Interview on the history of KLEAR', interviewed by Emma Penney, KLEAR, Kilbarrack, April 2017.
3. *Dictionary of the Irish Language: Based mainly on Old and Middle Irish materials; historical note and abbreviations* (Dublin: Royal Irish Academy, 1913), p. 76.
4. Angela Bourke, 'The Irish Traditional Lament and the Grieving Process', *Women's Studies International Forum, Special Issue: Feminism in Ireland*, vol. 11, no. 4 (New York: Pergamon Press, 1988), p. 289.
5. Michael Givoni, *The Care of the Witness: A contemporary history of testimony in crises* (New York: Cambridge University Press, 2016), p. 151.
6. O'Neill, 'Interview on the history of KLEAR'.
7. Ibid.
8. Megan Boler, 'Interview with Megan Boler: From "Feminist Politics of Emotions" to the "Affective Turn"', in Michalinos Zembylas and Paul A. Schutz (eds), *Methodological Advances in Research on Emotion and Education* (Zurich: Springer, 2016), pp. 17–30 (p. 19).
9. Máire Bradshaw, 'Interview on the history of the Cork Women's Poetry Circle', interviewed by Emma Penney, Cork, June 2018.
10. Mary Daly, *Women and Poverty* (Dublin: Attic Press, 1989), p. 8.
11. Ibid., p. 10.
12. Ibid., p. 25.
13. Cathleen O'Neill, *Telling It Like It Is* (Dublin: Combat Poverty Agency Press, 1992).
14. O'Neill, 'Poverty Is', in *Telling It Like It Is*, p. iii.
15. Jacqueline Rose, *On Not Being Able to Sleep: Psychoanalysis and the modern world* (London: Random House, 2010), p. 12.
16. O'Neill, 'Poverty Is', p. iii.
17. O'Neill, 'Interview on the history of KLEAR'.
18. Cathleen O'Neill, 'Feminist Fatigue', in Ailbhe Smyth, *Feminism in Ireland* (New York: Pergamon Press: 1988), p. 68.
19. Ibid.
20. O'Neill, *Telling It Like It Is*, p. ix.
21. O'Neill, 'Interview on the history of KLEAR'.
22. Daly, *Women and Poverty*, p. 107.
23. Gerry Moriarty, 'Community Arts and the Quality Issue', in Sandy Fitzgerald (ed.), *An Outburst of Frankness: A community arts reader* (Dublin: New Island Books, 2004), p. 149.
24. O'Neill, 'Interview on the history of KLEAR'.
25. Nora Gibney in 'Kilbarrack Sisters Still Doing it For Themselves', *The Irish Times*, 6 November 2001, p. 13.
26. Siobhán Holland, 'Our History in the Making', in James H. Murphy (ed.), *The Oxford History of the Book Volume IV: The Irish book in English* (London: Oxford University Press, 2011), p. 163.
27. Rebecca Pelan, *Two Irelands: Literary feminisms north and south* (New York: Syracuse University Press, 2005), p. 5.
28. Women's Community Press, File. No. B1137, Literature / Publishing, The Arts Council of Ireland Archives, 70 Merrion Square, Dublin. ArtsCo/WCP/B1137.

29 Charlotte McIvor, 'A Portrait of the Citizen as Artist: Community arts, devising and contemporary Irish theatre practice', in Charlotte McIvor and Siobhán O'Gorman (eds), *Devised Performance in Irish Theatre: Histories and contemporary practice* (Dublin: Carysfort Press, 2015).
30 Ibid.
31 Ibid.
32 Kate Shilton and Ramesh Srinivasan, 'Participatory Appraisal and Arrangement for Multicultural Archival Collections', *ARCHIVARIA* 63, spring 2007, pp. 87–101 (p. 95).
33 Brian Singleton, *Masculinities and the Contemporary Irish Theatre* (London: Palgrave Macmillan, 2011), p. 13.
34 *If You Can Talk ... You Can Write* (Dublin: Women's Community Press with the Kilbarrack women's writing group, 1983) is reported to be the first community anthology from Kilbarrack but it actually falls in the middle of the group's publishing history: *From Wits End to Humble Beginnings* (Dublin: Women's Community Press with the Kilbarrack women's writing group, 1981); *If You Can Talk ... You Can Write*; *By the Way Did I Tell You ...* (Dublin: Women's Community Press with the Kilbarrack women's writing group, 1984); *Notions* (1987) and *Telling It Like It Is* (1992). The third anthology of writing, from 1984, carries the imprint of the 'KLEAR Publishing Group', however, writers from Kilbarrack continued to contribute to Women's Community Press publications including *Write up Your Street* (1985), which contains writing by Kilbarrack women.

AFTERWORD: THE FUTURE OF IRISH WOMEN POETS: A NEW LANGUAGE

1 Eavan Boland, 'Mise Éire', in *New Collected Poems* (Manchester: Carcanet, 2005), p. 129.
2 Nokukhanya Dlamini, 'Scars', in Stephen Rea and Jessica Traynor (eds), *Correspondences: An anthology to call for an end to direct provision* (Correspondences Press, 2019), p. 95.
3 Anne Enright, 'Call yourself George: Gender representation in the Irish literary landscape', in *No Authority: Writings from the laureateship* (UCD Press, 2019), p. 86.
4 Ethna MacCarthy, *Poems*, ed. by Eoin O'Brien and Gerald Dawe (Dublin: Lilliput Press, 2019).
5 Moynagh Sullivan, 'Irish Poetry After Feminism: In search of "male poets"', in Justin Quinn (ed.), *Irish Poetry after Feminism* (Buckinghamshire: Colin Smythe, 2008), pp. 22–3.
6 Eric Falci, 'Rethinking Form (Yet Again) in Contemporary Irish Poetry', *Irish University Review*, 50.1, Special Issue: Golden Jubilee – Irish Studies Now, spring 2020, p. 184.
7 Annemarie Ní Churreáin, 'Postscript', in *Correspondences*, p. 32.

Index

Note: Page locators in bold refer to the main section of that particular poet.

1798 Rebellion, the, 68

'A PROPOS TO RADIO' (poem), 90–1
Abbey Theatre School of Acting, the, 113
Ackerley, J.R., 121
Adam, Jean, 22
Adorno, Theodor, 40
'Advent' (poem), 96, 97
Agricultural Co-operative Movement, the, 37
Ahmed, Sara, 60, 64
'Áilleacht Tír Chonaill' (poem), 112–13
Akhmatova, Anna, 86
'Alba' (poem), 8, 101, 102
Alcock, Mary, 34
'All Souls Eve' (poem), 74–5
All That Fall (radio play), 95
Amis, Kingsley, 124, 128
'Anarchism: What it really stands for' (essay), 60–1
'Ancient Garden' (poem), 136–7
Are You Somebody? (book), 128
'Argument to Book the Fourth' (poem), 34
Arts Council, the, 144, 152, 154
As You Like It (play), 31
Atlantic Rhymes and Rhythms (collection), 37

'ATTEMPT AT COMMENCING' (poem), 88–9
Attic Press, 149, 153
Austen, Jane, 28
Avis, Patricia, 10, **119–28**

'Ballad of Lost Lochlann' (poem), 72–3
'Ballad of St. Simon's' (poem), 97
Barbauld, Anna Laetitia, 18
Barber, Mary, 34
Barbican Writers' Group, the, 10, 130
'Barcelona' (poem), 100
Battersby, Eileen, 4–5
Battier, Henrietta, 26
BBC Radio, 114
Beaver Row Press, 143
Beckett, Samuel, 8, 59, 92–3, 94, 95, 96, 98, 99, 100–1
'Bed of Forget-Me-Nots, A' (poem), 54
Bell, The (journal), 80, 105, 107, 108
Bhuí Ní Laoire, Máire, 34
Biagini, Eugenio, 48
Bigger, F.J., 69, 71, 72
Bishop, Elizabeth, 12
'Black Horseman, The' (poem), 55
Bloodaxe Books national poetry competition, the, 131
Boland, Eavan, 141, 156, 162

Boler, Megan, 149
Book of Gilly: Four months out of a life (book), 40
Book of Irish Verse, A (collection), 55
Booth, James, 123–4
Boran, Pat, 144
Bourke, Angela, 148
Boyle Haberstroh, Patricia, 137, 140
Boyle O'Reilly, John, 49–50
Bradshaw, Máire, 149
Brady, Deirdre, 87–8
Breen, Mary Catherine, 29–30
Brennan, Máire, 114
Buckiad, a Mock-Heroic Poem, The (poem), 28, 33
'Buckiad, The' (poem), 33
'Bull, The' (poem), 115
Burns, Robert, 22, 23
Butler, Hubert, 125

Cadle, Nathaniel, 62
Cambridge Companion to Irish Poets, The (book), 3
Cambridge History of Irish Literature, The (book), 9
Campbell, Matthew, 50, 54
'Canal Bank Walk' (poem), 126
Carnduff, Thomas, 80
'carrikaturas' of Olivia Elder, 14, 17, 19
Cartwright, Isabelle, 134
Casement, Roger, 54–5
'Cean Duv Deelish' (poem), 55, 56
'Chain' (poem), 131
Chart, D.A., 81
Chelsea Householder, A (book), 39
Chesterton, G.K., 50
'Choice, The' (poem), 54–5
Church of Ireland tithes, 30
Cimino, Glenda, 143
Clare, John, 116

Clarke, Austin, 7, 77, 91, 96, 97, 107, 108
Cloncurry, Lord, 37
Clyde, Tom, 125
Coady, Michael, 33
Collected Early Works of Lola Ridge (collection), 6, 59
Collins, Lucy, 3, 80, 81, 87, 91, 103–4
'Colony, The' (poem), 77
Colum, Padraic, 96
Combat Poverty Agency, the, 149, 152
Coming of the Earls and Other Verse, The (collection), 7, 73
Conroy, Roisín, 153
Cooper, Jeanne Foster, 81
Cork Women's Poetry Circle, 149
Crane, Hart, 64
critical reviews, 39–40, 108–9, 140

Daly, Mary, 149–50, 152
Dance of Fire (collection), 60
'Dark is the Tomb' (poem), 54
Darwin, Charles, 39
Davies, Sarah W., 133
Davis, Leith, 23
Davitt, Michael, 47
Dawe, Gerald, 96
Dawn and Afterglow (collection), 77, 82
de Almeida, Hermione, 128
de Beauvoir, Simone, 121, 122
de Vere, Aubrey, 49
Deane, John F., 130, 140
Debussy, Claude, 94, 99
'December 1948' (poem), 95
December Bride (book), 78
Dedalus Press, 144
dialogue in poetry, 18
Dickinson, Emily, 116
'Dieppe' (poem), 94

Index

'Dirge' (poem), 29
'Dirge of the Munster Forest, 1581' (poem), 41, 42
Dlamini, Nokukhanya, 156
Dobrée, Bonamy, 123
Dolmen Press, 125
Dominick's Trials (book), 44
Donovan, Katie, 80
Doran, Mary, 153
'DR. SWIFT The Happy Life of a Country Person' (poem), 32
Dream of Fair to Middling Women (book), 100
Dublin literary society, 25, 26
Dublin Magazine (magazine), 96, 97
Dublin Poets & Artists (broadsheet), 91
Dublin University Review (journal), 44
'Dunciad, The' (poem), 33

Easter Rising, the, 53, 54, 55, 57, 62
Eccles, Isaac Ambrose, 26
Edgeworth, Maria, 28
'Eh, Joe' (TV drama), 98
Elder, John, 18
Elder, Olivia, 4, **13–19**, 158
'Electrocution' (poem), 62–3
'Elegy Written in a Country Churchyard' (poem), 22
Embers (radio play), 100
emigration, 44–5, 50
'Emma Goldman' (poem), 62
Emmet, Robert, 54, 68
Enlightenment, the, 40
'Enniskillen' (poem), 10–11, 129–30, 131–2
Enright, Anne, 157
Entomologist's Monthly Magazine (magazine), 38

equality in Irish publishing, 11, 12
see also patriarchal bias in the publishing industry; women in Irish writing and publishing
ESRI (Economic and Social Research Institute), the, 150
Eustace, Clotilda, 26
Eustace, Sir Maurice, 26
'Evergreen' (poem), 96–7
'Exile' (poem), 94, 96

Falci, Eric, 159
Fallon, Padraic, 37
Fallon, Peter, 144
feminine and sexual themes, 122–3, 141–2
'Feminist Fatigue' (short story), 151–2
Fenian uprising, the, 44
Festival of Britain poetry contest, the, 77, 79
Field Day Anthology of Irish Writing, The (book), 2, 34–5, 137, 140
Finnegan, Frances, 28, 29
Fired! Irish Women Poets and the Canon (digital platform), 3, 157
Fitzgerald, Lord Edward, 54
'Flight' (short story), 99–100
Flynn, Leontia, 140
Fogarty, Anne, 91
Fortnightly Review (journal), 50
Forty North, Fifty West (collection), 88
Fox's Covert, The (collection), 87
Fraser, G.S., 123
Freeman's Journal (newspaper), 14
French Revolution, the, 31
Freud, Sigmund, 141
'Frog' (poem), 110
From Wits End to Humble Beginnings (book), 153

Gaelic League, the, 45
Gallagher, Bernadette, 19
Gallery Press, 143, 144
'Garden Epitaphs' (poem), 135
Gayfield Press, the, 87–8, 91
Gébler, Ernest, 125
gender issues, 7–8, 148–9
'Ghetto, The' (poem), 58–9, 61
Ghetto and Other Poems, The (collection), 59, 60
Gibney, Norrie, 152–3
Gillespie, Elgy, 117–18
Gilpin, George H., 128
Ginsberg, Allen, 64
'Give me the Lark' (poem), 116–17
Givoni, Michael, 148
Gladstone, William, 6, 46, 47–8, 50
Gladstone sonnets, the (poems), 43–4, 46, 47, 48–9, 51
Glück, Louise, 33
Goldman, Emma, 60–1, 62
Goldsmith, Oliver, 29–30, 34
Grania (book), 36
Gray, Thomas, 22
Greacen, Robert, 96
Great Famine, the, 46–7
Greene, Angela, 10–11, **129–37**
Greene, Austin, 131, 133
Gregory, Padraic, 69
Grierson, Constantia, 34
Griffith, Elizabeth, 26
Griffith, Richard, 26
Gwynn, Stephen, 48, 49

Hanna Bell, Sam, 78
Hansson, Heidi, 39
Harrison, Patricia, 108, 109
Harte, Jack, 130
Harvey, Francis, 116
'He Wishes for the Cloths of Heaven' (poem), 53

Hellfire Club, the, 33
Hello Eternity! (collection), 87
Herbert, Dorothea, 4–5, **27–35**
Herron, Madge, 9–10, **110–18**, 159
Herron, Patricia, 110, 112, 117
Hewitt, John, 7, 77, 81, 96
Higgins, F.R., 97
History of Modern Irish Women's Literature, A (book), 9, 34–5
Hobson, Bulmer, 72
Holland, Siobhán, 153
Home Rule, the, 46, 48
Homer, 33
Honest Ulsterman, The (journal), 131
Horizon (magazine), 108
Horkheimer, Max, 40
Hughes, Eamonn, 82
Hyde, Douglas, 49

If You Can Talk … You Can Write (book), 153, 154
IFI (Irish Feminist Information), 153
Iliad (poem), 33
Imagism, 116
'In a Transitory Beauty' (poem), 104–5, 106–7
Inalienable Heritage, The (collection), 37, 40
Inglis, Brian, 119–20, 125
'Insomnia' (poem), 94
Introspections: The poetry & private world of Dorothea Herbert (collection), 28
IRB (Irish Republican Brotherhood), the, 72
Ireland, Denis, 80
Iremonger, Valentin, 96, 107–8
Irish Constitution, the, 87
Irish Examiner (newspaper), 95
Irish Journal of Medical Science (journal), 98

Index

Irish 'labouring-class' and women's poetry, the, 22–3
Irish language poetry, 111, 112–13, 116, 117, 148
Irish Literary and Cultural Revival, the, 37, 52, 69–70, 160
Irish Monthly (magazine), 45, 48, 49
Irish Press, The (newspaper), 113, 130, 131
Irish Review (newspaper), 69
Irish Times, The (newspaper), 92, 94, 95, 96, 97, 101, 105, 119–20, 125
Irish Women's Writing (1880–1920) Network (digital platform), 3
Irish Writing No. III (anthology), 97

Jennings, Elizabeth, 33
Joyce, James, 100
Jungian psychoanalysis, 105

'Kaimak' (short story), 94–5
Kathleen Ni Houlihan (nationalist symbol), 56–7
Kavanagh, Patrick, 91, 96, 121, 125, 126, 131
Kavanagh, Rose, 6, 53
Keating, Kenneth, 11
Kelly, A.A., 86
'Kelvin Barry' (poem), 62
Keogh, M.C., 45
Kirkland, Richard, 82
Kirwan, Elizabeth, 37
Kirwan, John, 37
KLEAR writing group, the, 11–12, 148, 149, 150–1, 152–3, 154, 155
Knowlson, James, 101, 102
Knox, Mary Ann, 18
Kociejowski, Marius, 114
Krapp's Last Tape (play), 101

Lady of the Hare, The (case study), 105
Lancet, The (journal), 101
Land War, the, 45, 46, 47, 48
Larkin, Philip, 120, 123–5, 128
Laughton, Freda, 9, 96, **103–9**, 161
Lawless, Emily, 5, **36–42**, 51, 56, 161
Layard, John, 105
'Le Deuxième Sexe' (poem), 119, 121–3, 124–5, 126
Leadbeater, Mary, 33
'Leave us religion' (poem), 84–6, 90–1
Lendennie, Jessie, 143
'Letting Go' (poem), 136
Leventhal, A.J. (Con), 94, 97
Leventhal-MacCarthy archive, the, 9
Levertov, Denise, 64
Light and Shade (book), 44
'Lines to a Friend' (poem), 27–9
Listener, The (magazine), 121, 123
Literature in Ireland (book), 56
Little, Janet, 22
Living a Feminist Life (book), 60
'Londonderry Air' (poem), 113–14
'Lost Garden, The' (poem), 134–5
Luke, John, 79
Lyons Castle, 37
Lyrics (collection), 49

Mac Liammóir, Micheál, 112
Macardle, Dorothy, 87
MacBeth, George, 114
MacCarthy, Denis Florence, 95
MacCarthy, Ethna, 8–9, **92–102**, 158
MacCurtain, Margaret, 90
MacDonagh, Thomas, 55, 56
MacNeice, Louis, 114, 123
Maelcho (book), 41–2
Major Lawrence, F.L.S. (book), 39
Malone Meurt/Malone Dies (book), 92–3

'Man-Eater, The' (poem), 141–2
'man from God knows where, The' (monologue), 68–9
Mandeville, Edward, 30
Marcus, David, 97, 130
Markievicz, Countess, 56–7
Marx, Karl, 141
Masefield, John, 55
Masque in Maytime (collection), 77, 82
Matchett, Rio, 64–5
Mauro, Evan, 63–4
Mayer, Bernadette, 64
McCarthy, Justin, 50
McDaid, Ailbhe, 11
McFadden, Roy, 77, 81
McGuckian, Medbh, 12, 140
McIvor, Charlotte, 154
McLaverty, Michael, 81
Meaney, Gerardine, 37, 104, 108, 109
MEAS (Measuring Equality in the Arts Sector), 11, 12, 144
Meehan, Paula, 90, 141, 143
Meeting the British (collection), 139
Merriman, Brian, 114
middle-class feminist publishing, 153–4, 155
Midnight Court, The (radio play), 114
Miller, Liam, 125
Milligan, Alice, 69, 70–1
Milne, Ewart, 88
Milton, John, 4, 14
'Mise Éire' (poem), 156
Missing Voices: Irish women poets of the 18th–20th centuries (seminar), 3
Modern Anglo-Irish Verse (collection), 69
Moira, Lady, 26
Monck, Mary, 34
Monteith, Charles, 121, 128
Moore, George, 50

Moran, Lynda, 11, **138–46**, 173
More, Hannah, 22
More Pricks than Kicks (short story), 100
Moriarty, Gerry, 112, 152
Morris, Catherine, 70
Morton, May, 7, **76–83**
Motion, Andrew, 123
Mount Cashell, Lady, 25–6
'Mountain Mist' (poem), 82
Muldoon, Paul, 139
Mulhall, Anne, 107, 108
Murphy, Richard, 120–1, 124, 125
Myles, Eileen, 64

Nation, The (newspaper), 37, 44
nationalist narrative of Irish poetry, 108
Nature (journal), 39
naturism and scientific knowledge, 38–41
'Nell Gwynn' (poem), 98
New Irish Poets (anthology), 96
New Lines (anthology), 125
New Poems (anthology), 123, 124
New Women Poets (anthology), 131
Ní Chuilleanáin, Eiléan, 9, 102
Ní Churreáin, Annemarie, 116, 161
Ní Dhomhnaill, Nuala, 12, 141
'Nightly Slim Adventures Slide' (poem), 105, 106–7
Nineteenth Century (journal), 45, 50
nonplus (magazine), 120, 125–6
'Nora' (poem), 56
North, The (pamphlet), 80
'Northern Dead, The' (poem), 73
Northern Whig (newspaper), 69

O'Brennan, Kathleen, 81
O'Brien, Charlotte Grace, 5–6, **43–51**

Index 189

O'Brien, Edna, 125
O'Brien, Kate, 77
O'Brien, William Smith, 5, 6, 44
O'Byrne, Cathal, 68
O'Casey, Sean, 77
O'Connor, Frank, 114
O'Connor, T.P., 45
O'Faolain, Nuala, 128
O'Faoláin, Seán, 80, 107
'Off the Wall' (poem), 147, 148, 149, 150, 151
'Old Toys' (poem), 101
'old woman' icon of Irish culture, the, 79
  see also Kathleen Ni Houlihan (nationalist symbol)
O'Neill, Cathleen, 11–12, **147–55**, 158
O'Nolan, Brian (Myles na gCopaleen), 125
O'Reilly, Caitríona, 12
Orwell, J.H., 97
Oxford History of the Book Volume IV: The Irish book in English (book), 153
oxyuriasis, 98

Paine, Thomas, 31, 33
Pall Mall Gazette (newspaper), 39, 44–5
Parnell, Charles Stewart, 45, 54
Parshley, Howard M., 121
'Parson's Fireside, The,' 31–2
'Patchwork Quilt, The' (poem), 52, 53, 54
patriarchal bias in the publishing industry, 141–6
Patriotism: A menace to liberty (book), 60
Paulin, Tom, 123
Pelan, Rebecca, 153

PEN International, 7, 77, 80–1
performance poetry *see* Herron, Madge
Picasso, Pablo, 115
Pillars of the House: An anthology of verse by Irish women (collection), 86
Pinsky, Robert, 64
'Played Out' (poem), 126–7
Playing the Harlot; or, Mostly Coffee (book), 128
Plunkett, Horace, 37, 50
PN Review (magazine), 114
Poems (collection), 8–9, 101
Poems, by Ellen Taylor, the Irish Cottager (collection), 18, 25
Poems from Ireland (anthology), 96
Poetics of Print: The private press tradition of Irish poetry, The (digital exhibition), 88
Poetry by Women in Ireland (anthology), 3–4
Poetry Ireland, 3
Poetry Ireland Review (journal), 131, 134
Poetry Now (anthology), 123
Poetry Now (radio programme), 114
Poetry of Mourning (book), 54
Poetry Round sessions, the, 114
Point of View: Some talks and disputations, The (collection), 37–8
political activism in poetry, 44–50, 59–62, 80, 82
  and Florence Mary Wilson, 69–73
Pope, Alexander, 4, 14, 32, 33
'Portrait of a Woman' (poem), 105–6, 107
'Poverty Is' (poem), 150, 1551
'Prayer to St Theresa, A' (poem), 111–12

'Preface' (poem), 32
Prescott, Sarah, 4
'Princess, The' (poem), 94
Provisional IRA, the, 131
pseudonyms, 14

Quinn, Antoinette, 126
Quinn, Justin, 91
Quin's Secret (play), 113

Racine, Jean, 97
Ramazani, Jahan, 54
Rank, Otto, 99
Reading the Sky (collection), 143
Red Flag (collection), 60, 62
Reid, Forrest, 82
Remembrance Sunday bombing, Enniskillen, 131–2
Repeal movement, the, 44
'Requiem' (poem), 101
Retrospections of Dorothea Herbert, The (memoir), 4–5, 28, 29, 33, 34, 35
Return and No Blame (collection), 143
'Reveille' (poem), 62
Rich, Adrienne, 64
Ridge, Lola, 6, **58–65**, 161
Rights of Man, The (book), 31, 33
'Rights of Woman, The' (poem), 30–1
Rodgers, W.R., 77, 114
Roe, Elizabeth, 34
Roe, John, 29, 33, 34
Róisín Dubh tradition, the, 56
Rose, Jacqueline, 150
Rossetti, Christina, 54
Rowley, Richard, 82
Royal Academy of Dramatic Art, London, 113
Rukeyser, Muriel, 64
Rumens, Carol, 131
Russell, Matthew, 49
Russell, Thomas, 68, 69
Russian revolution, the, 62

Sacco, Nicola, 62–3
Sad Years, The (collection), 6, 53, 54, 55
Salkeld, Blanaid, 8, **84–91**, 158, 159, 161
Salkeld, Cecil, 86, 87
'Sally the Waiting Maid's Complaint' (poem), 31
Salmon Poetry, 10, 131, 143, 144
SAOL writing group, the, 11, 148
Sappho, 33
Sarsfield, Patrick, 54
satire, 14, 17, 31, 32
Schiller, Friedrich, 49
scientific knowledge and naturism in poetry, 38–41
'Sea-Folk, The' (poem), 66–8, 75
Second Sex, The (book), 121, 122
sexism and canon formation, 64
Shakespeare, William, 31, 49
'shame of existing,' the, 141
'She Winds the Clock' (poem), 133–4
Sheil, George, 113
Sheridan Lefanu, Alicia, 26
Shilton, Kate, 154
Shorter, Clement K., 53, 55, 57
Sichel, Edith, 40
Sigerson, George, 52, 56
Sigerson Shorter, Dora, 6, **52–7**, 158, 160
Silence and the Blue Night (collection), 10, 131, 133, 135, 137
Silk Hats and No Breakfast: Notes on a Spanish journey (book), 97
Singleton, Brian, 155
'Sixteen Dead Men' (poem), 54
Smith, Terence, 97
Smyth, Ailbhe, 80

Index

social status of women in Ireland, the, 87, 150, 151–2
'Something Else' (poem by Lynda Moran), 138–40, 142
'Something Else' (poem by Paul Muldoon), 139
Spanish Civil War, the, 97
'Spindle and Shuttle' (poem), 7, 76, 77–80, 82–3
'Spires' (poem), 61
'Split the Lark – and you'll find the Music' (poem), 116
Srinivasan, Ramesh, 154
Starkie, Enid, 121
state funding of feminist groups, 152, 153–4
Stevenson, Anne, 64
Stopford Green, Alice, 51
'Storm, The' (poem), 32
Strang, Colin, 120
'Stranger, The' (poem), 145–6
subscribers to Ellen Taylor's work, 25–6
Sullivan, Moynagh, 87, 90, 159
Sun-Up (collection), 60
Sung to the Spinning Wheel (collection), 77
Svoboda, Terese, 60, 64, 65
Swift, Jonathan, 14–15
Swinburne, Algernon, 50

Tale of Venice: A Drama, A (collection), 49
Taylor, Ellen, 4, **20–6**
Telling It Like It Is (book), 150, 151–2
Tennyson, Alfred Lord, 94
testimony and traditions in storytelling, 148, 149–50
...the engine is left running (collection), 8, 84–6, 89–91

'They Did Not See Thy Face' (poem), 56
Thompson, Edward, 53
Thwaite, Anthony, 123
Tickell, Thomas, 26
'Tidings, The' (poem), 62
Tighe, Mary, 26
'To a Mountain Daisy' (poem), 23
'To a Shade' (poem), 54
'To a Tuft of White Bog-Cotton, Growing in the Tyrol' (poem), 40, 41, 42
'To Alexander Berkman' (poem), 62
'To Larkin' (poem), 62
'To that Rare and Deep-Red Burnet-Moth only to be met with in the Burren' (poem), 36, 38
To the Many (book), 64–5
'To the Same [i.e. Miss M.B.] Novbr 29th' (poem), 14–18
Tobin, Daniel, 59
Tone, Theobald Wolfe, 54
Tracy, Honor, 97
Traits and Confidences (book), 38
Transitory House, A (collection), 9, 103, 104
transnationalist perspectives in Irish women's poetry, 59, 65, 161
Trauma of Birth, The (book), 99
Tricolour, The (collection), 56, 57
Trio Poetry (anthology), 131
Truth About Lucy, The (collection), 11, 138, 139, 140, 141, 143, 145, 146
Tuberculosis in Childhood (newspaper article), 97–8
Tynan, Katharine, 6, 53, 57

Ulster linen industry, the, 77–80
Ulster Plantation, the, 77

Ulster-Scots vernacular in Irish poetry, 67, 68–9, 73–5
Uninvited, The (play), 99
University Review (journal), 126

'Vagrant Heart, A' (poem), 53–4
Vanzetti, Bartolomeo, 62–3
verse in the eighteenth-century Ulster Presbyterian community *see* Elder, Olivia
Vesey, Elizabeth, 25
'Viaticum' (poem), 92–4, 96
'Villa, The' (poem), 29, 30
'Village Adieu: A Farewell Poem, The' (poem), 29
Vindication of the Rights of Woman, A (book), 31

Waiting for Godot (play), 98
Walsh, Maurice, 81
'Wasteland' (poem), 131
WCP (Women's Community Press), 153, 154
Wheatley, David, 6
'While to the Sun the Swan' (poem), 103, 104
White, H.O., 77
Whiteboys, the, 30
Wilson, Florence Mary, 7, **66–75**
Wilson, Frederick, 69, 71
Wilson, Gordon, 132
Wilson, Marie, 132

Wilson, Niall, 72, 73
Wiltshire, Elinor Vere, 125
Wingfield, Sheila, 91
With the Wild Geese (collection), 37
Wollstonecraft, Mary, 26
'Woman with Child, The' (poem), 108–9
Women and Poverty (book), 149–50
'Women and the Creative Will' (poem), 59
Women Creating Women: Contemporary Irish women poets (book), 137, 140
women in Irish writing and publishing, 2–3, 7–8, 12, 107, 140, 141–4, 156–7
Women's Writers' Club, the, 87
working-class women and funding for publishing, 154, 155
World Health Organisation, the, 95
World War I, 72
Write Up Your Street (anthology), 149
'Written Because of Sarah W. Davies' (poem), 133
'Written by the BARROW Side' (poem), 20–1, 23–4

Yearsley, Ann, 22
Yeats, Jack Butler, 91
Yeats, W.B., 6, 37, 40, 53, 54, 55, 69
Young Ireland uprising, the, 44
Young Ulster (journal), 80